Lecture Notes of the Institute for Computer Sciences, Social Informatics and Telecommunications Engineering   **539**

The LNICST series publishes ICST's conferences, symposia and workshops.

LNICST reports state-of-the-art results in areas related to the scope of the Institute. The type of material published includes

- Proceedings (published in time for the respective event)
- Other edited monographs (such as project reports or invited volumes)

LNICST topics span the following areas:

- General Computer Science
- E-Economy
- E-Medicine
- Knowledge Management
- Multimedia
- Operations, Management and Policy
- Social Informatics
- Systems

Evangelia Kalyvianaki · Marco Paolieri
Editors

Performance Evaluation Methodologies and Tools

16th EAI International Conference,
VALUETOOLS 2023
Crete, Greece, September 6–7, 2023
Proceedings

 Springer

Editors
Evangelia Kalyvianaki
University of Cambridge
Cambridge, UK

Marco Paolieri 🆔
University of Southern California
Los Angeles, CA, USA

ISSN 1867-8211   ISSN 1867-822X   (electronic)
Lecture Notes of the Institute for Computer Sciences, Social Informatics
and Telecommunications Engineering
ISBN 978-3-031-48884-9   ISBN 978-3-031-48885-6   (eBook)
https://doi.org/10.1007/978-3-031-48885-6

This Springer imprint is published by the registered company Springer Nature Switzerland AG
The registered company address is: Gewerbestrasse 11, 6330 Cham, Switzerland

Paper in this product is recyclable.

Preface

We are delighted to introduce the proceedings of the 16th edition of the European Alliance for Innovation (EAI) International Conference on Performance Evaluation Methodologies and Tools (VALUETOOLS 2023).

The conference took place in Heraklion, Crete during September 6–7, 2023, bringing together researchers, developers, and practitioners from around the world and from different communities including computer science, networks and telecommunications, operations research, optimization, control theory, and manufacturing. The focus of VALUETOOLS 2023 was on methodologies and practices in modeling, performance evaluation, and optimization of complex systems.

The 27 members of the International Program Committee (PC) helped to provide at least 3 reviews for each of the 30 submitted contributions (19 research papers, 4 tool papers, 3 work-in-progress papers, and 1 vision paper). Based on the reviews and PC discussions, 11 high-quality papers (9 research papers, 1 tool paper, and 1 work-in-progress paper) were accepted to be presented during the conference. The overall acceptance rate for the conference was 37%. The contributions, which appear as papers in the ensuing proceedings, were organized into four thematic sessions: *Games and Optimization*; *Simulation*; *Networking and Queues*; *Tools*. The Best Paper award was announced at the conference.

A highlight of VALUETOOLS 2023 was the presence of two invited speakers, Aad van Moorsel and Maria Papadopouli, whom we thank for their participation and insightful presentations.

We would like to thank all the authors who entrusted their best work to VALUE-TOOLS 2023, making this event possible and allowing a high-quality program and a fruitful event. We also thank the program committee members and the additional reviewers for their hard work and for sharing their valued expertise with the VALUETOOLS community. A special thanks goes to the General Chairs, William Knottenbelt and Katinka Wolter, for the continued support and encouragement, and to Radka Vasileiadis and the EAI team for local organization, promotion, and coordination of the conference.

August 2023

Evangelia Kalyvianaki
Marco Paolieri

Organization

General Chairs

William Knottenbelt   Imperial College London, UK
Katinka Wolter   Freie Universität Berlin, DE

Program Committee Chairs

Evangelia Kalyvianaki   University of Cambridge, UK
Marco Paolieri   University of Southern California, US

Publication Chair

Diego Perez   Linnaeus University, SE

Local Organization and Publicity

Radka Vasileiadis   European Alliance for Innovation
Patricia Gabajova   European Alliance for Innovation

Steering Committee

Eitan Altman   INRIA, FR
Xiren Cao   Hong Kong University of Science & Technology,
                                      HK
Christos G. Cassandras   Boston University, US
Imrich Chlamtac   EAI and University of Trento, IT
William Knottenbelt   Imperial College London, UK
Kishor Trivedi   Duke University, US
Qianchuan Zhao   Tsinghua University, CN

Program Committee

Konstantin Avrachenkov	INRIA Sophia Antipolis, FR
Onno J. Boxma	Technical University Eindhoven, NL
Laura Carnevali	University of Florence, IT
Giuliano Casale	Imperial College London, UK
Josu Doncel	University of the Basque Country, ES
Douglas Down	McMaster University, CA
Rachid El Azouzi	University of Avignon, FR
Dieter Fiems	Ghent University, BE
Jean-Michel Fourneau	Université de Versailles, FR
Giuliana Franceschinis	Università del Piemonte Orientale, IT
Reinhard German	University of Erlangen-Nuremberg, DE
Marco Gribaudo	Politecnico di Milano, IT
Yezekael Hayel	University of Avignon, FR
Jane Hillston	University of Edinburgh, UK
Esa Hyytiä	University of Iceland, IS
Vana Kalogeraki	Athens University of Economics and Business, GR
Alexandros Koliousis	Northeastern University London, UK
Catalina Llado	University of the Balearic Islands, ES
Kostas Magoutis	University of Crete, GR
Luo Mai	University of Edinburgh, UK
Nihal Pekergin	University Paris-Est Créteil, FR
Anne Remke	University of Münster, DE
Sabina Rossi	Università Ca' Foscari di Venezia, IT
Jens B. Schmitt	TU Kaiserslautern, DE
Evgenia Smirni	College of William and Mary, US
Sabine Wittevrongel	Ghent University, BE
Armin Zimmermann	Technische Universität Ilmenau, DE

Additional Reviewers

Verena Menzel	University of Twente, NL
Benedetta Picano	University of Florence, IT
Riccardo Reali	University of Florence, IT
Leonardo Scommegna	University of Florence, IT
Jonas Stübbe	University of Münster, DE
Lisa Willemsen	University of Twente, NL

Contents

Tools

Games and Optimization

An Anti-jamming Game When None Player Knows Rival's Channel Gain

Andrey Garnaev$^{(\boxtimes)}$ and Wade Trappe

WINLAB, Rutgers University, North Brunswick, NJ, USA
garnaev@yahoo.com, trappe@winlab.rutgers.edu

Abstract. We consider a user's communication with a receiver in presence of a jammer, in the most competitive situation for user and jammer when they do not have access to complete information on channel gains of each other although they could have access to exact information on their own channel gains. The problem is modeled as a Bayesian power control game between user and jammer as players. Incomplete information is modeled as statistical data over possible channel gains (also referred as channel states). Since channel gain is a function on the distance to the receiver, this also covers scenarios where the user and jammer could know its own location via global positioning system (GPS), but none of them know the exact location of the other. A novel approach is suggested to derive equilibrium of such problems in closed form for two communication metrics: signal-to-interference-plus-noise ratio (SINR) metric, reflecting regular data transmission, and latency metric, reflecting emergency data transmission. In particular, it is shown that the user's equilibrium strategies corresponding to the latency metric is more sensitive to the a priori statistical information, as compared to the SINR metric. This reflects an advantage of implementing latency metric in case of availability of exact information on network parameters, and an advantage of implementing SINR metric in case of lack of such its availability.

Keywords: Jamming · SINR · Latency · Bayesian equilibrium

1 Introduction

The shared and open-access nature of the wireless medium renders wireless networks vulnerable to hostile interference or jamming. To design anti-jamming strategy in such a background, non-cooperative game theory has been widely employed due to in such problems each agent (say, a user who aims to communicate with the receiver and a jammer who aims to obstruct the user's communication via jamming) has its own objective [5,9,12,15,16,18–20]. While the above cited works about anti-jamming problems assume that each player, user and jammer, has complete information about own (network and communication) parameters as well as about such parameters of the rival, there are works where

© ICST Institute for Computer Sciences, Social Informatics and Telecommunications Engineering 2024
Published by Springer Nature Switzerland AG 2024. All Rights Reserved
E. Kalyvianaki and M. Paolieri (Eds.): VALUETOOLS 2023, LNICST 539, pp. 3–17, 2024.
https://doi.org/10.1007/978-3-031-48885-6_1

none of the players, user and jammer, could have access to the exact information about some own network parameters, or only one of them might have access to the exact information about own parameters [2,3,6,8,10,11,13,14,17]. For example, the players might not know exact values of some parameters involved in payoffs [2,3,6,10,11,14,17], the player might not know whether the other player is selfish or malicious [13], the player might not know whether the other player implements behavior's strategies or not [8]. Meanwhile in the real-world most competitive scenarios, the user as well as the jammer might have exact information about itself but do not have complete information about the rival. Such a scenario is the most competitive since the advantage that each player could gain via access to exact information about itself, could be used against the player by the rival due to lack of information for the player about the rival. To the best knowledge of the authors such anti-jamming problems have not been studied in literature.

Motivation of the research: All the above cited papers have been addressed to anti-jamming scenarios where either only one of the players (user or jammer) has access to exact information or none of them has such an access. Meanwhile, in the real-world scenarios related to anti-jamming problems under incomplete information on channel gains, both players, user and jammer, might have access to exact information about itself but do not have such access about the other. It is motivated, for example, by the fact that the channel gain is a function on the distance to the receiver, and each player, user and jammer, might have complete information about its own location via GPS, but none of them might not know another player's location. To model access of the player to exact information about its location, a player's type has to be assigned per location. That is why such a problem leads to an increase in its dimension and complexity in contrast to those studied in literature. Such an increase in complexity calls for development of a new approach to design anti-jamming strategies and methods to verify whether such a designed anti-jamming strategy could maintain stability in communication.

The main contributions of this paper are as follows: (i) A Bayesian game approach is employed to model a power control anti-jamming problem for different access of the players (user and jammer) to information (exact or only statistical) about channel states. (ii) A novel approach is developed allowing to find in closed form equilibrium strategies with such incomplete information for two communication metrics: SINR metric, reflecting regular data transmission, and latency metric, reflecting emergency data transmission. (iii) Stability of designed anti-jamming strategies are verified via proving uniqueness of equilibrium. (iv) An advantage of implementing latency metric in case of availability of exact information on network parameters as well as an advantage of implementing SINR metric in case of a lack of its availability are revealed via showing that user's equilibrium strategies corresponding to the latency metric is more sensitive to the a priori statistic information, as compared to the SINR metric.

2   The Communication Model

Let us consider a single carrier transmission scheme with two agents: a *user* and an *adversary*. The adversary is a jammer, who intends to degrade the user's communication by generating interference. User's resource is its transmission power P, $P \in [0,\overline{P}]$, and jammer's resource is its jamming power J, $J \in [0,\overline{J}]$. In contrast to [7,19], where communication channel and jammer's channel of each player are fixed and known to both players, we assume that: (a) communication channel can be in one of K states corresponding to fading gains $h_1,\ldots,h_K$, with probabilities $\alpha_1,\ldots,\alpha_K$, respectively, and (b) jammer's channel can be in one of M states corresponding to fading gains $g_1,\ldots,g_M$, with probabilities $\beta_1,\ldots,\beta_M$, respectively. Each of the players knows its own channel state, meanwhile regarding rival's channel state it only knows set of feasible states and corresponding a priori probabilities. Without loss of generality, let us assume that the gains of the user's channel and jammer's channel are arranged in increasing order, i.e.,

$$h_0 \triangleq 0 < h_1 < h_2 < \ldots < h_K < h_{K+1} \triangleq \infty, \tag{1}$$

$$g_0 \triangleq 0 < g_1 < g_2 \ldots < g_M < g_{M+1} \triangleq \infty. \tag{2}$$

In the following, by *type-k user* ($k \in \mathcal{K} \triangleq \{1,\ldots,K\}$) we refer to a user if its channel state k occurs, and let P_k be its strategy, and $\boldsymbol{P} \triangleq (P_1,\ldots,P_K)$.[1] By *type-m jammer* ($m \in \mathcal{M} \triangleq \{1,\ldots,M\}$) we refer to a jammer if its channel state m occurs, and let J_m be its strategy, and $\boldsymbol{J} \triangleq (J_1,\ldots,J_M)$.

In this section we consider SINR as communication metric. Then, the type-k user's payoff reflects trade-off between its SINR and transmission cost and given as follows:

$$v_{U,k}(P_k,\boldsymbol{J}) \triangleq \sum_{m\in\mathcal{M}} \beta_m \frac{h_k P_k}{N + g_m J_m} - C_P P_k = (h_k T(\boldsymbol{J}) - C_P) P_k, \tag{3}$$

where N is the background noise variance and C_P is user's transmission cost per power unit and

$$T(\boldsymbol{J}) \triangleq \sum_{m\in\mathcal{M}} \beta_m/(N + g_m J_m). \tag{4}$$

The type-m jammer's payoff is given as follows:

$$v_{J,m}(\boldsymbol{P},J_m) \triangleq -\sum_{k\in\mathcal{K}} \alpha_k \frac{h_k P_k}{N + g_m J_m} - C_J J_m = \frac{H(\boldsymbol{P})}{N + g_m J_m} - C_J J_m, \tag{5}$$

where C_J is jamming cost per power unit and

$$H(\boldsymbol{P}) \triangleq \sum_{k\in\mathcal{K}} \alpha_k h_k P_k. \tag{6}$$

---

[1] We use bold font in vector's notations.

Intuition behind $T(\boldsymbol{J})$ is that it is expected inverse total noise when all jammer's types apply strategies $\boldsymbol{J}$. Meanwhile $H(\boldsymbol{P})$ is that it is the expected power generated by all user's types implementing strategies $\boldsymbol{P}$.

Each of user's and jammer's types want to maximize its payoff. Thus, we look for Bayesian equilibrium [4]. In other words, we look for such vector of user's types strategies $\boldsymbol{P} = (P_1, \dots, P_K)$ and vector of jammer's types strategies $\boldsymbol{J} = (J_1, \dots, J_K)$ that each of these strategies is the best response to the others, i.e.,

$$P_k = \mathrm{BR}_{U,k}(\boldsymbol{J}) \triangleq \mathrm{argmax}\{v_{U,k}(\tilde{P}_k, \boldsymbol{J}) : \tilde{P}_k \in [0, \overline{P}]\}, \; k \in \mathcal{K}, \tag{7}$$

$$J_m = \mathrm{BR}_{J,m}(\boldsymbol{P}) \triangleq \mathrm{argmax}\{v_{J,m}(\boldsymbol{P}, \tilde{J}_m) : \tilde{J}_m \in [0, \overline{J}]\}, \; m \in \mathcal{M}. \tag{8}$$

These $K + M$ real-value best response equations can be rewritten as two vector-value equations:

$$\boldsymbol{P} = \mathbf{BR}_U(\boldsymbol{J}) \text{ and } \boldsymbol{J} = \mathbf{BR}_J(\boldsymbol{P}), \tag{9}$$

where

$$\mathbf{BR}_U(\boldsymbol{J}) \triangleq (\mathrm{BR}_{U,1}(\boldsymbol{J}), \dots, \mathrm{BR}_{U,K}(\boldsymbol{J})), \tag{10}$$

$$\mathbf{BR}_J(\boldsymbol{P}) \triangleq (\mathrm{BR}_{J,1}(\boldsymbol{P}), \dots, \mathrm{BR}_{J,M}(\boldsymbol{P})). \tag{11}$$

Let us denote by Γ this game.

Proposition 1. *In game Γ there is at least one equilibrium.*

Please find the proof in Appendix.

3   Equilibrium

In this section solving best response equation (9) we establish the condition when equilibrium is unique or multiple equilibria arise.

3.1   The Players' Best Responses

In the following proposition we provide the players' best responses in closed form.

Proposition 2. *For a fixed $\boldsymbol{J}$, type-k user's best response is given as follows*

$$BR_{U,k}(\boldsymbol{J}) \begin{cases} = 0, & T(\boldsymbol{J}) < C_P/h_k \\ \in [0, \overline{P}], & T(\boldsymbol{J}) = C_P/h_k, \\ = \overline{P} & T(\boldsymbol{J}) > C_P/h_k. \end{cases} \tag{12}$$

For a fixed $\boldsymbol{P}$, type-m jammer's best response is given as follows

$$BR_{J,m}(\boldsymbol{P}) = \begin{cases} 0, & H(\boldsymbol{P}) \le A_m, \\ \sqrt{\dfrac{H(\boldsymbol{P})}{C_J g_m}} - \dfrac{N}{g_m}, & A_m < H(\boldsymbol{P}) < B_m, \\ \overline{J} & B_m \le H(\boldsymbol{P}), \end{cases} \tag{13}$$

where

$$A_m \triangleq C_J N^2 / g_m \ and \ B_m \triangleq C_J (N + g_m \overline{J})^2 / g_m. \qquad (14)$$

Please find the proof in Appendix.

It is clear that, by (14),

$$A_m < B_m \qquad (15)$$

and

$$0 < \sqrt{\frac{H(\boldsymbol{P})}{C_J g_m}} - \frac{N}{g_m} < \overline{J} \ for \ A_m < H(\boldsymbol{P}) < B_m. \qquad (16)$$

Thus, (13) defines jammer's types best responses correctly.

3.2   Structure of User Types' Equilibrium Strategies

In the following proposition we derive in the parameterized form, given by (18) below, all plausible candidates to be user types' equilibrium strategies. In particular, it means that there are no user types' equilibrium strategies which are not given by (18) for a specific value of its parameter x. Intuition behind this parameter x in such form is that it allows to identify threshold user's type which separates user's types implementing the maximal and minimal (zero) transmission power as well as to specify the transmission power implemented by this threshold user's type. Finally, we derive the K-dimension vector equation to obtain the value of this parameter. Such an approach (method) to design equilibrium and investigate its uniqueness via parameterizing all plausible candidates to be equilibrium we call a parameterization method.

Proposition 3. *$(\boldsymbol{P}, \boldsymbol{J})$ is an equilibrium in game Γ if and only if there is an $x \in [0, K\overline{P}]$ such that*

$$\boldsymbol{P} = \boldsymbol{P}(x) \triangleq (P_1(x), \dots P_K(x)) \ and \ \boldsymbol{J} = \mathbf{BR}_J(\boldsymbol{P}(x)), \qquad (17)$$

where for $x \in [0, K\overline{P}]$ vector $(P_1(x), \dots P_K(x))$ is given as follows:

$$P_k(x) \triangleq \begin{cases} 0, & k < \lfloor x/\overline{P} \rfloor + 1, \\ (\lfloor x/\overline{P} \rfloor + 1)\overline{P} - x, & k = \lfloor x/\overline{P} \rfloor + 1, \ for \ k \in \mathcal{K}, \\ \overline{P}, & k > \lfloor x/\overline{P} \rfloor + 1 \end{cases} \qquad (18)$$

where $\lfloor \xi \rfloor$ is the greatest integer less than or equal to ξ. Moreover, x is the root in $[0, K\overline{P}]$ of the following K-dimension vector equation:

$$P_k(x) = \begin{cases} 0, & \mathcal{T}(x) < C_P / h_k, \\ \in [0, \overline{P}], & \mathcal{T}(x) = C_P / h_k, \ k \in \mathcal{K}, \\ \overline{P}, & \mathcal{T}(x) > C_P / h_k, \end{cases} \qquad (19)$$

where

$$T(x) = \sum_{m \in I_0(x)} \frac{\beta_m}{N} + \sum_{m \in I(x)} \frac{\beta_m}{\sqrt{g_m}} \sqrt{\frac{C_J}{\mathcal{H}(x)}} + \sum_{m \in \overline{I}(x)} \frac{\beta_m}{N + g_m \overline{J}} \qquad (20)$$

with

$$\mathcal{H}(x) \triangleq H(\boldsymbol{P}(x)), \qquad (21)$$
$$I_0(x) \triangleq \{m \in \mathcal{M} : a_m \leq x\}, \qquad (22)$$
$$I(x) \triangleq \{m \in \mathcal{M} : b_m < x < a_m\}, \qquad (23)$$
$$\overline{I}(x) \triangleq \{m \in \mathcal{M} : x \leq b_m\}, \qquad (24)$$

where

$$a_m \triangleq \begin{cases} K\overline{P}, & \mathcal{H}(0) \leq A_m \\ \mathcal{H}^{-1}(A_m), & \mathcal{H}(0) > A_m \end{cases} \text{ and } b_m \triangleq \begin{cases} 0, & \mathcal{H}(0) \leq B_m, \\ \mathcal{H}^{-1}(B_m), & \mathcal{H}(0) > B_m. \end{cases} \qquad (25)$$

Please find the proof in Appendix.

Let us explain intuition behind functions $\mathcal{H}(x)$ and $T(x)$ implemented in Proposition 3. By (6) and (21), $\mathcal{H}(x)$ is the expected power generated by all user's types implementing strategies $\boldsymbol{P}(x)$, and, by (6), (18) and (21),

$$\mathcal{H}(x) \text{ is strictly decreasing from } \mathcal{H}(0) = \overline{P} \sum_{k \in \mathcal{K}} \alpha_k h_k \text{ to } \mathcal{H}(K\overline{P}) = 0. \qquad (26)$$

Thus, by (26), a_m and b_m are correctly defined by (25).

By (4), (13) and (20)–(25), we have that $T(\mathbf{BR}_J(\boldsymbol{P}(x))) = T(x)$. Thus, $T(x)$ is the expected inverse total noise when the jammer's types apply best response to user's types strategies $\boldsymbol{P}(x)$. Moreover, $T(x)$ is non-decreasing continuous function. Since $T(x)$ might be constant within some sub-intervals it might lead to multiple solutions of K-dimension vector equation (19) if and only if there is a k such that $x = k\overline{P}$ is solution of (19). In this case multiple equilibrium strategies arise for the only type-k user.

3.3   Equilibrium in Closed Form

By Proposition 1, in game Γ, there is at least one equilibrium. In the following theorem we find equilibrium as well as establish condition when equilibrium is unique. Moreover, we prove that the jammer types' equilibrium strategies are always unique while multiple user types' equilibrium strategies might arise for the only user's type.

Theorem 1. *In game Γ let $(\boldsymbol{P}, \boldsymbol{J})$ be an equilibrium. Then $\boldsymbol{P} = \boldsymbol{P}(x)$ and $\boldsymbol{J} = \mathbf{BR}_J(\boldsymbol{P}(x))$ with $x \in [0, K\overline{P}]$, where $\boldsymbol{P}(x)$ given by (18). Moreover, such x is defined as follows:*

(a) If

$$C_P/h_1 < T(0) \tag{27}$$

then $x = 0$;
(b) If

$$T(K\overline{P}) < C_P/h_K \tag{28}$$

then $x = K\overline{P}$;
(c) If (27) and (28) do not hold then there is an unique $\tilde{k}$ such that either (29) or (30) given below hold and
(c-i) if

$$C_P/h_{\tilde{k}} < T(\tilde{k}\overline{P}) < C_P/h_{\tilde{k}-1} \tag{29}$$

then $x = \tilde{k}\overline{P}$;
(c-ii) if

$$T(\tilde{k}\overline{P}) \le C_P/h_{\tilde{k}} \le T((\tilde{k}+1)\overline{P}) \tag{30}$$

then x is the root in $[\tilde{k}\overline{P}, (\tilde{k}+1)\overline{P}]$ of the equation

$$T(x) = C_P/h_{\tilde{k}}. \tag{31}$$

This x can be found via the bisection method.

Please find the proof in Appendix.

Finally note that $T(x)$ is non-decreasing continuous function. This and Theorem 1 imply that if x is given by this theorem and there is no $[a, b]$ such that $x \in [a, b]$ and $T(t)$ is constant in $[a, b]$ then user's types equilibrium strategies are unique. Otherwise, $P(t)$ with $t \in [a, b]$ is also equilibrium.

4   Latency Metric

For further illustration of the suggested parameterization method, let us consider latency communication metric modeled by the inverse SINR [9]. It might be interesting to note that SINR and negative latency might be included into a uniform scale of user's communication utilities via α-fairness utility with $\alpha = 0$ and $\alpha = 2$, respectively [1]. The user wishes to find the trade-off between a reduction in latency of the signal at the receiver and transmission power cost. Then, the k-type user's payoff is given as follows:

$$v_{U,k}^L(P_k, J) \triangleq - \sum_{m=1}^{M} \beta_m \frac{N + g_m J_m}{h_k P_k} - C_P P_k = -\frac{W(J)}{h_k P_k} - C_P P_k, \tag{32}$$

where

$$W(\boldsymbol{J}) \triangleq N + \sum_{m \in \mathcal{M}} \beta_m g_m J_m. \tag{33}$$

The type-m jammer's payoff is given as follows

$$v^L_{J,m}(\boldsymbol{P}, J_m) \triangleq \sum_{k=1}^{K} \alpha_k \frac{N + g_m J_m}{h_k P_k} - C_J J_m = N R(\boldsymbol{P}) + (g_m R(\boldsymbol{P}) - C_J) J_m, \tag{34}$$

where

$$R(\boldsymbol{P}) \triangleq \sum_{k \in \mathcal{K}} \alpha_k / (h_k P_k). \tag{35}$$

Intuition behind $W(\boldsymbol{J})$ is that it is the expected total noise when the jammer's types apply jamming strategies $\boldsymbol{J}$. Meanwhile, $R(\boldsymbol{P})$ is that it is the expected inverse power generated by all user's types implementing strategies $\boldsymbol{P}$.

Let us denote by Γ^L such Bayesian game with user's and jammer's payoffs given by (32) and (34), respectively.

Proposition 4. *In game Γ^L there is at least one equilibrium.*

Please find the proof in Appendix.

4.1   The Best Responses in Game Γ^L

In this section we provide the players' best responses in closed form.

Proposition 5. *For a fixed $\boldsymbol{J}$, the type-k user best responses is*

$$BR^L_{U,k}(\boldsymbol{J}) = \min\{\sqrt{W(\boldsymbol{J})/(h_k C_P)}, \overline{P}\}. \tag{36}$$

For a fixed $\boldsymbol{P}$, the type-m jammer best response is:

$$BR^L_{J,m}(\boldsymbol{P}) = \begin{cases} 0, & R(\boldsymbol{P}) < C_J/g_m, \\ \in [0, \overline{J}], & R(\boldsymbol{P}) = C_J/g_m, \\ \overline{J}, & R(\boldsymbol{P}) > C_J/g_m. \end{cases} \tag{37}$$

Please find the proof in Appendix.

4.2   Structure of Jammer Types' Equilibrium Strategies

In the following proposition we derive in the parameterized form, given by (39) below, all plausible candidates to be jammer types' equilibrium strategies. In particular, it means that there are no jammer types' equilibrium strategies which are not given by (39) for a specific value of its parameter y. Intuition behind this parameter y in such form is that it allows to identify threshold jammer's type which separates jammer's types implementing the maximal and minimal (zero) jamming power as well as to specify the jamming power implemented by this threshold jammer's type. Finally, we derive M-dimension vector equation to obtain the value of this parameter.

Proposition 6. (P, J) *is an equilibrium in game* Γ^L *if and only if there is a* $y \in [0, M\overline{J}]$ *such that*

$$J = J(y) \triangleq (J_1(y), \ldots J_M(y)) \text{ and } P = \mathbf{BR}_U^L(J(y)), \tag{38}$$

where for a fixed $y \in [0, M\overline{J}]$ *vector* $(J_1(y), \ldots J_M(y))$ *is given as follows:*

$$J_m(y) \triangleq \begin{cases} 0, & m < \lfloor y/\overline{J} \rfloor + 1, \\ (\lfloor y/\overline{J} \rfloor \overline{J} + 1)\overline{J} - y, & m = \lfloor y/\overline{J} \rfloor + 1, \text{ for } m \in \mathcal{M}. \\ \overline{J}, & m > \lfloor y/\overline{J} \rfloor + 1 \end{cases} \tag{39}$$

Moreover, such y *is solution in* $[0, M\overline{J}]$ *of the following* M*-dimension vector equation:*

$$J_m(y) = \begin{cases} 0, & \mathcal{R}(y) < C_J/g_m, \\ \in [0, \overline{J}], & \mathcal{R}(y) = C_J/g_m, \ m \in \mathcal{M}, \\ \overline{P}, & \mathcal{R}(y) > C_J/g_m, \end{cases} \tag{40}$$

where

$$\mathcal{R}(y) \triangleq \sum_{k \in I^L(y)} \alpha_k \sqrt{\frac{h_k C_P}{W(J(y))}} + \sum_{k \in \overline{I}^L(y)} \frac{\alpha_k}{h_k \overline{P}} \tag{41}$$

with

$$I^L(y) \triangleq \left\{ k \in \mathcal{K} : W(J(y)) \le h_k C_P \overline{P}^2 \right\}, \tag{42}$$

$$\overline{I}^L(y) \triangleq \left\{ k \in \mathcal{K} : h_k C_P \overline{P}^2 < W(J(y)) \right\}. \tag{43}$$

Please find the proof in Appendix.

Let us explain intuition behind functions $W(J(y))$ and $\mathcal{R}(y)$ implemented in Proposition 6. By (33), $W(J(y))$ is total noise when the jammer's types apply jamming strategies $J(y)$. By (35), (36) and (41)–(43), we have that $R(\mathbf{BR}_U(J(y))) = \mathcal{R}(y)$. Thus, $\mathcal{R}(y)$ the expected inverse power generated by all user's types when the user's types apply best response to jammer's types strategies $J(y)$.

4.3   Equilibrium in Closed Form

By Proposition 4, in game Γ^L there is at least one equilibrium. In the following theorem we find equilibrium as well as establish its uniqueness.

Theorem 2. *Let* (P^L, J^L) *be an equilibrium in game* Γ^L. *Then* $J^L = J(y)$ *and* $P^L = \mathbf{BR}_U(J^L(y))$ *with* $y \in [0, M\overline{J}]$, *where* $J(y)$ *given by (39). Moreover, such* y *is defined as follows:*

(a) If

$$C_J/g_1 < \mathcal{R}(0) \qquad (44)$$

then $y = 0$;
  (b) If

$$\mathcal{R}(M\overline{J}) < C_J/g_M \qquad (45)$$

then $y = M\overline{J}$;
  (c) If (44) and (45) do not hold then there is an unique $\tilde{m}$ such that either
(46) or (47) given below hold and
  (c-i) if

$$C_J/g_{\tilde{m}} < \mathcal{R}(\tilde{m}\overline{J}) < C_J/g_{\tilde{m}-1} \qquad (46)$$

then $y = \tilde{m}\overline{J}$;
  (c-ii) if

$$\mathcal{R}(\tilde{m}\overline{J}) \leq C_J/h_{\tilde{m}} \leq \mathcal{R}((\tilde{m}+1)\overline{J}) \qquad (47)$$

then y is the root in $[\tilde{m}\overline{J}, (\tilde{m}+1)\overline{J}]$ of the equation

$$\mathcal{R}(y) = C_J/g_{\tilde{m}}. \qquad (48)$$

This y can be found via the bisection method.

Please find the proof in Appendix.

Since $\mathcal{R}(y)$ is either strictly increasing or constant, equilibrium is unique except the only case if $\mathcal{R}(y)$ is constant in $[0, M\overline{J}]$.

5   Discussion of the Results

The complexity to design an equilibrium of game Γ, by Theorem 1, is $\kappa = \log_2(\overline{P}/\epsilon)$, where ϵ is the tolerance of the bisection method. The complexity to design an equilibrium of game Γ^L is similar, and, by Theorem 2, it equals to $\kappa^L = \log_2(\overline{J}/\epsilon)$. Thus, in game Γ, the impact of the maximal transmission power on the complexity to design an equilibrium is larger compare with the impact of the maximal jamming power. While, in game Γ^L, we can observe the inverse influence. To illustrate the obtained equilibrium strategies in Theorem 1 and Theorem 2, let us consider the network with background noise $N = 0.2$, and transmission and jamming costs $C_P = C_J = 1$. We compare the equilibrium strategies for scenario where the channels can be in two states: good and bad, i.e., $K = M = 2$, and let fading gains are $(g_1, g_2) = (0.3, 1) = (h_1, h_2)$. Also let the total powers resource of the players be $\overline{P} = \overline{J} = 5$, and the a priori probabilities are parameterized by probability for the first state to occur, i.e., $(\alpha_1, \alpha_2) = (\alpha, 1 - \alpha)$ and $(\beta_1, \beta_2) = (\beta, 1 - \beta)$. Figure 1 illustrates that

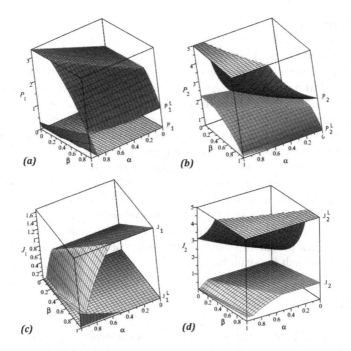

Fig. 1. (a) P_1 and P_1^L, (b) P_2 and P_2^L, (c) J_1 and J_1^L and (d) J_2 and J_2^L.

the user with latency as communication utility is more sensitive to the a priori probabilities compare with the user with latency as communication utility. This is reflected by an increase in zone where the corresponding strategies are constant, and, thus do not react on small variation of the a priori probabilities. The jammer's sensitiveness on the a priori probabilities is higher for SINR as communication utility. Thus, SINR metric assumes less information requirements for the user, and, so, communication with such metric might be easier to maintain for the user. An increase in probability that the user's channel is in good state leads to a decrease in applied transmission power for all user's types in both metrics. An increase in probability that the jammer's channel is in good state leads to a decrease in applied jamming power for all jammer's types in both metrics. The user with SINR metric applies higher transmission power if the user's channel is in good state compare with bad state. Moreover, if the user's channel is in bad state the user might prefer not to communicate with the receiver (Fig. 1(a), Fig. 1(b) and (12)). The user with latency metric, independent on in which state the channel is, keeps on communicating with the receiver. Moreover, when the channel is in good state, the user can transmit at lower power, while the user need to increase their power when the channel worsens to keep on communicating (Fig. 1(a), Fig. 1(b) and (36)).

6   Conclusions

The optimal power control anti-jamming strategy has been designed in a game-theoretical framework for the most competitive scenario where the user and the jammer could have access to exact information about own channel state and only statistical information about rival's channel states. A novel approach, called parameterization method, has been developed to design equilibrium strategies in such problems with incomplete information. Based on this parameterization method, equilibrium strategies have been found in closed form and compared for two communication metrics: SINR and latency metrics reflecting regular and emergency data transmission, respectively. In particular, it has been established that user's equilibrium strategies corresponding to latency metric is more sensitive to varying a priori probabilities, as compared to the SINR. This reflects an advantage of implementing latency metric in case of availability of exact information on network parameters, and an advantage of implementing SINR metric in case of lack of such its availability.

Appendix

Proof of Proposition 1: Since $v_{J,m}(\boldsymbol{P}, J_m)$ is concave in J_m, and $v_{U,k}(P_k, \boldsymbol{J})$ is linear in P_k, and set of feasible strategies of each player is compact, the result follows from Nash theorem [4]. ∎

Proof of Proposition 2: By (3), $v_{U,k}(P_k, \boldsymbol{J})$ is linear in P_k. Then, (12) follows from (3) and (7). By (5), we have that

$$\frac{\partial v_{J,m}(\boldsymbol{P}, J_m)}{\partial J_m} = \frac{g_m H(\boldsymbol{P})}{(N + g_m J_m)^2} - C_J. \tag{49}$$

Since $v_{J,m}(\boldsymbol{P}, J_m)$ is concave in J_m, by (8) and (49), we have that

$$\text{BR}_{J,m}(\boldsymbol{P}) = \begin{cases} 0, & \frac{\partial v_{J,m}(\boldsymbol{P}, 0)}{\partial J_m} \leq 0, \\ \frac{\partial v_{J,m}(\boldsymbol{P}, J_m)}{\partial J_m} = 0, & \frac{\partial v_{J,m}(\boldsymbol{P}, \overline{J})}{\partial J_m} < 0 < \frac{\partial v_{J,m}(\boldsymbol{P}, 0)}{\partial J_m}, \\ \overline{J}, & 0 \leq \frac{\partial v_{J,m}(\boldsymbol{P}, \overline{J})}{\partial J_m}. \end{cases} \tag{50}$$

Substituting (49) into (50) and taking into account (6) and (14) imply (13). ∎

Proof of Proposition 3: By (1) and (12), for a fixed $\boldsymbol{J}$ there exists an unique $\tilde{k}(\boldsymbol{J}) \in \{0, 1, \ldots, K, K+1\}$ such that

$$\text{BR}_{U,k}(\boldsymbol{J}) = \begin{cases} 0, & k < \tilde{k}(\boldsymbol{J}), \\ \in [0, \overline{P}], & k = \tilde{k}(\boldsymbol{J}), \text{ or } \text{BR}_{U,k}(\boldsymbol{J}) = \begin{cases} 0, & k < \tilde{k}(\boldsymbol{J}), \\ \overline{P} & k \geq \tilde{k}(\boldsymbol{J}). \end{cases} \\ \overline{P} & k > \tilde{k}(\boldsymbol{J}) \end{cases} \tag{51}$$

Thus, user's types equilibrium strategies have to have the form $\boldsymbol{P}(x)$ given by (18) with an $x \in [\tilde{k}(\boldsymbol{J})\overline{P}, (\tilde{k}(\boldsymbol{J}) + 1)\overline{P})$. To derive an equation to find such x, note that, by (9), $\boldsymbol{P}(x)$ is user's types equilibrium strategies if and only if

$$\boldsymbol{P}(x) = \mathbf{BR}_U(\mathbf{BR}_J(\boldsymbol{P}(x)). \tag{52}$$

By (4), (13) and (20), we have that

$$T(\mathbf{BR}_J(\boldsymbol{P}(x))) = \mathcal{T}(x), \tag{53}$$

with $I_0(x) \triangleq \{m \in \mathcal{M} : \mathcal{H}(x) \le A_m\}$, $I(x) \triangleq \{m \in \mathcal{M} : A_m < \mathcal{H}(x) < B_m\}$ and $\overline{I}(x) \triangleq \{m \in \mathcal{M} : B_m \le \mathcal{H}(x)\}$. By (25) and (26) these sets $I_0(x)$, $I(x)$ and $\overline{I}(x)$ can be present in equivalent form given by (22)–(24). Then substituting (12) and (53) into right side of fixed point equation (52), and (18) into its right side imply (19), and the result follows. ∎

Proof of Theorem 1: Let $\boldsymbol{P}(x)$ be an equilibrium. Then, by Proposition 3, there are $\tilde{k}$ and $x \in [\tilde{k}\overline{P}, (\tilde{k}+1)\overline{P})$ such that

$$P_k(x) = \begin{cases} 0, & k < \tilde{k}, \\ \in [0, \overline{P}], & k = \tilde{k}, \\ \overline{P} & k > \tilde{k} \end{cases} \quad \text{or } P_k(x) = \begin{cases} 0, & k < \tilde{k}, \\ \overline{P} & k \ge \tilde{k} \end{cases} \tag{54}$$

with

$$P_{\tilde{k}}(x) = (\tilde{k}+1)\overline{P} - x \tag{55}$$

and

$$P_k(x) = \begin{cases} 0, & \mathcal{T}(x) < C_P/h_k, \\ \in [0, \overline{P}], & \mathcal{T}(x) = C_P/h_k, \quad \text{for } k \in \mathcal{K}. \\ \overline{P}, & \mathcal{T}(x) > C_P/h_k, \end{cases} \tag{56}$$

Note that, by (20),

$$\mathcal{T}(x) \text{ is non-decreasing continuous function.} \tag{57}$$

Thus, by (56), if (27) holds then $x = 0$, and (a) follows. If (28) holds then $x = K\overline{P}$, and (b) follows. Let (27) and (28) do not hold. Let user's types equilibrium strategies are given by the right formula in (54). Then, by (55), $x = \tilde{k}\overline{P}$, and, thus, by (56), (29) holds, and (c-i) follows.

Let user's types equilibrium strategies are given by the left formula in (54). Then, by (55), $\tilde{k}\overline{P} < x < (\tilde{k}+1)\overline{P}$, and by (56), $\mathcal{T}(x) = C_P/h_{\tilde{k}}$. This equation has a root in $[\tilde{k}\overline{P}, (\tilde{k}+1)\overline{P}]$ if and only if (30) holds, and (c-ii) follows. ∎

Proof of Proposition 4: It is clear that $v_{U,k}^L(P_k, \boldsymbol{J})$ is concave in P_k and $v_{J,m}^L(\boldsymbol{P}, J_m)$ is linear in J_m. Thus, by Nash theorem [4], equilibrium exists. ∎

Proof of Proposition 5: By (34), $v_{J,m}^L(\boldsymbol{P}, J_m)$ is linear in J_m. Then, (37) follows from (34). Further, by (34), we have that

$$\frac{\partial v_{U,k}^L(P_k, \boldsymbol{J})}{\partial P_k} = \frac{W(\boldsymbol{J})}{h_k P_k^2} - C_P. \tag{58}$$

Since $v_{U,k}^L(P_k, \boldsymbol{J})$ is concave in P_k and $v_{U,k}^L(0, \boldsymbol{J}) = -\infty$ we have that

$$\mathrm{BR}_{U,k}^L(\boldsymbol{J}) = \begin{cases} \dfrac{\partial v_{U,k}^L(P_k, \boldsymbol{J})}{\partial P_k} = 0, & \dfrac{\partial v_{U,k}^L(\overline{P}, \boldsymbol{J})}{\partial P_k} < 0, \\ \overline{P}, & 0 \leq \dfrac{\partial v_{U,k}^L(\overline{P}, \boldsymbol{J})}{\partial P_k}. \end{cases} \tag{59}$$

Substituting (58) into (59) implies (36). By (34), $v_{J,m}^L(\boldsymbol{P}, J_m)$ is linear in J_m, and, then, (37) immediately follows from (34). ∎

Proof of Proposition 6: By (2) and (37), for a fixed $\boldsymbol{P}$ there exists an unique $\tilde{m}(\boldsymbol{P}) \in \{0, 1, \ldots, M, M+1\}$ such that

$$\mathrm{BR}_{J,m}^L(\boldsymbol{P}) = \begin{cases} 0, & m < \tilde{m}(\boldsymbol{P}), \\ \in [0, \overline{J}], & m = \tilde{m}(\boldsymbol{P}), \\ \overline{J} & m > \tilde{m}(\boldsymbol{P}) \end{cases} \quad \text{or} \quad \mathrm{BR}_{J,m}^L(\boldsymbol{P}) = \begin{cases} 0, & m < \tilde{m}(\boldsymbol{P}), \\ \overline{J} & m \geq \tilde{m}(\boldsymbol{P}). \end{cases} \tag{60}$$

Thus, jammer's types equilibrium strategies have to have the form $\boldsymbol{J}(y)$ given by (39) with $y \in [\tilde{m}(\boldsymbol{P})\overline{J}, (\tilde{m}(\boldsymbol{P}) + 1)\overline{J})$. To derive an equation to find such y, note that, $\boldsymbol{J}(y)$ is jammer's types equilibrium strategies if and only if

$$\boldsymbol{J}(y) = \mathrm{BR}_J^L(\mathrm{BR}_U^L(\boldsymbol{J}(y))). \tag{61}$$

By (35), (36) and (41)–(43), we have that $R\left(\mathbf{BR}_U(\boldsymbol{J}(y))\right) = \mathcal{R}(y)$. Then this, (37), (39) and (61) and (39) imply (40), and the result follows. ∎

Proof of Theorem 2: By (33) and (39), $W(\boldsymbol{J}(y))$ is strictly decreasing in $[0, M\overline{J}]$, by (41)–(43), $\mathcal{R}(y)$ is either constant or strictly increasing in $[0, M\overline{J}]$. Then the result follows from Proposition 6. ∎

References

1. Altman, E., Avrachenkov, K., Garnaev, A.: Generalized α-fair resource allocation in wireless networks. In: Proceedings of 47th IEEE Conference on Decision and Control, pp. 2414–2419 (2008)
2. Altman, E., Avrachenkov, K., Garnaev, A.: Jamming in wireless networks under uncertainty. Mobile Netw. Appl. **16**, 246–254 (2011)
3. Aziz, F., Shamma, J., Stuber, G.L.: Jammer type estimation in LTE with a smart jammer repeated game. IEEE Trans. Veh. Technol. **66**, 7422–7431 (2017)
4. Fudenberg, D., Tirole, J.: Game Theory. MIT Press, Boston, MA (1991)

5. Gao, Y., Xiao, Y., Wu, M., Xiao, M., Shao, J.: Game theory-based anti-jamming strategies for frequency hopping wireless communications. IEEE Trans. Wirel. Commun. **17**, 5314–5326 (2018)

6. Garnaev, A., Hayel, Y., Altman, E.: A Bayesian jamming game in an OFDM wireless network. In: Proceedings of 10th International Symposium on Modeling and Optimization in Mobile, Ad Hoc and Wireless Networks (WIOPT), pp. 41–48 (2012)

7. Garnaev, A., Petropulu, A., Trappe, W., Poor, H.V.: A power control game with uncertainty on the type of the jammer. In: Proceedings of IEEE Global Conference on Signal and Information Processing (GlobalSIP) (2019)

8. Garnaev, A., Petropulu, A., Trappe, W., Poor, H.V.: A jamming game with rival-type uncertainty. IEEE Trans. Wirel. Commun. **19**, 5359–5372 (2020)

9. Garnaev, A., Petropulu, A., Trappe, W., Poor, H.V.: A multi-jammer game with latency as the user's communication utility. IEEE Commun. Lett. **24**, 1899–1903 (2020)

10. He, G., Debbah, M., Altman, E.: k-player Bayesian waterfilling game for fading multiple access channels. In: Proceedings of 3rd IEEE International Workshop on Computational Advances in Multi-Sensor Adaptive Processing (CAMSAP), pp. 17–20 (2009)

11. Inaltekin, H., Wicker, S.B.: Random access games: Selfish nodes with incomplete information. In: Proceedings of IEEE Military Communications Conference (MIL-COM) (2007)

12. Li, Y., Xiao, L., Liu, J., Tang, Y.: Power control Stackelberg game in cooperative anti-jamming communications. In: Proceedings of 5th International Conference on Game Theory for Networks, pp. 1–6 (2014)

13. Sagduyu, Y.E., Berry, R., Ephremides, A.: MAC games for distributed wireless network security with incomplete information of selfish and malicious user types. In: Proceedings of International Conference on Game Theory for Networks (2009)

14. Scalabrin, M., Vadori, V., Guglielmi, A.V., Badia, L.: A zero-sum jamming game with incomplete position information in wireless scenarios. In: Proceedings of 21th European Wireless Conference, pp. 1–6 (2015)

15. Wang, K., Yuan, L., Miyazaki, T., Chen, Y., Zhang, Y.: Jamming and eavesdropping defense in green cyber-physical transportation systems using a stackelberg game. IEEE Trans. Industr. Inf. **14**, 4232–4242 (2018)

16. Xiao, L., Xie, C., Chen, T., Dai, H., Poor, H.V.: A mobile offloading game against smart attacks. IEEE Access **4**, 2281–2291 (2016)

17. Xu, Y., Ren, G., Chen, J., Luo, Y., Jia, L., Liu, X., Yang, Y., Xu, Y.: A one-leader multi-follower Bayesian-Stackelberg game for anti-jamming transmission in UAV communication networks. IEEE Access **6**, 21697–21709 (2018)

18. Yang, D., Xue, G., Zhang, J., Richa, A., Fang, X.: Coping with a smart jammer in wireless networks: A Stackelberg game approach. IEEE Trans. Wirel. Commun. **12**, 4038–4047 (2013)

19. Yang, D., Zhang, J., Fang, X., Richa, A., Xue, G.: Optimal transmission power control in the presence of a smart jammer. In: Proceedings of IEEE Global Communications Conference (GLOBECOM), pp. 5506–5511 (2012)

20. Yu, L., Wu, Q., Xu, Y., Ding, G., Jia, L.: Power control games for multi-user anti-jamming communications. Wirel. Netw. **25**, 2365–2374 (2019)

Selfish Mining in Public Blockchains: A Quantitative Analysis

Daria Smuseva(✉)[iD], Andrea Marin[iD], and Sabina Rossi[iD]

Università Ca' Foscari Venezia, Venice, Italy
{daria.smuseva,marin,sabina.rossi}@unive.it

Abstract. Blockchains are digital ledgers of transactions that aim to be decentralized, secure, and tamper-proof. To achieve this goal, they rely on a consensus algorithm, with the most well-known being the proof-of-work (PoW) algorithm. In PoW, a group of specialized users known as miners invest a significant amount of energy to secure the blockchain ledger. Miners are incentivized to participate in the network through the potential rewards they can earn, which are based on the number of blocks they are able to consolidate and add to the chain. An important characteristic of the PoW algorithm is that miners' rewards must be statistically proportional to the amount of computational power (and hence energy) invested in this process. In this work, we study the selfish miner attack by means of a stochastic model based on a quantitative process algebra. When a successful attack occurs, a miner or mining pool is able to receive more rewards than they should, at the expense of other miners. The model analysis allows us to derive the conditions under which the attack becomes convenient for the miners.

Keywords: Blockchain security · Stochastic process algebra · Selfish mining attack

1 Introduction

A blockchain is a digital ledger that is decentralized and distributed, where records are stored in blocks. Transactions are added to the network after being validated by a group of specialized users called *miners*, who bundle them into blocks. Once a transaction is added to the blockchain, it becomes highly resistant to alteration or deletion, making the records permanent and immutable.

Each blockchain network employs a consensus protocol to achieve consensus on the validity of transactions. The most commonly used consensus protocol is the Proof-of-Work (PoW) protocol, initially introduced in the original Bitcoin blockchain [14]. This protocol requires miners to compete to solve a complex computational problem, with the first miner to solve it receiving a reward. The primary advantage of PoW is that any attempt to modify transactions in the

© ICST Institute for Computer Sciences, Social Informatics and Telecommunications Engineering 2024
Published by Springer Nature Switzerland AG 2024. All Rights Reserved
E. Kalyvianaki and M. Paolieri (Eds.): VALUETOOLS 2023, LNICST 539, pp. 18–32, 2024.
https://doi.org/10.1007/978-3-031-48885-6_2

ledger becomes prohibitively expensive for malicious actors, as they must re-mine all subsequent blocks, making it computationally infeasible.

The Bitcoin blockchain features a lightweight scripting language that allows users to specify transaction validity conditions. Advanced blockchains, such as Ethereum [3], have introduced Turing-complete scripting languages that enable users to encode any computation as a script. The computational framework of scriptable cryptocurrencies has been referred to as *consensus computer* (see [10]). Miners within consensus computers are responsible for two primary functions: verifying the correct construction of blocks, and assessing the validity of transactions included within each block. While verifying the correct block construction is relatively straightforward, validating transactions within a block can take significantly more time due to the execution of corresponding code fragments. However, miners are incentivized to verify these scripted transactions to support the common good of the cryptocurrency.

In most of public blockchains with PoW consensus mechanism, miners who successfully solve a cryptopuzzle are given the chance to record a set of transactions and collect a cryptocurrency reward. The greater the mining power a miner employs, the higher the likelihood of being the first to solve the puzzle. This reward structure acts as an incentive for miners to allocate their resources towards the system, ultimately upholding the decentralized nature of the currency.

The PoW protocol requires that most miners operate honestly and follow the prescribed protocol. However, if a group of colluding miners controls the majority of the mining power in the network, the currency's decentralized nature is lost, and the colluding group governs it. This scenario could result in the prohibition of certain transactions, or even all transactions.

Empirical evidences and game theoretical models have revealed that Bitcoin miners are strategic in nature and frequently form mining pools [9]. These pools are created to reduce the variance of each member's income rate, given that rewards are dispersed at infrequent, random intervals. All members of the pool contribute to the solution of each cryptopuzzle and receive rewards in proportion to their level of involvement.

Initially, it was assumed that there is no advantage for colluding miners to organize into ever-increasing pools and it poses no threat to the system [2]. However, in [5] the authors have described a strategy that can be used by a minority pool to obtain more revenue than the pool's fair share, that is, more than its ratio of the total mining power.

The Selfish Mining strategy is based on the idea of a mining pool keeping its discovered blocks confidential and intentionally creating a fork, i.e., two branches, in the blockchain. Meanwhile, honest miners continue to mine on the public chain, unaware of the pool's private branch. Whenever the pool discovers more blocks, it strengthens its lead on the public chain and continues to keep its blocks secret. When the public branch approaches the pool's private branch in length, the selfish miners reveal blocks from their private chain to the public one, causing the public chain to become the shorter branch and their private chain to become the longer one.

This strategy results in a wastage of resources for honest miners who follow the blockchain protocol by solving cryptopuzzles that serve no objective. Although both honest and selfish miners squander some resources, honest miners bear a higher percentage of the wastage. Moreover, the rewards obtained by the selfish pool exceed its portion of the network's mining power, providing it with a competitive edge and encouraging rational miners to join the selfish mining pool.

To completely understand the selfish miner attack, we must consider some important facts. Firstly, the selfish mining attack does not compromise the integrity of the blockchain, i.e., the validity and immutability of the data is still preserved. Secondly, several factors contribute to the success of a selfish miner attack, including the ability of the mining pool to efficiently and rapidly propagate its blocks. Therefore, even if the pool is unable to create a longer chain than the one mined by fair miners, there is still a chance that it can propagate its block quickly enough to make it the official branch of the fork.

In this work, we take a quantitative approach to analyze the selfish mining attack by presenting a model expressed with a Markovian process algebra, namely the Performance Evaluation Process Algebra (PEPA) [7]. With respect to previous studies, we consider the effect of the verification time on the selfish mining strategy. Since with the introduction of smart contacts this may be not negligible, as discussed in the seminal work [5], our model is applicable to a broader range of scenarios. Our findings suggest that slower verification times provide an advantage to the selfish miners.

The paper is structured as follows. In Sect. 2, we review the state of the art. Section 3 describes the mining process and the selfish mining attack. Moreover, we briefly introduce PEPA to keep the paper self-contained. In Sect. 4, we describe the model and in Sect. 5, we show the exact solution of its lumping. This allows us to derive the conditions under which the selfish mining attack is rationally convenient for miners. Finally, Sect. 6 concludes the paper.

To the best of our knowledge, this is the first work that models the selfish miner attack by means of a Markovian process algebra.

2   Related Work

The selfish mining attack in Bitcoin was studied in [4–6] where a Markovian model was proposed to demonstrate that a mining pool with a sufficiently large fraction of computational power f (but lower than 50%) can receive a higher fraction of rewards than f. Although the attack does not affect the integrity of the transactions stored in the ledger, the authors emphasize that the economic mechanism that supports the mining process is critical to the blockchain's security. Furthermore, the overproduction of chain forks caused by the selfish mining behaviour, causes a waste of hash power reducing the security of the ledger. With respect to this work, our results are more general since we account for the block verification time which was regarded as negligible in [4–6]. We show that this parameter has a significant impact on selfish miners' expected reward.

Selfish mining has faced criticism in [17] where the author assumes that the attack becomes convenient when the selfish pool can mine two consecutive blocks while fair miners are still working on one block. However, this assumption over-looks the fact that the mining pool can announce its first block as soon as a fair miner announces a consolidated block. This gives the pool a chance to win the race for making its branch of the fork successful, even if it fails to mine the second block in time. However, the success of this strategy heavily relies on the network connectivity and the propagation time of the blocks announced by the pool.

The impact of selfish mining attacks on the Bitcoin network is extensively studied in [13]. The authors show that the impact of selfish mining on the network performance is noticeable and that the expected number of forks observed in the blockchain is higher than what would be expected if all miners were fair. This suggests that the selfish miner attack is still a major problem in blockchains.

Quantitative analysis has been widely employed in blockchain studies to gain insights into various aspects of blockchain systems such as performance, security, and scalability. Through quantitative analysis, researchers have been able to evaluate the behavior of blockchain networks, understand the dynamics of transaction processing, and identify potential vulnerabilities in the system. For instance, in [15] the authors propose a queueing model and apply it to study the performance of Bitcoin blockchain.

Building on [16], where PEPA process algebra was used to model and analyze the Verifier's Dilemma in the Ethereum Classic blockchain, we apply PEPA to model a public blockchain with PoW and investigate the Selfish Mining attack while taking into account the block verification time.

3   Background

In this section, we provide an overview of the selfish miner attack problem, as well as a brief introduction to the notation and important aspects of PEPA.

3.1   Selfish Mining

When two miners create a block with the same prior block, the chain splits into two branches, resulting in a *fork*. Miners can add valid blocks to either branch, mining on whichever they choose. However, to maintain a consistent chain, min-ers follow a globally-agreed upon sequence of transactions. The protocol requires miners to pick the longest chain and add blocks to it. If a miner's successful min-ing result is discarded from the network, they lose the potential reward.

Assuming a PoW-based blockchain network where the majority of miners follow the honest mining strategy, a colluding minority pool may adopt the selfish mining strategy. The key idea behind selfish mining is to compel honest miners to expend their resources on a branch of the blockchain that ultimately will not be included in the final chain.

In order to increase their revenue, selfish miners keep their mined blocks private, which results in the creation of a private branch causing the bifurcation of the blockchain. The pool gradually reveals blocks from the private branch, causing honest miners to switch to the newly revealed blocks and abandon the shorter public branch. This results in the invalidation of the honest miners' past efforts on the public branch and empowers the selfish pool to accumulate greater reward by incorporating a greater proportion of its blocks into the blockchain.

As the selfish mining pool has only a fraction of the total mining power, its private branch cannot remain longer than the public branch indefinitely. Therefore, when the public branch becomes longer, the selfish mining pool adopts it and starts mining on top of the current public head.

When the selfish miners discover a new block, instead of publishing it they keep it private and keep mining. If the selfish miners find a second block before the honest miners can reveal their first block, the selfish pool will have a longer private branch and will lead the public chain. Even if the honest miners reveal their first block at this point, the selfish pool will still receive a reward for publishing their two blocks on the private branch. However, since the selfish pool has less hash power, there is a high likelihood that the public branch will eventually become longer than the private branch.

When the selfish pool has a one-block lead and a honest miner discovers a block on the public branch, the selfish pool will immediately publish the private branch, triggering a race between the two branches. The selfish miners will extend their private branch while the honest miners will choose which branch to mine on based on notification propagation. At this point, there are three possible outcomes: the selfish pool successfully mines the second block on their first block, making their branch longer and earning revenue for both blocks; a honest miner builds a block after the pool's first block, allowing the pool to earn revenue from the first block and the honest miner to earn revenue from the second block; or the pool gets nothing if honest miners mine a block after their own block.

3.2   PEPA

We use the Performance Evaluation Process Algebra (PEPA) [7] to investigate the effects of Selfish mining on miners' behavior in public blockchains. PEPA is a compositional modeling language that is supported by a tool that can be applied to Eclipse, known as the PEPA Eclipse Plug-in. One of the main advantages of using PEPA is that it has an underlying stochastic process, which is a continuous time Markov process under certain assumptions.

In PEPA, a system specification comprises a group of active agents or components that work together through activities to accomplish the desired system behavior. The syntax of PEPA terms is determined by the following grammar:

$$S ::= (\alpha, r).S \mid S + S \mid A \qquad P ::= P \underset{L}{\bowtie} P \mid P/L \mid S$$

where S denotes a *sequential component*, while P denotes a *model component* which can be obtained as the cooperation of sequential terms. The meaning of the operators is the following: $(\alpha, r).S$ performs the activity (α, r) with action type α and rate r and subsequently behaves as S. $S_1 + S_2$ specifies a system which may behave either as S_1 or as S_2. The meaning of a constant A is given by a defining equation such as $A \stackrel{def}{=} P$ which gives the constant A the behaviour of the component P. The component P/L behaves as P except that any activity of type within the set L is relabelled with the *unknown type* τ. The cooperation combinator $\underset{L}{\bowtie}$ represents an interaction between two components, which is determined by the *cooperation set* L of action types. Activities with action types in the cooperation set L, called *shared* activities, require the synchronisation of the components. It is assumed that each component proceeds independently with the activities whose types do not occur in the cooperation set L. The duration of a shared activity is reflected by the rate of the slower participant. If in a component an activity has the *unknown rate* $\top$, then the rate of the shared activity will be that of the other component.

The stationary throughput of action a, denoted as X_a, is calculated as the sum of the stationary probabilities of all states where action a is enabled, each multiplied by the respective rate.

4   Analysis of the Selfish Mining Strategy

In this section, we present a PEPA model for a blockchain network with PoW consensus mechanism with fair miners and one selfish miner with arbitrary hash power. We assume that all miners have the same computational power γ, and verification is performed in an exponentially distributed time with mean β^{-1}.

4.1   PEPA Model for Networks of All Fair Miners

We first inspect the behaviour of miners who follow the blockchain consensus protocol by verifying all new blocks in the network. Let $M_1, \ldots, M_K$ be a network of K fair miners. The specification of a single fair (verifying) miner, say M_1, can be expressed in PEPA as

$$M_1 \stackrel{def}{=} (m_1, \gamma).M_1 + (m_2, \top).V_1 + \ldots + (m_K, \top).V_1$$

$$V_1 \stackrel{def}{=} (v_2, \beta).M_1 + \ldots + (v_K, \beta).M_1 + (m_2, \top).V_1 + \ldots + (m_K, \top).V_1$$

Miner M_1 mines a new block with action type m_1 and rate γ. Then, it returns to its initial state and it starts to mine another block. Whenever M_1 gets a block from the network through an activity $(m_j, \top)$ with $j \in \{2, \ldots, K\}$, then it starts the verification process and moves to state V_1.

We assume that all miners possess an equal proportion of computational power, and thus they perform verification in a synchronous manner. The block announced by a miner M_i is verified by all the other miners with rate β and action type v_i. It is evident that miners verify all blocks on the network, except for the block they have created themselves. During the verification phase, M_1

Table 1. PEPA model of a network with K fair miners

$$M_i \quad \stackrel{def}{=} \quad (m_i, \gamma).M_i + \sum_{j \neq i}(m_j, \top).V_i$$

$$V_i \quad \stackrel{def}{=} \quad \sum_{j \neq i}(v_j, \beta).M_i + \sum_{j \neq i}(m_j, \top).V_i$$

$$Network \quad \stackrel{def}{=} \quad (..((M_1 \underset{L \cup L_{12}}{\bowtie} M_2) \underset{L \cup L_3}{\bowtie}) \underset{L \cup L_4}{\bowtie} ...) \underset{L \cup L_K}{\bowtie} M_K$$

where $i, j \in \{1, \ldots, K\}$ and $L = \{m_1, \ldots, m_K\}, L_{12} = \{v_3, \ldots, v_K\},$
$L_j = \{v_1, \ldots, v_K\} \setminus \{v_j\}$ for $j \geq 3$

can still get new blocks from the rest of the network through an activity $(m_j, \top)$ with $j \in \{2, \ldots, K\}$.

The specification of a network composed by $K \geq 3$ fair miners is reported in Table 1. Notice that, according to the operational semantics of PEPA, if miner M_i announces a block, m_i is received by all miners except M_i. Thus, all miners moves to state V_j with $j \neq i$, while M_i is still mining. Now, according to the synchronization operation specified in Table 1, all miners in V_j synchronize on the intersection of all synchronizing sets that is exactly equal to $\{v_i\}$, hence once the verification is completed, they all simultaneously move to the mining phase due to action v_i, as required.

The derivation graph of the model in Table 1 is depicted in Fig. 1.

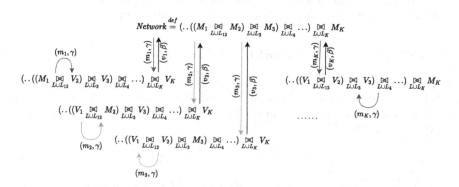

Fig. 1. Derivation graph of the model in Table 1

4.2   PEPA Model for Networks of Fair and Selfish Miners

Suppose the network contains a selfish mining pool that controls the amount of hash power $w\gamma$, and it uses action types m_{S_1} and m_{S_2} to mine blocks. The PEPA specification of a network with K honest miners and one selfish miner M_S, representing the mining pool, is presented in Table 2. The action type m_{S_1}

Table 2. PEPA model of a network with K fair miners and one selfish pool M_S

$$M_{F_i} \stackrel{def}{=} (m_{F_i}, \gamma).M_{F_i} + \sum_{j \neq i}(m_{F_j}, \top).V_i + (m_{S_2}, \top).V_{i_S}$$

$$V_i \stackrel{def}{=} \sum_{j \neq i}(v_j, \beta).M_{F_i} + \sum_{j \neq i}(m_{F_j}, \top).V_i$$

$$V_{i_S} \stackrel{def}{=} (v_S, \beta).M_{F_i} + (m_{S_2}, \top).V_{i_S}$$

$$M_S \stackrel{def}{=} (m_{S_1}, w\gamma).C + \sum_i (m_{F_i}, \top).V_S$$

$$C \stackrel{def}{=} (m_{S_2}, w\gamma).M_S + \sum_i (m_{F_i}, \top).V_S$$

$$V_S \stackrel{def}{=} \sum_i (v_i, \beta).M_S + \sum_{j \neq i}(m_{F_j}, \top).V_S$$

$$Network \stackrel{def}{=} M_S \underset{L \cup V}{\bowtie} (..((M_{F_1} \underset{L \cup V_{12}}{\bowtie} M_{F_2}) \underset{L \cup V_3}{\bowtie} M_{F_3})...) \underset{L \cup V_K}{\bowtie} M_{F_K})$$

where $\quad i, j \in \{1, \dots, K\}$ and $L = \{m_{S_2}, m_1, \dots, m_K\}, V = \{v_1, \dots, v_K\},$

$V_{12} = \{v_S, v_3, \dots, v_K\}, V_j = \{v_S, v_1, \dots, v_K\} \setminus \{v_j\}$ for $j \geq 3$

refers to the first block mined by the selfish pool, which is kept private, creating a separate branch, while m_{S_2} describes the second successful block mined by the selfish pool. Once the second block is produced, two blocks are revealed from the private branch to the public, causing the rest of the network to enter the verification phase and switch from the shorter public branch to the recently revealed blocks. This behavior is captured in the model by the fact that all nodes in the network synchronize on the action type v_S when the second block of the selfish pool is announced.

Observe that, for the sake of simplicity, in our model the selfish miner discloses two blocks from their private branch to the public. Nonetheless, the model can be extended to encompass a longer queue of blocks.

Figure 2 represents the derivation graph of the model in Table 2, while Fig. 3 represents its underlying Markov chain.

4.3 Lumped Model

The detailed model that represents the state of each miner is not scalable, as the total number of miners in a blockchain is typically very large. To address this issue, we propose using a representation based on aggregation through lumping [1,8,11,12] all fair miners into an environment.

Let K be the number of fair miners. The PEPA specification of the lumped model is represented in Table 3, its derivation graph is depicted in Fig. 4 and the underlying CTMC is reported in Fig. 5.

Component E_F represents the behaviour of K fair miners which mine new blocks with action type m_{E_F} and rate $K\gamma$. Hence, $K\gamma$ is the total hash power held by fair miners. When a new block is produced by one fair miner, the environment

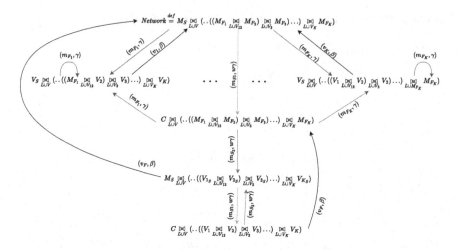

Fig. 2. Derivation graph of the model in Table 2

moves to state V_{E_F} where the miner that has proposed the block starts mining the next block, while the others verify the newly shared block. When the selfish pool reveals a block with action m_{S_2} then the environment moves to state V_{E_S} and verifies it with action v_S. The PoW race policy requires summing the rates of miners. However, the verification phase is not subject to the race policy and operates at the single miner rate β. Since all miners perform the same operations with equal computational power, the aggregated speed remains β. Additionally, since the time for solving PoW is independent and exponentially distributed by design, the aggregation of the rates is exact.

Meanwhile, the selfish miner M_S creates its first block with action type m_{S_1} and rate $w\gamma$. However, it keeps its mined block private, secretly creating a fork. The second block is created in the cheating phase C with action type m_{S_2} and rate $w\gamma$. At this point the selfish miner strategically reveals two blocks from the private branch to the public, causing the honest miners to switch to the recently revealed blocks and abandon the shorter public branch. Once the selfish miner gets a block from the network, it starts the verification process V_S. The verification of a block occurs with action v_{E_F} and rate β.

The *Lumped_Network* component is obtained as the cooperation of E_F and M_S over the set of actions L.

4.4   Performance Indices

We assume that the reward that miners gain is proportional to their *effective throughput*, which represents the proportion of their computational power that is used for mining after taking into account the necessary validation of new blocks. This effective throughput is lower than the originally invested hash power, as all miners in our model are fair and validate new blocks.

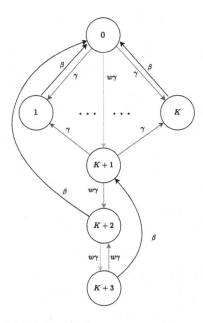

Fig. 3. Markov chain of the model underlying the derivation graph in Fig. 2

Table 3. Lumped PEPA model of a network with K fair miners aggregated in E_F and one selfish miner

E_F	$\stackrel{def}{=}$	$(m_{E_F}, K\gamma).V_{E_F} + (m_{S2}, \top).V_{E_S}$
V_{E_F}	$\stackrel{def}{=}$	$(v_{E_F}, \beta).E_F + (m_{E_F}, \gamma).V_{E_F}$
V_{E_S}	$\stackrel{def}{=}$	$(v_S, \beta).E_F + (m_{S2}, \top).V_{E_S}$
M_S	$\stackrel{def}{=}$	$(m_{S1}, w\gamma).C + (m_{E_F}, \top).V_S$
C	$\stackrel{def}{=}$	$(m_{S2}, w\gamma).M_S + (m_{E_F}, \top).V_S$
V_S	$\stackrel{def}{=}$	$(v_{E_F}, \beta).M_S + (m_{E_F}, \top).V_S$
$Lumped\_Network$	$\stackrel{def}{=}$	$E_F \underset{L}{\bowtie} M_S$
where		$L = \{m_{E_F}, m_{S2}, v_{E_F}\}$

Note that in our model two scenarios of successful selfish mining are captured. Action type m_{S1} refers to the production of the first block in the private branch. With certain probabilities p and $(1-p)$ the block is accepted or rejected by the network, respectively. Thus, for the calculation of the effective throughput we need to consider the throughput of m_{S1} being able to impose the block without producing the second, meaning $X_p = p(X_{m_{S1}} - X_{m_{S2}})$. Action type m_{S2} refers

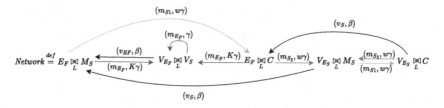

Fig. 4. Derivation graph of the model in Table 3

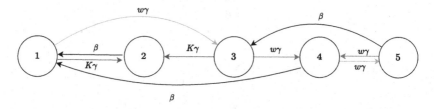

Fig. 5. Markov chain of the model underlying the derivation graph in Fig. 4

to the production of the second block, and it should be noted that whenever the selfish pool successfully propagates their private branch with two blocks, they receive a reward for both of them. Therefore, the total reward of the selfish pool is given by $X_S = 2X_{mS2} + X_p = (2 - p)X_{mS2} + pX_{mS1}$.

Every time the selfish pool successfully propagates its private branch with two blocks, one block mined by a fair miner in the network is discarded. Thus, the fair environment has an effective throughput given by

$$X_{EF} = X_{m_{EF}} - X_{mS2} - X_p = X_{m_{EF}} - (1 - p)X_{mS2} - pX_{mS1}.$$

Consequently, the effective throughput of one fair miner is given by

$$X_F = \frac{X_{EF}}{K} = \frac{X_{m_{EF}} - (1 - p)X_{mS2} - pX_{mS1}}{K}.$$

The effective throughput of the selfish pool per unit of hash power invested in the mining process can be obtained as:

$$X_S^N = \frac{X_S}{w} = \frac{(2 - p)X_{mS2} + pX_{mS1}}{w}.$$

Finally, we introduce the revenue of the selfish pool that is calculated as

$$R = \frac{X_S}{X_S + X_{EF}}.$$

As we may see, R measures the fraction of rewards obtained by a selfish pool.

Table 4. Parameters used for the case study

Parameter	Value
K	100 fair miners
γ	8.3×10^{-4} blocks/s
β	0.314 s^{-1}
w	100

5 Stationary Analysis and Numerical Evaluation

In this section, we give explicit expressions for the steady-state probabilities and reason about the conditions under which a selfish mining pool has a advantage over fair miners.

5.1 Steady-State Probabilities

The limited number of states of the lumped process allows us to derive the steady-state probability distribution explicitly. The symbolic expression of the steady-state probabilities of the Markov chain underlying the *Lumped_Network* depicted in Table 3 are:

$$\pi_1 = \frac{\beta(\beta(K+w)+\gamma w(2\,K+w))}{G}, \quad \pi_2 = \frac{\gamma K(\beta(K+2w)+\gamma w(2\,K+3w))}{G}$$

$$\pi_3 = \frac{\beta w(\beta+2\gamma w)}{G}, \quad \pi_4 = \frac{\gamma w^2(\beta+\gamma w)}{G}, \quad \pi_5 = \frac{\gamma^2 w^3}{G},$$

where the normalizing constant is

$$G = \gamma K^2(\beta+2\gamma w) + K(\beta+\gamma w)(\beta+3\gamma w) + 2w(\beta+\gamma w)^2.$$

For instance, if we use the parameters specified in Table 4, we obtain:

$\pi_1 \approx 0.475964$, $\pi_2 \approx 0.1946725$, $\pi_3 \approx 0.260505$, $\pi_4 \approx 0.0569526$, $\pi_5 \approx 0.011907$.

Notice that, from the steady-state probability distribution, we can compute the performance metrics described in Sect. 4.4.

5.2 The Convenience of Selfish Behaviors

It should be clear that it is not easy for a mining pool to understand if a selfish behaviour is profitable. Intuitively, if the probability to generate two consecutive blocks in the time in which fair miners consolidate a single block is negligible, then the selfish pool would have a lower revenue than fair miners. Moreover, it is also unclear how the verification time impacts on this considerations.

In this subsection, we try to unveil some of the aspects that play a role in driving the decision of a rational mining pool about behaving in a selfish manner.

To make a fair comparison, let v be the fraction of hash power controlled by the selfish mining pool, i.e., $v = w/(w + K)$. We must assume that $v < 0.5$, otherwise the blockchain would be vulnerable to the 50% attack and hence would not be considered secure for more severe reasons than the selfish miner attack. In Figs. 6a, 6c, 6e, we compare the effective throughput of a single fair miner with the normalized effective throughput of a selfish miner for $p = 0.2$, $p = 0.5$ and $p = 0.8$. The other network parameters are those of Table 4. We notice that when the mining pool is able to quickly propagate its blocks as soon as a fair block is announced, the fraction of hash power that it has to control to overtake fair miners' profit becomes smaller.

Figures 6b, 6d, 6f show the revenue of the selfish pool as function of the fraction of controlled hash power. This is compared with the revenue it would obtain in a network where everyone (including the pool itself) is fair, i.e., when its revenue is equal to the fraction of controlled hash power. This experiments are coherent with the ones in [5,13] where the authors do not consider the impact of the verification times. This is somehow expected since, in our case, $\beta >> \gamma$.

It is useful now to investigate the impact of the verification time on the point in which the selfish mining pool has an advantage over the fair miners. Formally, let w^* be the minimum positive solution in w of the equation $X_F = X_S^N$ and let $v^* = w^*/(w^* + K)$, i.e., the minimum fraction of hash power that must be controlled by the selfish pool to take advantage by the attack.

Figure 7 shows v^* as function of β. This analysis shows that slower verification times drastically reduce the demand of hash power for the greedy miners. As a consequence, blockchains with smart contracts that require longer block verification times are even more exposed to the selfish miner attack than Bitcoin, where β is very high.

6   Conclusion

In conclusion, our study provides a quantitative analysis of the selfish miner attack in blockchain systems based on a stochastic model expressed with the Performance Evaluation Process Algebra. We have shown that the verification time of the transactions affects the rationality of the attacker, and we have derived the conditions under which the attack becomes convenient for selfish miners. This work contributes to the understanding of the selfish miner attack and can help in the development of more robust and efficient blockchain systems. Further research can explore the extension of our model to consider more complex scenarios and the application of our findings in real-world blockchain systems.

Acknowledgements. This work is partially supported by the Project NiRvAna: Noninterference and Reversibility Analysis in Private Blockchains (20202FCJMH) funded by MUR Progetti di Ricerca di Rilevante Interesse Nazionale (PRIN 2020), and by the project SERICS (PE00000014) under the

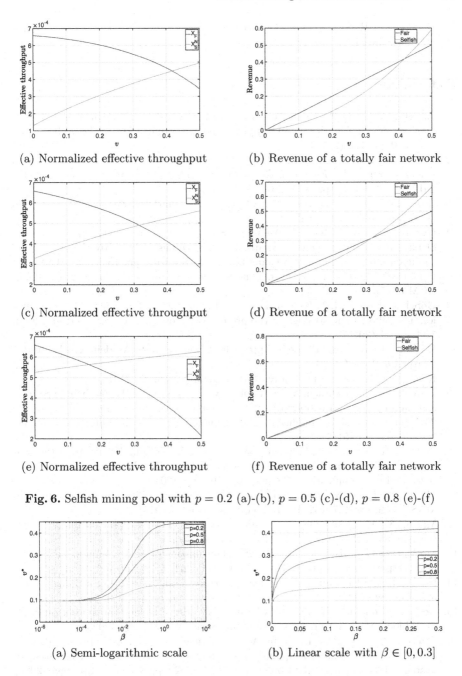

Fig. 6. Selfish mining pool with $p = 0.2$ (a)-(b), $p = 0.5$ (c)-(d), $p = 0.8$ (e)-(f)

Fig. 7. How different β affects the minimum fraction of selfish miners at which they overtake the revenue with the different probability

MUR National Recovery and Resilience Plan funded by the European Union - NextGenerationEU.

References

1. Alzetta, G., Marin, A., Piazza, C., Rossi, S.: Lumping-based equivalences in Markovian automata: Algorithms and applications to product-form analyses. Inf. Comput. **260**, 99–125 (2018)
2. Barber, S., Boyen, X., Shi, E., Uzun, E.: Bitter to better-how to make bitcoin a better currency. In: Financial Cryptography and Data Security Conference, FC 2012, pp. 399–414. Springer (2012)
3. Buterin, V., et al.: Ethereum: a next-generation smart contract and decentralized application platform (2014)
4. Carlsten, M., Kalodner, H., Weinberg, S.M., Narayanan, A.: On the instability of bitcoin without the block reward. In: Proceedings of the 2016 ACM SIGSAC Conference on Computer and Communications Security, pp. 154–167 (2016)
5. Eyal, I., Sirer, E.G.: Majority is not enough: Bitcoin mining is vulnerable. Commun. ACM **61**(7), 95–102 (2018)
6. Göbel, J., Keeler, H.P., Krzesinski, A.E., Taylor, P.G.: Bitcoin blockchain dynamics: The selfish-mine strategy in the presence of propagation delay. Perform. Eval. **104**, 23–41 (2016)
7. Hillston, J.: A Compositional Approach to Performance Modelling. Cambridge University Press (1996)
8. Kemeny, J.G., Snell, J.L.: Finite Markov Chains. Springer (1976)
9. Lewenberg, Y., Bachrach, Y., Sompolinsky, Y., Zohar, A., Rosenschein, J.S.: Bitcoin mining pools: a cooperative game theoretic analysis. In: Proceedings of the 2015 International Conference on Autonomous Agents and Multiagent Systems, pp. 919–927 (2015)
10. Luu, L., Teutsch, J., Kulkarni, R., Saxena, P.: Demystifying incentives in the consensus computer. In: Proceedings of the 22nd ACM SIGSAC Conference on Computer and Communications Security, pp. 706–719 (2015)
11. Marin, A., Rossi, S.: On the relations between lumpability and reversibility. In: MASCOTS, pp. 427–432. IEEE Computer Society (2014)
12. Marin, A., Rossi, S.: On the relations between Markov chain lumpability and reversibility. Acta Informatica **54**(5), 447–485 (2017)
13. Motlagh, S.G., Mišić, J., Mišić, V.B.: The impact of selfish mining on bitcoin network performance. IEEE Trans. Netw. Sci. Eng. **8**(1), 724–735 (2021)
14. Nakamoto, S.: Bitcoin: a peer-to-peer electronic cash system. Decentralized Business Review (2008)
15. Rossi, S., Malakhov, I., Marin, A.: Analysis of the confirmation time in proof-of-work blockchains. Futur. Gener. Comput. Syst. **147**, 275–291 (2023)
16. Smuseva, D., Malakhov, I., Marin, A., van Moorsel, A., Rossi, S.: Verifier's dilemma in ethereum blockchain: A quantitative analysis. In: Quantitative Evaluation of Systems: 19th International Conference, QEST 2022, pp. 317–336. Springer (2022)
17. Wright, C.S.: The fallacy of the selfish miner in bitcoin: an economic critique. Available at SSRN: https://ssrn.com/abstract=3151923 (2018)

Improving Sample Efficiency in Evolutionary RL Using Off-Policy Ranking

S. R. Eshwar$^{(\boxtimes)}$ ⓘ, Shishir Kolathaya ⓘ, and Gugan Thoppe ⓘ

Indian Institute of Science, Bangalore, India
{eshwarsr,shishirk,gthoppe}@iisc.ac.in

Abstract. Evolution Strategy (ES) is a potent black-box optimization technique based on natural evolution. A key step in each ES iteration is the ranking of candidate solutions based on some fitness score. In the Reinforcement Learning (RL) context, this step entails evaluating several policies. Presently, this evaluation is done via on-policy approaches: each policy's score is estimated by interacting several times with the environment using that policy. Such ideas lead to wasteful interactions since, once the ranking is done, only the data associated with the top-ranked policies are used for subsequent learning. To improve sample efficiency, we introduce a novel off-policy ranking approach using a local approximation for the fitness function. We demonstrate our idea for two leading ES methods: Augmented Random Search (ARS) and Trust Region Evolution Strategy (TRES). MuJoCo simulations show that, compared to the original methods, our off-policy variants have similar running times for reaching reward thresholds but need only around 70% as much data on average. In fact, in some tasks like HalfCheetah-v3 and Ant-v3, we need just 50% as much data. Notably, our method supports extensive parallelization, enabling our ES variants to be significantly faster than popular non-ES RL methods like TRPO, PPO, and SAC.

Keywords: Reinforcement learning · Evolutionary strategies · Off-policy ranking · ARS · TRES

1 Introduction

In optimization, features of the objective function such as linearity, convexity, or differentiability are often non-existent, unknown, or impossible to detect. An

ESR was supported by the Prime Minister's Research Fellowship (PMRF). SK was supported by the SERB Core Research Grant CRG/2021/008115. GT was supported in part by DST-SERB's Core Research Grant CRG/2021/00833, in part by IISc Start-up grants SG/MHRD-19-0054 and SR/MHRD-19-0040, and in part by the "Pratiksha Trust Young Investigator" award.

E. Kalyvianaki and M. Paolieri (Eds.): VALUETOOLS 2023, LNICST 539, pp. 33–50, 2024.
https://doi.org/10.1007/978-3-031-48885-6_3

Evolution Strategy (ES) [10], due to its derivative-free nature, is a go-to alternative in such scenarios. [17] introduced the first competitive ES method in Reinforcement Learning (RL). However, that technique's efficacy hinges on several intricate concepts and the application of neural networks to parameterize policies. These intricacies encompass converting rewards into rankings and utilizing these rankings for computing updates, partitioning the action space to promote exploration, and adopting policies parameterized by neural networks with virtual batch normalization.

Fortunately, two recent ES methods—the Augmented Random Search (ARS) [13] and Trust Region Evolution Strategy (TRES) [12]—have shown that (deterministic) linear policies and a suitably modified basic random search are often effective enough. In that, they can help to cut down the running times by an order of magnitude. Our work introduces novel off-policy adaptations of ARS and TRES. These adaptations maintain similar computation times as the original techniques but require notably less data (sometimes as little as 50%).

The formal motivation for our work is to explore ES algorithms in RL that minimize agent-environment interactions. Clearly, this would be of significance in practical RL. A vital example is robotics, where collecting samples is very expensive since the process involves active calibration, maintenance, and safety checks for every component, and overlooking these can result in unsafe behaviours.

We now describe how existing ES methods for RL operate and also point out the key step at which they are sample-inefficient. Recall that, in each iteration, a generic ES method i.) obtains a bunch of candidate solutions from some sampling distribution, ii.) ranks them using some fitness score based on the objective function, and iii.) uses the top-ranked ones to update the sampling distribution for use in the next iteration. In the context of RL, a candidate solution is a specific policy, while its fitness is the associated value function. Existing techniques such as ARS and TRES use an on-policy approach to find this fitness score: interact with the environment using every policy whose score needs to be estimated. Since multiple policies need to be ranked in each iteration, current ES approaches end up with significantly high interactions. Notably, most of this data is discarded in each iteration except those related to the top-ranked policies.

Our proposed idea to improve sample efficiency is to replace the above wasteful ranking approach with an off-policy alternative. Our new approach involves two key ideas: the fitness function choice, and the use of a kernel approximation to estimate the same. Their details are as follows.

1. **Fitness Function**: Instead of using the value function $\eta(\tilde{\pi})$ of a candidate policy $\tilde{\pi}$ as its fitness score, we use its approximation $L_\pi(\tilde{\pi})$ defined in terms of a different policy π called the behavior policy [21, (6)]. Indeed, any policy ranking based on a value-function approximation is sub-optimal. However, it is also the key factor enabling our off-policy ranking. The data generated by the *single* policy π can now be used to rank all the candidate policies!
2. **Kernel Approximation**: $L_\pi(\tilde{\pi})$ is estimated in [21] via importance sampling (see (40) in ibid). This idea works only when both π and $\tilde{\pi}$ are stochastic. However, ARS's sample efficiency crucially relies on the candidate policies

being deterministic. To circumvent this deterministic-stochastic gap, we propose to alternatively smooth the deterministic policies using a suitable kernel function. This approach is loosely inspired from [7,8], which extends ideas from discrete contextual bandit settings to the continuous case.

Key Contributions: The main highlights of this work are as follows.

1. We propose novel variants of ARS and TRES; see Algorithms 1 and [3, Algorithm A1]. Their main feature is off-policy ranking: data from one behavior policy is used to identify the best among multiple candidate policies. We emphasize that this is the first usage of off-policy ranking in any ES method. Moreover, our idea is extremely simple to implement and directly applies to deterministic policies. Also, while we use this idea for ARS and TRES, it is extendable to other ES methods.
2. Our simulations on MuJoCo tasks (Sect. 4) show that our variants reach reward thresholds in running times comparable to the original ARS and TRES. Notably, we often need just 50–80% as much data. This is significant when enivornmental interactions are hard or expensive, e.g., robotics.
3. We also do sensitivity to seed and hyperparameter tests similar to [13]. Our results are similar in spirit to what was obtained in ibid. That is, the median trajectory crosses the reward threshold in most environments, confirming that our algorithm is robust to seed and hyperparameter choices. This contrasts behaviors of non-ES methods, e.g., DDPG [11], TRPO [18], PPO [19].

2   Preliminaries

Here, we describe our RL setup and provide an overview of the original ARS and TRES algorithms.

2.1   RL Setup and Important Definitions

The primary goal in RL is to estimate a control policy that empowers an agent to effectively perform a task involving sequential decision making. Formally, our setup is that of an MDP. At each time-step t, the agent notes the current state of its environment as $s_t \in \mathcal{S}$ (state space), and then executes an action $a_t \in \mathcal{A}$ (action space) sampled from its current policy $(\pi_t(a|s_t))_{a \in \mathcal{A}}$ (which is a distribution). The environment then transitions to a new state $s_{t+1} \sim \mathbb{P}(s'|s, a)$, where $\mathbb{P}$ is the transition function of the MDP, and the agent receives an associated scalar reward $r_t = r(s_t, a_t)$. The aforementioned goal then is to find a policy that has the largest average reward, i.e., one that solves

$$\max_{\pi} \eta(\pi), \tag{1}$$

where

$$\eta(\pi) := \lim_{H \to \infty} \frac{1}{H} \mathbb{E}_{\tau \sim P_\pi(\tau)} \left[\hat{\eta}(\pi) \right].$$

In the above relation, $\hat{\eta}(\pi) \equiv \hat{\eta}_H(\pi, \tau) = \sum_{t=0}^{H-1} r(s_t, a_t)$ and $P_\pi(\tau)$ is the likelihood of a trajectory $\tau = \{(s_0, a_0, r_0), (s_1, a_1, r_1), \ldots\}$ under the policy π.

Note that the sequence of states observed under a fixed policy π forms a Markov chain. If this chain has a stationary distribution d_π and

$$d_\pi(s) = \lim_{H \to \infty} \frac{1}{H} \sum_{t=0}^{H-1} \mathbb{P}_{\tau \sim P_\pi(\tau)}(s_t = s), \tag{2}$$

then $\eta(\pi) = \mathbb{E}_{s \sim d_\pi, a \sim \pi}[r(s, a)]$.

In our later discussions, we will also be using some terms related to the value function such as the state-bias function (V_π), action-bias function (Q_π), and the advantage function (A_π). These are given by

$$V_\pi(s) := \mathbb{E}_{\tau \sim P_\pi(\tau)} \left[\sum_{t=0}^{\infty} (r(s_t, a_t) - \eta(\pi)) | s_0 = s \right]$$

$$Q_\pi(s, a) := \mathbb{E}_{\tau \sim P_\pi(\tau)} \left[\sum_{t=0}^{\infty} (r(s_t, a_t) - \eta(\pi)) | s_0 = s, a_0 = a \right]$$

and $A_\pi(s, a) := Q_\pi(s, a) - V_\pi(s)$, respectively.

2.2   Review of ARS and TRES

ARS belongs to a family of iterative black-box optimization methods called random search [14]. Basic Random Search (BRS) is the simplest member of this family and is also where the origins of ARS lie. For ease of exposition, we first explain BRS's approach to solving (1). Throughout this subsection, we restrict our attention to finite-horizon MDPs where the search space is some parameterized family of policies. Note that this is often the case in practical RL and is also what we deal with in our MuJoCo simulations.

For the above setup, by fixing a large H, the problem in (1) translates to

$$\max_\theta \mathbb{E}_\tau[\hat{\eta}(\pi_\theta)] \equiv \max_\theta \mathbb{E}_\tau[\hat{\eta}_H(\pi_\theta, \tau)]. \tag{3}$$

In general, this objective function need not be smooth. To circumvent this issue, BRS looks at its smooth variant and then uses the idea of a stochastic gradient ascent. Specifically, the alternative objective considered is $\mathbb{E}_\delta \mathbb{E}_\tau[\hat{\eta}(\pi_{\theta+\nu\delta})]$, where ν is a suitably fixed scalar, and δ is a random perturbation made up of i.i.d. standard Gaussian entries. Further, in each iteration, the gradient of this function is estimated via a finite-difference method. That is, N random directions $\delta_1, \ldots, \delta_N$ are first generated in the parameter space, $\hat{\eta}(\pi_{\theta+\nu\delta_k})$ and $\hat{\eta}(\pi_{\theta-\nu\delta_k})$ are then estimated by interacting with the environment using $\pi_{\theta+\nu\delta_k}$ and $\pi_{\theta-\nu\delta_k}$ for each k, and finally $\frac{1}{N} \sum_{k=1}^{N} [\hat{\eta}(\pi_{\theta+\nu\delta_k}) - \hat{\eta}(\pi_{\theta-\nu\delta_k})] \delta_k$ is used as a proxy for the gradient at θ. BRS's update rule, thus, has the form $\theta_{j+1} = \theta_j + \frac{\alpha}{N} \sum_{k=1}^{N} [\hat{\eta}(\pi_{\theta_j+\nu\delta_k}) - \hat{\eta}(\pi_{\theta_j-\nu\delta_k})] \delta_k$ for some parameter $\alpha > 0$.

Mania et al. [13] developed ARS by making the following changes to BRS. To begin with, they restricted the search space to a class of deterministic and linearly parameterized policies: a policy now is represented by a matrix M and the vector Ms denotes the deterministic action to be taken at state s under that policy. Further, three modifications were made to the update rule of BRS. The first was to scale the gradient estimate by the standard deviation of the $\hat{\eta}$ values; this yields the ARS-V1 algorithm. The second was to normalize the states, given as input to the policies, so that all state vector components are given equal importance; this yields ARS-V2. The final modification was to pick some $b < N$ and use only the b best-performing search directions for estimating the gradient in each iteration. The first and the third step yield the ARS-V1t algorithm, while the combination of all three gives ARS-V2t. The ARS-V2t variant is of most interest to us and its update rule has the form $M_{j+1} = M_j + \frac{\alpha}{b\sigma_R} \sum_{k=1}^{b} [\hat{\eta}(\pi_{j,(k),+}) - \hat{\eta}(\pi_{j,(k),-})]\delta_{(k)}$, where σ_R is the standard deviation of the $2b$ $\hat{\eta}$ values, $\delta_{(k)}$ denotes the k-th largest direction decided based on the value of $\max\{\hat{\eta}(\pi_{j,k,+}), \hat{\eta}(\pi_{j,k,-})\}$ for different k choices, and $\pi_{j,k,+}(s) = (M_j + \nu\delta_k)\mathrm{diag}(\Sigma_j)^{-1/2}(s - \mu_j)$ and $\pi_{j,k,-}(s) = (M_j - \nu\delta_k)\mathrm{diag}(\Sigma_j)^{-1/2}(s - \mu_j)$ with μ_j and Σ_j being the mean and covariance of the $2bHj$ states encountered from the start of the training.

The reason for focusing on ARS-V2t is that, in MuJoCo tasks, it typically outperforms the other ARS variants and also the previous state-of-the-art approaches such as TRPO [18], PPO [19], DDPG [11], the ES method from [17], and the Natural Gradient method from [16]. This shows that normalization of states, and then ranking and only picking the best directions for updating parameters often helps in improving the sample efficiency.

Nevertheless, in each iteration, ARS uses an on-policy technique to estimate $\hat{\eta}(\pi_{j,k,+})$ and $\hat{\eta}(\pi_{j,k,-})$ for each k so that the b best-performing directions can be identified. Because of this, we claim that ARS still does more interactions with the environment than what is needed. Also, in each iteration, it discards data that do not correspond to the top-ranked policies.

TRES [12] is another state-of-the-art ES method that has been shown to outperform methods such as TRPO, PPO, and the ES method from [17]. While broadly similar, the major differences between TRES and ARS is in the choice of the objective function. Instead of using a simple sum of rewards on a single trajectory as in (3), TRES uses a novel local approximation ([12, (25)]) to the value function that matches the latter up to the first-order. The main advantage of this alternative choice is that it guarantees monotonic improvement in successive policy estimates. Also, this new objective function enables TRES to use the same data from top performing directions to update the parameters multiple times in the same iteration. This is not possible with the objective function used in ARS, and is claimed to be core reason for improving sample efficiency. A detailed review of TRES is given in [3, Appendix B].

Algorithm 1 Off-policy ARS

1: **Setup:** State space $\mathbb{R}^n$, Action Space $\mathbb{R}^p$
2: **Hyperparameters:** step-size α, number of directions sampled per iteration N, standard deviation of the exploration noise ν, number of top-performing directions to use b, bandwidth to use for kernel approximation h, number of behaviour policy trajectories to run n_b
3: **Initialize:** $M_0 = \mathbf{0} \in \mathbb{R}^{p \times n}$, $\mu_0 = \mathbf{0} \in \mathbb{R}^n$, $\Sigma_0 = \mathbf{I}_n \in \mathbb{R}^{n \times n}$ (identity matrix), $j = 0$
4: **while** ending condition not satisfied **do**
5:     Sample $\delta_1, \delta_2, \ldots, \delta_N$ in $\mathbb{R}^{p \times n}$ with i.i.d. Standard Gaussian entries
6:     Run n_b trajectories using policy parameterized by M_j, resulting in N_d interactions
7:     Sort the directions δ_k based on $f_{\pi_j}(\delta_k, h)$ scores (using (7)), denote by $\delta_{(k)}$ the k-th largest direction, and by $\pi_{j,(k),+}$ and $\pi_{j,(k),-}$ the corresponding policies
8:     Collect $2b$ rollouts of horizon H and their corresponding return $(\hat{\eta}(\cdot))$ using the $2b$ policies of the b best direction

$$\pi_{j,(k),+}(s) = (M_j + \nu\delta_{(k)})\text{diag}(\Sigma_j)^{-1/2}(s - \mu_j)$$

$$\pi_{j,(k),-}(s) = (M_j - \nu\delta_{(k)})\text{diag}(\Sigma_j)^{-1/2}(s - \mu_j)$$

9:     Make the update step:

$$M_{j+1} = M_j + \frac{\alpha}{b\sigma_R}\sum_{k=1}^{b}[\hat{\eta}(\pi_{j,(k),+}) - \hat{\eta}(\pi_{j,(k),-})]\delta_{(k)},$$

where σ_R is the standard deviation of $2b$ returns used in the update step.
10:    Set μ_{j+1}, Σ_{j+1} to be the mean and covariance of the $2bH(j+1)$ states encountered since the start of the training
11:    $j \leftarrow j + 1$
12: **end while**

---

3   Off-Policy ARS and TRES

Here, we provide a detailed description of our proposed approach to improve upon the wasteful on-policy ranking step in ARS. We use the same idea also to improve upon TRES, but leave these details to [3, Appendix C].

Intuitively, in each iteration of our ARS variant, we plan to identify a suitable deterministic policy, interact with the environment using just this *single* policy, and then use the resultant data to rank the $2N$ deterministic policies $\{\pi_{j,k,+}, \pi_{j,k,-} : 1 \leq k \leq N\}$. As a first step, we come up with a way to approximate the value function of a deterministic policy $\tilde{\pi}$ in terms of another deterministic policy π. We focus on deterministic policies here since ARS's performance crucially depends on this determinism.

If π and $\tilde{\pi}$ were stochastic in nature, then such an approximation has already been given in [21], which itself is inspired from similar estimates given in [6] and [18]. We now discuss the derivation of this approximation.

Consider the average reward RL setup described in Sect. 2.1. Suppose that, for every stationary policy π, the induced Markov chain is irreducible and aperiodic and, hence, has a stationary distribution d_π satisfying (2). In this framework, [21, Lemma 1] showed that the value functions of the two stochastic policies π and $\tilde{\pi}$ satisfy

$$\eta(\tilde{\pi}) = \eta(\pi) + \mathbb{E}_{s \sim d_{\tilde{\pi}}, a \sim \tilde{\pi}} [A_\pi(s, a)]. \tag{4}$$

Given this relation, a natural question to ask is whether $\eta(\tilde{\pi})$ can be estimated using just the data collected by interacting with the environment using π. The answer is no, mainly because the expectation on the RHS is with respect to the states being drawn from $d_{\tilde{\pi}}$. In general, this distribution is unknown a priori and is also hard to estimate unless you interact with the environment with $\tilde{\pi}$ itself.

Inspired by [6] and [18], [21] proposed using

$$L_\pi(\tilde{\pi}) := \eta(\pi) + \mathbb{E}_{s \sim d_\pi, a \sim \tilde{\pi}} [A_\pi(s, a)] \tag{5}$$

as a proxy for the RHS in (4) to overcome the above issue. Two notable benefits arise from the aforementioned approximation. The first is that $L_\pi(\tilde{\pi})$, since it uses d_π instead of $d_{\tilde{\pi}}$, can be estimated from only environmental interactions involving π. Second, and importantly, [21, Lemmas 2, 3] showed that $|L_\pi(\tilde{\pi}) - \eta(\tilde{\pi})|$ is bounded by the total variation distance between π and $\tilde{\pi}$. Thus, when π and $\tilde{\pi}$ are sufficiently close, an estimate for $L_\pi(\tilde{\pi})$ is also one for $\eta(\tilde{\pi})$. Hence, $L_\pi(\tilde{\pi})$ paves the way for estimating $\eta(\tilde{\pi})$ in an off-policy fashion, i.e., using data from a different policy π. Henceforth, we refer to the policy chosen for interaction (e.g., π above) as the behavior policy and the one whose value needs to be estimated (e.g., $\tilde{\pi}$ above) as the target policy.

We now extend the above idea to the case with deterministic policies, which we emphasize is one of our main contributions. While the idea may look simple on paper, the actual extension is not at all straightforward. The key issue is that, in the case of stochastic policies, the idea of importance sampling and, in particular, the relation

$\mathbb{E}_{s \sim d_\pi, a \sim \tilde{\pi}} [A_\pi(s, a)] = \mathbb{E}_{s \sim d_\pi, a \sim \pi} \left[\frac{\tilde{\pi}(a|s)}{\pi(a|s)} A_\pi(s, a) \right]$ is used for estimating the second term in (5). However, for deterministic policies, the ratio $\tilde{\pi}(a|s)/\pi(a|s)$ will typically be 0, which means the estimate for the second term will also almost always be zero. Hence, this importance sampling idea for estimating $L_\pi(\tilde{\pi})$ fails for deterministic policies.

The alternative we propose is to modify the definition of $L_\pi(\tilde{\pi})$ so that it becomes useful even for deterministic policies. Specifically, we redefine $L_\pi(\tilde{\pi})$ as

$$L_\pi(\tilde{\pi}) = \eta(\pi) + \mathbb{E}_{s \sim d_\pi, a \sim \pi} \left[\frac{K_h(\|a - \tilde{\pi}(s)\|)}{K_h(\|a - \pi(s)\|)} A_\pi(s, a) \right], \tag{6}$$

where $K_h(u) = h^{-1} K(u/h)$ and $K : \mathbb{R} \to \mathbb{R}$ denotes a suitably chosen kernel function satisfying $\int K(u) du = 1$ and $\int u K(u) du = 0$. This approach is loosely inspired from [7,8] which look at extending policy evaluation and control algorithms from discrete contextual bandit settings to the continuous case.

While there are multiple choices for K, we use $K(u) = e^{-u^2}$ in this work. Substituting this definition in (6) gives

Table 1. Comparison of median number of interactions for ARS, TRES, OP-ARS and OP-TRES on MuJoCo locomotion tasks to achieve prescribed reward thresholds (Th). Intx represents the number of interactions in order of 10^3. % column represents the percentage of data required by our method compared to the original method. The * in Ant-v3 signifies the interleaving of on-policy evaluations. The # signifies 16 seeds were used instead of 8 in Walker2d environment for ARS and OP-ARS. We use the following abbreviations in the table below: SW = Swimmer, HO = Hopper, HC = HalfCheetah, WA = Walker2d, AN = Ant, HU = Humanoid

Env	Th	ARS			OP-ARS		TRES			OP-TRES	
		N	b	Intx	Intx	%	N	b	Intx	Intx	%
SW	325	2	1	520 (580)	**440**	85	4	2	800 (560)	800	100
HO	3120	8	4	883 (1098)	**765**	86	–	–	–	–	–
HC	3430	32	4	4480 (3840)	2400	53	16	8	2720 (2400)	**1275**	46
WA#	4390	40	30	18802 (23151)	**14414**	76	–	–	–	–	–
AN	3580	60	20	10492 (17711)	15071*	143	40	20	10849 (10409)	**6165**	56
HU	6000	350	230	40852 (23594)	**14260**	35	–	–	–	–	–

$$L_\pi(\tilde{\pi}) = \eta(\pi) + \mathbb{E}_{s \sim d_\pi}\left[e^{-\|\pi(s)-\tilde{\pi}(s)\|^2/h^2} A_\pi(s, \pi(s))\right]$$

The reason for the above choice of K is that it performs quite well in simulations and also provides a clean intuitive explanation for $L_\pi(\tilde{\pi})$. That is, $L_\pi(\tilde{\pi})$ assigns a higher value to a policy $\tilde{\pi}$ if it takes actions similar to π at all those states s where $A_\pi(s, \pi(s))$ is large. In summary, $L_\pi(\tilde{\pi})$ given above provides us with the desired expression to approximate the value function of a deterministic target policy with only the data from a deterministic behavior policy.

We now discuss incorporating this expression in ARS to improve its sample efficiency. In particular, we now show how we can rank the $2N$ policies $\{\pi_{j,k,+}, \pi_{j,k,-}\}$, generated randomly in each iteration of ARS, in an off-policy fashion. The first thing we need to decide is the choice of the behavior policy for interacting with the environment. Recall from the discussion below (5) that $|\eta(\tilde{\pi}) - L_\pi(\tilde{\pi})|$ is small when π and $\tilde{\pi}$ are sufficiently close. Now, since the policy parameterized by M_j is close to each of the $2N$ policies specified above, it is the natural choice for the behavior policy and, indeed, this is what we use.

In summary, our ranking in each iteration works as follows:

1. Interact with the environment using the behavior policy $\pi_j \equiv \pi_{M_j}$ on n_b number of trajectories. Each trajectory here is presumed to have H many time steps (or less in case of premature termination). Suppose these interactions result in N_d (s_t, a_t, r_t, s_{t+1}) transitions overall.
2. Estimate $Q_{\pi_j}(s_t, a_t)$, $0 \le t \le N_d - 1$, using the definition given in Sect. 2.1.

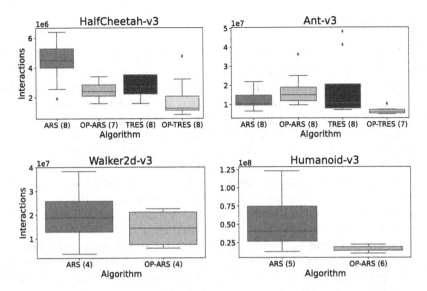

Fig. 1. Box plots of number of interactions required to reach the reward threshold in ARS, TRES, OP-ARS and OP-TRES. The number next to the algorithm's name represents the number of seeds in which the threshold was reached.

3. Estimate

$$f_{\pi_j}(\delta_k, h) = \mathbb{E}[e^{-\|\nu\delta_k s\|^2/h^2} Q_{\pi_j}(s, a)] \approx \frac{1}{N_d} \sum_{t=0}^{N_d-1} [e^{-\|\nu\delta_k s\|^2/h^2} Q_{\pi_j}(s_t, a_t)]$$

(7)

for each $1 \leq k \leq N$. Note that $f_{\pi_j}(\delta_k, h)$ is a proxy for the expression in (6). In that, it ignores all the constant terms: those that depend only on the behavior policy π_j.

4. Use the above estimates to rank $\{\pi_{j,k,+}, \pi_{j,k,-}\}$.

Once the b best–performing directions are identified, the rest of our ARS variant more or less proceeds as the original. That is, we come up with better estimates of the value-functions of these top policies in an on-policy fashion and improve upon M_j along the lines discussed in Sect. 2.2. The complete details are given in Algorithm 1. A detailed section discussing the differences in the original ARS from our off-policy variant is given in Appendix A.

We end our discussion here by pointing out that the original ARS used $2N$ interaction trajectories, each of length roughly H, in each iteration. In our variant, we only need $2b + n_b$ many trajectories. When $b < N$, this difference is what leads to the significant reduction in interactions seen in our simulations.

4   Experiments

We compare ARS and TRES with our proposed off-policy variants on benchmark MuJoCo [20] tasks available in OpenAI gym [1]. We show that these variants (henceforth, called OP-ARS and OP-TRES) i.) take significantly less number of interactions to reach rewards thresholds, ii.) are robust to random seeds and hyperparameter choices, and iii.) have very low running times. Separately, in Appendix C, we show that OP-ARS outperforms ARS even on Linear Quadratic Regulator. Finally, we discuss some limitations of our proposed approach.

Expt. 1 (Sample efficiency): Because an ES method is stochastic, the intermediate policies that are learned will be different on each run. Hence, to have a robust comparison, we initiate all random number generators and OpenAI gym environments as a function of a single seed, and then study the performance of our algorithms for eight uniformly random seeds. Further, after every ten iterations of our Algorithm, we compute the value function of the current policy (e.g., the policy parameterized by M_j in Algorithm 1) by averaging the total reward obtained over 100 trajectories.

The sample complexity of our ES methods on each of the eight seeds is the first time the value function of the learned policy is above a certain reward threshold. We use the same thresholds that were used in [13]. The comparison of sample complexity estimates for ARS, TRES, OP-ARS, and OP-TRES is given in Table 1, Figs. 1, and 2.

In Table 1, the 'Env' and 'Th' columns represent the environment names and its corresponding thresholds. The median of sample complexity estimates is provided under the column titled 'Intx' for different N and b choices. In particular, the values in round brackets are for the case where b random directions are chosen and data from all the b directions is used for updating the policy parameter. The ones outside are for the case where N directions are chosen and data from only the top performing b directions is used for parameter update. Finally, the numbers under % denote the percentage of data required by OP-ARS (resp. OP-TRES) to reach the threshold compared to ARS (resp. TRES). Clearly, the median estimates (see bold text in Table 1) for our variants are significantly lower than those of ARS and TRES.

In Table 1, observe that there are two scenarios: either sampling only b directions and using all of them for parameter update is better (see HalfCheetah and Humanoid in ARS, and HalfCheetah and Ant in TRES) or sampling N directions and then picking the top-performing b directions is better (e.g., Swimmer, Hopper, Walker2d, and Ant in ARS). The former scenario corresponds to the case when the overhead of evaluating the additional $N - b$ directions is costlier than the benefit of exploring more directions and using the best performing ones. In both scenarios, by circumventing this overhead issue via off-policy ranking, OP-ARS and OP-TRES significantly cuts down on sample complexity. Note that Humanoid-v3 is considered the most challenging MuJoCo environment.

While Table 1 shows that the median of the timesteps needed for the first crossover happens much earlier in our off-policy variants, it doesn't fully capture the variance. We address this in Figs. 1 and 2. Figure 1 consists of box plots of the number of interactions required to reach the threshold in ARS, TRES, OP-ARS and OP-TRES. The number of seeds on which each method reached the threshold is mentioned next to the algorithm's name. Clearly, the variance in our approach is either less or comparable to original algorithms. The advantage is particularly significant for OP-TRES in Ant-v3 and for OP-ARS in Humanoid-v3.

In Fig. 2, the overall progress of various algorithms is shown for different seeds. In particular, the horizontal green dotted lines represent the specific reward thresholds, while the different curves correspond to different seeds. The blue and red dots on the curves represent the first timestep where the threshold is reached. Finally, the star represents the median of all the dots marked over various runs. The plots clearly show that our methods reach the threshold significantly faster than the original methods in most cases.

Due to space constraints we have represented the figures only from few environments, the figures of all the remaining environments can be found in [3, Appendix I]. The details about the environment is given in [3, Appendix D] and the implementation details are given in [3, Appendix E].

Expt. 2 (Random Seeds and Hyperparameter choices): The top row of Fig. 3 shows the performance of OP-ARS over 100 random seeds sampled from $[0, 10000]$. We see that the median (thick blue line) crosses the threshold in most of the environments, demonstrating robustness to seeds.

Next, we discuss the sensitivity of OP-ARS to the two new hyperparameters we introduce: h (the bandwidth choice in kernel approximation) and n_b (the number of trajectories generated using the behaviour policy). For this, we first identify multiple choices for h and n_b, wherein the performance of the proposed algorithms is reasonable (see Appendix B). Next, we run our algorithm under all possible combinations of these hyperparameter choices. The performance graphs (refer to the lower row of Fig. 3) align with those observed in the 100-seed test conducted earlier, thus confirming that the algorithm's performance remains largely unaffected by hyperparameter selections. This implies that the specific values of hyperparameters do not significantly impact the process of learning. This is in sharp contrast to behaviors of deep reinforcement learning methodologies which often display high sensitivity to hyperparameters; e.g., in DDPG, slight adjustments often disrupts the learning process [2,4,5]. We don't look at the sensitivity of OP-ARS to other hyperparameters such as ν, α, N, b. Such a study has been done in [13] for ARS and the role of these parameters in both ARS and our off-policy variant are similar.

Expt. 3 (Comparison to non-ES methods): Table 2 shows the quality of the policy obtained after a fixed number of environmental interactions under various RL methods. While the outputs among ES methods are always comparable, there are certain environments, e.g., HalfCheetah and Humanoid, where non-ES methods such as SAC and/or DDPG truly outperform others. The key reason is

Table 2. The maximum average policy return after running the algorithms for 1 million timesteps (2 million for Humanoid-v3). The abbreviations SW, ..., HU have similar expansions as in Table 1.

Algorithm	SW	HO	HC	WA	AN	HU
ARS	358	3308	3147	2481	1246	657
OP-ARS	345	3308	2890	1759	1084	881
TRES	346	–	2713	–	1310	–
OP-TRES	344	–	3559	–	1208	–
TRPO	367	3753	4838	5346	4568	4329
PPO	367	1018	6682	4368	3909	1153
DDPG	42	2775	12025	3928	721	263
A2C	201	1028	2885	395	-38	472
SAC	353	3644	11434	4952	5588	6949

Table 3. Wall clock time required to reach the standard threshold (see Table 1). HU 5% means 5% of the standard threshold for HU. The notation − means that the corresponding thresholds were not reached.

Algorithm	SW	HO	HC	WA	AN	≈ HU				
						5%	10%	15%	25%	100%
ARS	40	48	42	364	322	30	112	454	696	1050
OP-ARS	52	80	110	366	665	34	79	205	400	625
TRES	32	–	37	–	581	–	–	–	–	–
OP-TRES	63	–	37	–	533	–	–	–	–	–
TRPO	267	1020	878	1656	–	357	2412	3789	3691	–
PPO	1658	–	1007	4390	5616	76	5803	24170	17106	–
DDPG	–	5300	349	6434	–	7	–	–	–	–
SAC	14692	6457	672	7704	10754	281	1374	1999	6293	24893

that these non-ES methods have been meticulously refined to extract the maximum information from a provided dataset. However, non-ES methods offer very little scope for parallelization. Accordingly, as Table 3 shows, the wall-clock times recorded to achieve different thresholds are remarkably high for non-ES methods (even when executed on GPUs) compared to our methods (which are executed on CPUs). In summary, our methods maintain comparable run times to ARS and TRES, but provide substantial advantage in terms of sample complexity.

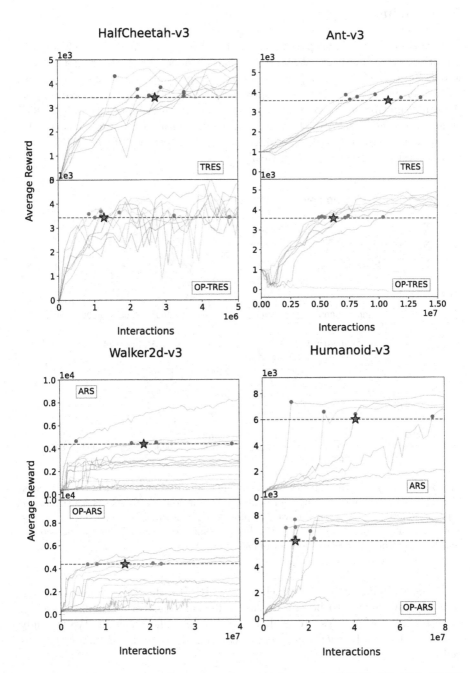

Fig. 2. Figures representing the trajectories of various runs of ARS, OP-ARS, TRES and OP-TRES algorithms where the number of interactions with the environment is plotted against the average reward.

5   Conclusion

This work proposes an off-policy ranking idea for improving sample efficiency in evolutionary RL methods. While traditional off-policy methods are not directly applicable to deterministic policies, we enable it using kernel approximations. Our experiments show that our proposed ARS and TRES variants have roughly the same run time as the original, but reach reward thresholds with only 50-80% as much interactions. We believe our approach is easily extendable to other ES or Random Search methods as well. A promising direction of future work would be to investigate the same theoretically.

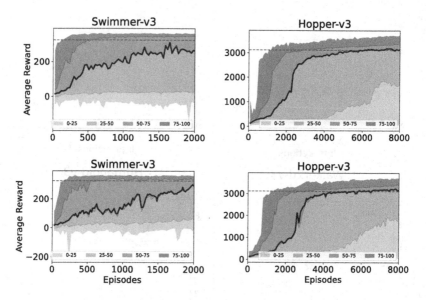

Fig. 3. The figures in the top row represent the evaluation of OP-ARS over 100 seeds. The figures in the bottom row represent the evaluation of OP-ARS's sensitivity to hyperparameters. The average reward is plotted against episodes. The thick blue line represents the median curve, and the shaded region corresponds to the percentiles mentioned in the legend (see bottom of each figure).

Recently, hybrid algorithms such as CEM-RL [15] that mix ES and Deep RL methods have shown to be more sample efficient than ES methods. However, there too all the policies are evaluated in an on-policy fashion. We strongly believe that our off-policy ranking idea can help in these hybrid algorithms as well.

A Differences in the Original ARS from Our Off-Policy Variant

In this section, we mention the key differences between the original ARS and our off-policy variant OP-ARS. Table 4 indicates the exact steps that differ between the algorithms and their implications.

Table 4. Key differences between ARS and our off-policy variant OP-ARS. The step column refers to the step number in Algorithm 1.

Step	ARS	OP-ARS	Implications
6	There is no corresponding step in ARS	Run n_b trajectories	The trajectories are run using policy parameterized by M_j (used as behavior data for off-policy evaluation)
8	Step 5 in ARS; collects **2N** rollouts	Collects only **2b** Rollouts (note that $b < N$)	We collect data required only for update step
7	Step 6 in ARS; sorts δ_k based on returns from the $2N$ trajectories	We sort δ_k based on the fitness function (7) derived using off-policy technique	We generate less data as we find the approximate ranking of δs using off-policy technique even before generating trajectories, unlike in ARS where trajectories are run for all $2N$ policies to find the rankings
9	Step 7 in ARS; uses $r(\pi)$ for the total reward received from policy π	We use $\hat{\eta}(\pi)$ to denote the total reward received from policy π	We use $\hat{\eta}(\cdot)$ to denote the total reward because we use $r(\cdot)$ for one-step reward
7, 8	Step 5, 6 in ARS; first collect data from $2N$ policies, then rank	We first rank; then collect only data from $2b$ policies	We generate less samples as mentioned earlier

B Hyperparameters

In this section, we would like to describe the set of hyperparameters used in our experiments. The ARS and TRES algorithms have a predefined set of hyperparameters, which have been fine-tuned in the corresponding papers. Hence, we use the same hyperparameters in our algorithms for most of the environments. Our off-policy variants OP-ARS and OP-TRES have two new hyperparameters: the number of trajectories to run using behavior policy n_b and the bandwidth in kernel function h. We experiment with varying values of n_b and h, as indicated in Table 5, as part of our hyperparameter exploration process. The most effective hyperparameters, denoted in bold, are employed to generate the outcomes presented in Table 1 and Fig. 1, including the images in the uppermost row of Fig. 3.

Table 5. Hyperparameter grid used in each environment

Env.(-v3)	OP-ARS				OP-TRES			
	N	b	n_b	h	N	b	n_b	h
Swimmer	2	1	1, **2**	1.0, 0.5, 0.25, **0.1**	4	2	**1**, 2	1.0, 0.5, 0.25, **0.1**
Hopper	8	4	1, **2**	1.0, 0.5, **0.25**, 0.1	–	–	–	–
HalfCheetah	32	4	1, **2**	**1.0**, 0.5, 0.25, 0.1	16	8	**1**, 2	1.0, **0.5**, 0.25, 0.1
Walker2d	40	30	1, **2**	1.0, **0.5**, 0.25, 0.1	–	–	–	–
Ant	60	20	**1**, 2	1.0, 0.5, **0.25**, 0.1	40	20	1, 2	1.0, **0.5**, 0.25, 0.1
Humanoid	350	230	1, **2**	1.0, 0.5, **0.25**, 0.1	–	–	–	–

C   LQR Experiments

In this section, we showcase the outcomes of our experiments conducted with the LQR environment. As elucidated in Sect. 4.3 of [13], there exist limitations inherent to MuJoCo robotic tasks. Particularly notable is the lack of knowledge concerning the optimal policies within these environments. This uncertainty extends to the comparison between the learned policy of their algorithm and the optimal policy. A viable approach involves applying the algorithms to straightforward, widely recognized environments with well-established optimal policies. In [13], the choice fell upon the Linear Quadratic Regulator (LQR) as the benchmarking environment due to its known dynamics. For a more in-depth understanding of this environment, additional insights can be found in [3, Appendix D.2].

We employ the same framework utilized by [13] to compare our approach with model-based Nominal Control, LSPI [9], and ARS [13]. As demonstrated in the work by [13], the Nominal method exhibits significantly greater sample efficiency than LSPI and ARS by orders of magnitude, underscoring the potential for enhancement. Our experiments corroborate this notion, revealing that our method surpasses ARS in terms of sample efficiency, as indicated in Fig. 4a. Furthermore, Fig. 4b underscores our algorithm's superiority over ARS in terms of stability frequency.

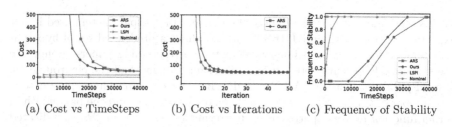

(a) Cost vs TimeSteps   (b) Cost vs Iterations   (c) Frequency of Stability

Fig. 4. Comparison of sample efficiency and stability of various algorithms on LQR.

References

1. Brockman, G., Cheung, V., Pettersson, L., Schneider, J., Schulman, J., Tang, J., Zaremba, W.: Openai gym. arXiv preprint arXiv:1606.01540 (2016)
2. Duan, Y., Chen, X., Houthooft, R., Schulman, J., Abbeel, P.: Benchmarking deep reinforcement learning for continuous control. In: International Conference on Machine Learning, pp. 1329–1338. PMLR (2016)
3. Eshwar, S., Kolathaya, S., Thoppe, G.: Improving sample efficiency in evolutionary RL using off-policy ranking arXiv:2208.10583 (2023)
4. Haarnoja, T., Zhou, A., Abbeel, P., Levine, S.: Soft actor-critic: Off-policy maximum entropy deep reinforcement learning with a stochastic actor. In: International Conference on Machine Learning, pp. 1861–1870. PMLR (2018)
5. Henderson, P., Islam, R., Bachman, P., Pineau, J., Precup, D., Meger, D.: Deep reinforcement learning that matters. In: Proceedings of the AAAI Conference on Artificial Intelligence, vol. 32 (2018)
6. Kakade, S., Langford, J.: Approximately optimal approximate reinforcement learning. In: In Proc. 19th International Conference on Machine Learning. Citeseer (2002)
7. Kallus, N., Uehara, M.: Doubly robust off-policy value and gradient estimation for deterministic policies. Advances in Neural Information Processing Systems 33 (2020)
8. Kallus, N., Zhou, A.: Policy evaluation and optimization with continuous treatments. In: International Conference on Artificial Intelligence and Statistics, pp. 1243–1251. PMLR (2018)
9. Lagoudakis, M.G., Parr, R.: Model-free least-squares policy iteration. Advances in neural information processing systems **14** (2001)
10. Li, Z., Lin, X., Zhang, Q., Liu, H.: Evolution strategies for continuous optimization: A survey of the state-of-the-art. Swarm Evol. Comput. **56**, 100694 (2020)
11. Lillicrap, T.P., Hunt, J.J., Pritzel, A., Heess, N., Erez, T., Tassa, Y., Silver, D., Wierstra, D.: Continuous control with deep reinforcement learning. In: ICLR (Poster) (2016)
12. Liu, G., Zhao, L., Yang, F., Bian, J., Qin, T., Yu, N., Liu, T.Y.: Trust region evolution strategies. In: Proceedings of the AAAI Conference on Artificial Intelligence. vol. 33, pp. 4352–4359 (2019)
13. Mania, H., Guy, A., Recht, B.: Simple random search of static linear policies is competitive for reinforcement learning. In: Proceedings of the 32nd International Conference on Neural Information Processing Systems. pp. 1805–1814 (2018)
14. Matyas, J.: Random optimization. Autom. Remote. Control. **26**(2), 246–253 (1965)
15. Pourchot, A., Sigaud, O.: Cem-rl: Combining evolutionary and gradient-based methods for policy search. arXiv preprint arXiv:1810.01222 (2018)
16. Rajeswaran, A., Lowrey, K., Todorov, E., Kakade, S.: Towards generalization and simplicity in continuous control. In: Proceedings of the 31st International Conference on Neural Information Processing Systems. pp. 6553–6564 (2017)
17. Salimans, T., Ho, J., Chen, X., Sidor, S., Sutskever, I.: Evolution strategies as a scalable alternative to reinforcement learning. arXiv preprint arXiv:1703.03864 (2017)
18. Schulman, J., Levine, S., Abbeel, P., Jordan, M., Moritz, P.: Trust region policy optimization. In: International conference on machine learning. pp. 1889–1897. PMLR (2015)

19. Schulman, J., Wolski, F., Dhariwal, P., Radford, A., Klimov, O.: Proximal policy optimization algorithms. arXiv preprint arXiv:1707.06347 (2017)
20. Todorov, E., Erez, T., Tassa, Y.: Mujoco: A physics engine for model-based control. In: 2012 IEEE/RSJ International Conference on Intelligent Robots and Systems. pp. 5026–5033. IEEE (2012)
21. Zhang, Y., Ross, K.W.: On-policy deep reinforcement learning for the average-reward criterion. In: International Conference on Machine Learning. pp. 12535–12545. PMLR (2021)

Efficiency of Symmetric Nash Equilibria in Epidemic Models with Confinements

Maider Sanchez and Josu Doncel[(✉)] [ID]

University of the Basque Country, UPV/EHU, 48940 Leioa, Spain
msanchez162@ikasle.ehu.eus, josu.doncel@ehu.eus

Abstract. We consider a non-cooperative game in the SIR model with confinements. Each member of the population is a player whose strategy is her probability of being protected from the epidemic. We assume that for each player, there is a cost of infection per unit time and a cost of being confined, which is linear and decreasing on her confinement strategy. The total cost is defined as the sum of her confinement and infection costs. We present a method for computing a symmetric Nash equilibrium for this game and study its efficiency. We conclude that the Nash equilibrium we obtain leads to fewer confinements than the strategy that minimizes the cost of the entire population.

Keywords: SIR model · Symmetric Nash equilibrium · Efficiency

1 Introduction

The recent epidemic caused by COVID19 disease shows the great importance of mathematical models applied in this field. Indeed, these models can be used to analyze how a population will behave in an epidemic as well as the effect of several factors on the evolution of the spread of the disease.

Non-cooperative game-theory studies the behavior of self-interested agents (or players) that are in interaction [10]. A crucial concept in this field is the Nash equilibrium which is defined as the set of strategies such that none of the players gets benefit from a unilateral deviation. The Nash equilibrium appears in a variate of applications such as complex stochastic networks. The SIR model is a stochastic network in which each member of the population under consideration belongs to one of the following states: susceptible (S), infected (I) or recovered (R). It was introduced in [8] and it has been considered in a large number of works since then (see the monographs [1,4]).

We consider the SIR model with confinements. This means that the susceptible population can be protected from getting the disease. We consider that the size of the population is N. We formulate a non-cooperative game in which each

This work has been partially supported by the Department of Education of the Basque Government, Spain through the Consolidated Research Group MATHMODE (IT1294-19) and by the Marie Sklodowska-Curie grant agreement No 777778.

E. Kalyvianaki and M. Paolieri (Eds.): VALUETOOLS 2023, LNICST 539, pp. 51–58, 2024.
https://doi.org/10.1007/978-3-031-48885-6_4

member of the population is a player. The strategy that each player selects is her confinement strategy, which consists of the probability of being protected from the epidemic. When this probability is equal to zero, we say that the player is fully exposed to the epidemic, whereas when it is equal to one, it is completely confined. Associated to each infected member of the population, there is a cost per unit time. We consider that there is also a cost of confinement associated to the susceptible population, which is linear and decreasing with the confinement strategy. The cost of each player is thus the sum of her infection and confinement costs. We consider a problem with an infinite time horizon and discounted cost.

We are interested in calculating the symmetric Nash equilibrium of this game. First, we formulate a Markov Decision Process to calculate the best response strategy of a player to the set of strategies of the rest of the players. Using value iteration and a simple fixed-point algorithm, we present how to compute a pure Nash equilibrium.

We also formulate a global optimization problem whose goal is to find the optimal confinement strategy, i.e., the confinement strategy to be applied to the entire susceptible population in order to minimize the total cost of the population. We also formulate this problem as a Markov Decision Process. Finally, we compare the optimal confinement strategy with the Nash equilibrium strategy. Our first conclusion is that both strategies are very similar. However, in the Nash equilibrium strategy achieves complete confinement (i.e. the situation where a player is completely protected from the epidemic) more often than the global minimum strategy. Moreover, the Nash equilibrium switches from full exposure to full protection in a line which does not depend on the proportion of susceptible population. This situation is not achieved in the global minimum strategy, where this change is given in a switching curve.

Several game-theory based models have been studied considering vaccinations in the SIR models, for instance [2,5,7,9]. However, confinements have been only studied using mean-field games in [3,12] and considering that the entire population can control the contact rate. Our work is different as we consider game with N players and only susceptible population can control her interaction with the others.

2   Model Description

We analyze the SIR model in which a population of N people evolve over time. We consider that time is discrete. In the SIR model, each of the people belonging to the population under study is in one of the following three states: susceptible (S), infected (I) or recovered (R). We denote by $m_S(t)$, $m_I(t)$ and $m_R(t)$ the proportion of the population that is in each state.

We now describe the dynamics of this population. An individual encounters other individual in a time slot with probability γ. If an individual that is susceptible encounters an infected individual, then it becomes infected. Moreover, an infected individual becomes recovered in the next time slot (i.e., it gets recovered in a time slot) with probability ρ. We consider that R is an absorbing state, which means that the recovered population does not change her state.

We consider that the susceptible population can avoid to get the infection by choosing her confining strategy π. More precisely, a strategy π is a function that represents the exposure probability of the susceptible population to the infection, i.e. it is the probability that a susceptible individual is exposed to the infection at time slot t. For instance, if $\pi(t) = 0$, the susceptible population gets confined at time t, which means that they cannot get the infection at time slot t; whereas if $\pi(t) = 1$, the susceptible population is fully exposed to the infection. Thus, we have that $\pi : \mathbb{N} \to [0,1]$.

In Fig. 1, we represent the Markov chain describing the dynamics of an individual in this model.

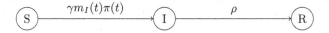

Fig. 1. The dynamics of an individual in the epidemic model under consideration. Each individual has three possible states: S (susceptible), I (infected) and R (recovered).

We focus on the evolution over time of the proportion of people in each state, which is described by the following equation:

$$\begin{cases} m_S(t+1) = m_S(t) - \gamma m_S(t) m_I(t) \pi(t) \\ m_I(t+1) = m_I(t) + \gamma m_S(t) m_I(t) \pi(t) - \rho m_I(t) \\ m_R(t+1) = m_R(t) + \rho m_I(t). \end{cases} \tag{1}$$

From this expression we derive several properties. For instance, we see that the proportion of people in state R is non-decreasing and also that, when $\pi(t) = 0$, the proportion of people in state S is constant and the proportion of people in state I is decreasing. Throughout this paper, we assume that $(m_S(0), m_I(0), m_R(0))$ is fixed. We also note that

$$(m_S(t), m_I(t), m_R(t)) = \left\{ \left(\frac{i}{N}, \frac{j}{N}, \frac{N-i-j}{N} \right) : i + j \leq N \right\}.$$

In the next section, we present a non-cooperative game for this model and in the following one, we analyze the efficiency of the Nash equilibrium.

3 Formulation of the Non-cooperative Game

3.1 Game Description

We consider a non-cooperative game in the SIR model with confinements that we presented above. In this game, each individual of the population is a player that can choose her confinement strategy, that is, each player can select, in each time slot, her probability of being protected from the infection (or confinement probability). We denote by $\pi_i(t)$ the confinement probability of Player i and by $\pi_{-i}(t)$ the confinement probability of the entire population except for Player i, with $i = 1, \ldots, N$. We denote by π_i the vector of the confinement probability chosen by Player i in each time slot and by π_{-i} the vector of the confinement probability chosen by the rest of the players.

We consider that an infected player incurs a cost of $c_I > 0$ per unit of time. Moreover, we assume that there is also a confinement cost for each player that depends linearly on her strategy. More precisely, when at time slot t the Player i selects the confinement strategy $\pi_i(t)$, there is a confinement cost which equals $c_L - \pi_i(t)$, where $c_L \geq 1$. As a result, the cost of Player i at time slot t is the sum of her confinement cost and her infection cost. We denote by $x_s^{\pi_i, \pi_{-i}}(t)$ the probability that Player i is in state s at time slot t, where $s \in \{S, I, R\}$. Therefore, if we denote by $C_i(\pi_i, \pi_{-i})$ the total cost of Player i is given by

$$C_i(\pi_i, \pi_{-i}) = \sum_{t=0}^{\infty} \delta^t((c_L - \pi_i(t)) x_S^{\pi_i, \pi_{-i}}(t) + c_I x_I^{\pi_i, \pi_{-i}}(t)), \quad \text{(COST-GAME)}$$

where $\delta \in (0, 1)$.

Remark 1. We would like to remark that [11] analyzed this model but considering the finite horizon case and they formulate a mean-field game (i.e., they consider that the number of players tends towards infinity). Our model differs significantly because we are considering a discounted cost infinite horizon case and, moreover, the number of players is finite and equal to N.

The best response of the Player i to π_{-i} is the confinement strategy that minimizes the above expression. That is,

$$BR_i(\pi_{-i}) = \arg \min_{\pi_i} C_i(\pi_i, \pi_{-i}) \qquad \text{(BR-i)}$$

A symmetric Nash equilibrium is a strategy such that none of the players gets benefit from unilateral deviation. This means that π is a symmetric Nash equilibrium if, for all $i = 1, \ldots, N$

$$\pi = BR_i(\pi), \qquad \text{(NASH-EQ)}$$

or alternatively, if for all $i = 1, \ldots, N$ and any other confinement strategy $\tilde{\pi}$,

$$C_i(\pi, \pi) \leq C_i(\tilde{\pi}, \pi).$$

The existence of a Nash equilibrium of this game follows from [6]. The computation of a Nash equilibrium is carried out using the set of instructions presented in Algorithm 1. Indeed, when the algorithm converges, we conclude that (NASH-EQ) is satisfied by π because all the players are symmetric (and therefore $BR_i(\pi) = BR_j(\pi)$ for $i \neq j$ and for every π). Therefore, in that case we can conclude that a pure Nash equilibrium has been found.

Algorithm 1 Fixed-point algorithm to compute a Nash equilibrium

---

Require: π_{-i}
  repeat
    $\tilde{\pi} \leftarrow \pi_{-i}$
    $\pi \leftarrow BR_i(\pi_{-i})$
  until $\pi = \tilde{\pi}$

3.2 Markov Decision Process Formulation

To obtain the best response of Player i to π_{-i}, we formulate a Markov Decision Process. To simplify the presentation, we consider that the size of the rest of the population is N (i.e., we consider a population of size $N+1$). The state of the Markov Decision Process is given by $(x, \frac{i}{N}, \frac{i}{N})$, where $x \in \{S, I, R\}$ and $i + j \neq N$, i.e., the first component represents the state of Player i and the rest of the components the possible values of the proportion of the susceptible and infected population. For a fixed strategy π, the strategy that minimizes (BR-i) (i.e., which is the best response of Player i to π) satisfies the following Bellman equations:

$$V_{k+1}^*\left(S, \frac{i}{N}, 0\right) = \min_{\pi_i}[c_L - \pi_i], \quad i = 0, 1, \ldots, N,$$

$$V_{k+1}^*\left(S, 0, \frac{i}{N}\right) = \min_{\pi_i}\left[c_L - \pi_i + \delta\left(\gamma\frac{j}{N}\pi_i V_k^*\left(I, 0, \frac{i}{N}\right)\right.\right.$$
$$\left.\left. + \rho\frac{j}{N}V_k^*\left(S, 0, \frac{j-1}{N}\right)\right)\right], i = 1, \ldots, N,$$

$$V_{k+1}^*\left(S, \frac{i}{N}, \frac{j}{N}\right) = \min_{\pi_i}\left[c_L - \pi_i + \delta\left(\gamma\frac{j}{N}\pi_i V_k^*\left(I, \frac{i}{N}, \frac{j}{N}\right)\right.\right.$$
$$+ \gamma\frac{j}{N}\pi\left(\frac{i}{N}, \frac{j}{N}\right)V_k^*\left(I, \frac{i-1}{N}, \frac{j+1}{N}\right)$$
$$\left.\left. + \rho\frac{j}{N}V_k^*\left(S, \frac{i}{N}, \frac{j-1}{N}\right)\right)\right], i, j = 1, \ldots, N,$$

$$V_{k+1}^*\left(I, \frac{i}{N}, 0\right) = c_I, \quad i = 0, 1, \ldots, N,$$

$$V_{k+1}^*\left(I, 0, \frac{i}{N}\right) = c_I + \delta\rho\frac{i}{N}V_k^*\left(I, 0, \frac{i-1}{N}\right), \quad i = 1, \ldots, N$$

$$V_{k+1}^*\left(I, \frac{i}{N}, \frac{j}{N}\right) = c_I + \delta\left(\gamma\frac{j}{N}\pi\left(\frac{i}{N}, \frac{j}{N}\right)V_k^*\left(I, \frac{i-1}{N}, \frac{j+1}{N}\right)\right.$$
$$\left. + \rho\frac{j}{N}V_k^*\left(I, \frac{i}{N}, \frac{j-1}{N}\right)\right), \quad i, j = 1, \ldots, N.$$

From the first expression, we conclude that when none of the people of the rest of the population are infected (i.e., when $m_I = 0$), the best response of Player i

to π is $\arg\min_{\pi_i}[c_i - \pi_i]$, which gives one, i.e., Player i is never confined when there are no infected people. Moreover, from the second expression, we conclude that when none of the people of the rest of the population is susceptible, the best response is the value of π_i that minimizes

$$c_L - \pi_i + \delta\left(\gamma\frac{j}{N}\pi_i V_k^*\left(I, 0, \frac{i}{N}\right) + \rho\frac{j}{N}V_k^*\left(S, 0, \frac{j-1}{N}\right)\right).$$

Finally, from the third expression, we conclude that, when there are susceptible and infected people in the rest of the population, the best response of Player i to π is the value of π_i that minimizes

$$c_L - \pi_i + \delta\left(\gamma\frac{j}{N}\pi_i V_k^*\left(I, \frac{i}{N}, \frac{j}{N}\right) + \gamma\frac{j}{N}\pi(\frac{i}{N}, \frac{j}{N})V_k^*\left(I, \frac{i-1}{N}, \frac{j+1}{N}\right)\right.$$
$$\left. + \rho\frac{j}{N}V_k^*\left(S, \frac{i}{N}, \frac{j-1}{N}\right)\right).$$

It is also remarkable that, in all the cases, the expression to be minimized so as to obtain the best response of Player i to π is linear in π_i. This implies that the best response, which can be in the interval $[0, 1]$, will be one of the two following values: zero or one.

4   Efficiency of Nash Equilibria

4.1   Global Optimum Confinement Strategy

We now focus on the global optimum confinement strategy, which is the value of π such that the cost of the population is minimized, i.e.,

$$\arg\min_\pi \sum_{t=0}^{\infty} \delta^t \left(c_I m_I(t) + (c_L - \pi)m_S(t)\right). \qquad \text{(GLOBAL-OPT)}$$

We know that the global optimum confinement strategy satisfies the following Bellman equations:

$$V_{k+1}^*(0, 0) = 0$$
$$V_{k+1}^*\left(\frac{i}{N}, 0\right) = \min_\pi[\frac{i}{N}(c_L - \pi)], \quad i = 1, \ldots, N$$
$$V_{k+1}^*\left(0, \frac{i}{N}\right) = c_I\frac{i}{N} + \delta\left(\rho V_k^*\left(0, \frac{i-1}{N}\right)\right), \quad i = 1, \ldots, N$$
$$V_{k+1}^*\left(\frac{i}{N}, \frac{j}{N}\right) = \min_\pi\left[c_I\frac{j}{N} + (c_L - \pi)\frac{i}{N} + \delta\left(\rho V_k^*\left(\frac{i}{N}, \frac{j-1}{N}\right)\right.\right.$$
$$\left.\left. + \gamma\frac{j}{N}\pi V_k^*\left(\frac{i-1}{N}, \frac{j+1}{N}\right)\right)\right], \quad i, j = 1, \ldots, N.$$

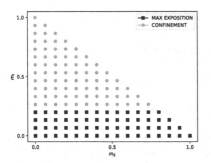 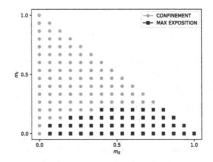

Fig. 2. Nash equilibrium strategy (left) and global optimum strategy (right) with N=15 and $c_I = 6$. The green dots represent that the probability of being protected from the epidemic is one, whereas blue squares that this probability is zero.

4.2 Efficiency Analysis

We now study the efficiency of the Nash equilibria of the formulated game, i.e., we compare the confinement strategy of (NASH-EQ) with that of (GLOBAL-OPT). We have performed extensive numerical experiments and here we present an example to illustrate the observed properties of all our experiments[1]. We consider $N = 15$, $c_I = 6$, $c_L = 2$, $\delta = 0.99$, $\gamma = 0.6$ and $\rho = 0.4$. The left plot of Fig. 2 shows the confinement strategy of the Nash equilibrium we obtained with Algorithm 1. We observe that the Nash equilibrium consists of being completely exposed to the epidemic (which is represented as MAX EXPOSITION in the plot) when the proportion of infected population is smaller or equal to 0.25 and being completely protected from the epidemic (which is represented as CONFINEMENT in the plot) otherwise. However, in the right plot of Fig. 2, we observe that the switching curve in which the optimal policy changes from being completely exposed to the epidemic to being completely confined is not a straight line (as in the Nash equilibrium case). Another interesting property of this experiment is that although both strategies are very similar, the Nash equilibrium strategy leads to less confinement (i.e., green dots are fewer in the left plot than in the right plot).

5 Future Work

This work is the first step of the research we plan to carry out in the future. Indeed, we would like to provide an analytical efficiency study of this model. Furthermore, we plan to study the conditions under which Algorithm 1 converges to a Nash equilibrium. Finally, we are interested in extending this model by considering that a recovered individual can become susceptible.

---

[1] The code to reproduce the experiments of this section is available at https://github.com/josudoncel/StudentsCode/tree/main/MaiderSanchezJimenez.

References

1. Anderson, R.M., May, R.M.: Infectious Diseases of Humans: Dynamics and Control. Oxford University Press (1992)
2. Bauch, C.T., Earn, D.J.: Vaccination and the theory of games. Proc. Natl. Acad. Sci. U.S.A. **101**(36), 13391–13394 (2004)
3. Cho, S.: Mean-field game analysis of sir model with social distancing. arXiv preprint arXiv:2005.06758 (2020)
4. Diekmann, O., Heesterbeek, J.A.P.: Mathematical epidemiology of infectious diseases: model building, analysis and interpretation, vol. 5. Wiley (2000)
5. Doncel, J., Gast, N., Gaujal, B.: A mean field game analysis of sir dynamics with vaccination. Probab. Eng. Inf. Sci. **36**(2), 482–499 (2022)
6. Fink, A.M.: Equilibrium in a stochastic n-person game. J. Sci. Hiroshima University, series ai (mathematics) **28**(1), 89–93 (1964)
7. Hubert, E., Turinici, G.: Nash-mfg equilibrium in a sir model with time dependent newborn vaccination (2016)
8. Kermack, W.O., McKendrick, A.G.: A contribution to the mathematical theory of epidemics. In: Proceedings of the Royal Society of London A: Mathematical, Physical and Engineering Sciences, vol. 115, pp. 700–721. The Royal Society (1927)
9. Laguzet, L., Turinici, G.: Global optimal vaccination in the sir model: properties of the value function and application to cost-effectiveness analysis. Math. Biosci. **263**, 180–197 (2015)
10. Nisan, N., Roughgarden, T., Tardos, E., Vazirani, V.V.: Algorithmic Game Theory. Cambridge University Press (2007)
11. Sagastabeitia, G., Doncel, J., Gast, N.: To confine or not to confine: a mean field game analysis of the end of an epidemic. Proceedings of Eleventh International Workshop on Practical Applications of Stochastic Modelling (PASM'22)
12. Yagiz Olmez, S., Aggarwal, S., Kim, J.W., Miehling, E., Başar, T., West, M., Mehta, P.G.: How does a rational agent act in an epidemic? arXiv e-prints pp. arXiv-2206 (2022)

Simulation

The Best of Both Worlds: Analytically-Guided Simulation of HPnGs for Optimal Reachability

Mathis Niehage[✉][ID] and Anne Remke[ID]

Westfälische Wilhelms-Universität, 48149 Münster, Germany
{mathis.niehage,anne.remke}@uni-muenster.de

Abstract. Efficient reachability analysis, as well as statistical model checking have been proposed for the evaluation of Hybrid Petri nets with general transitions (HPnG). Both have different (dis-)advantages. The performance of statistical simulation suffers in large models and the number of required simulation runs to achieve a relatively small confidence interval increases considerably. The approach introduced for analytical reachability analysis of HPnGs however, becomes infeasible for a large number of random variables. To overcome these limitations, this paper applies statistical simulation for optimal reachability defined as *until* property in Stochastic Time Logic to a pre-computed symbolic state-space representation of HPnGs, i.e., the Parametric Location Tree (PLT), which has previously been used for model checking HPnGs. A case study on a water tank model shows the feasiblity of the approach and illustrates its advantages w.r.t. the original simulation and analysis approaches.

Keywords: Statistical simulation · State-space representation · Hybrid Petri nets with general transitions

1 Introduction

The dependability of critical infrastructures like water and energy distribution is of utmost importance to society and industry. Improving their dependability requires the efficient evaluation of complex models that combine discrete and continuous behaviour with stochasticity to model the duration of failure and repair times. Such models are so-called stochastic hybrid models (SHM) and a large variety of such models exists with different expressivity. Hybrid Petri nets with general transitions (HPnGs) [17] extend classical Petri nets by introducing continuous places and transitions, thus allowing to model hybrid behaviour, as well as general transitions whose firing time is distributed according to a probability density function. HPnGs have proven to be very useful for evaluating dependability of critical infrastructures [15, 16] and (dis-)charging strategies of battery storage, e.g., in smart homes and electric vehicles [34, 36].

E. Kalyvianaki and M. Paolieri (Eds.): VALUETOOLS 2023, LNICST 539, pp. 61–81, 2024.
https://doi.org/10.1007/978-3-031-48885-6_5

Nondeterminism is often used to model concurrency or to account for under-specification in the model. As a modeling feature, nondeterminism is tradition-ally present in automata models and preserved in most (non-stochastic) hybrid automata formalisms. In contrast, stochastic Petri net models often resolve non-determinism through probabilistic choices [6], as the combination of nondeter-minism and stochastic behaviour poses a serious challenge when evaluating such models. Existing analytical approaches for the computation of reachability prob-abilities in SHM heavily rely on discretization and over-approximation. They either discretize the state-space [1,12] or the support of random variables [18]. All analytical approaches face the problem of state-space explosion, when increasing the number of random variables [7,44], the number of continuous variables or the number of nondeterministic decisions in the model. Simulative approaches rarely address the optimal resolution of nondeterminism, especially for SHM, as they suffer from high computational costs when attempting to identify optimal schedulers due to the need to exhaustively explore the state space.

The contribution of this paper is an analytically-guided simulation for HPnGs. We pursue a simulation-based approach, which builds on a pre-computed symbolic state-space representation as PLT [27]. The PLT has previously been used for model checking HPnGs analytically [25]. Instead, we efficiently simulate paths through the PLT, using the information stored sym-bolically in every node of the PLT to speed up simulation. We show that a bijec-tive function exists, which maps each path in the HPnG to a path in the PLT (and vice-versa). We further provide algorithms for analytically-guided simula-tion that allow us to optimize reachability probabilities defined as *until* property in Stochastic Time Logic in HPnGs for different scheduler classes, by restricting the information available to the scheduler. The advantage of the analytically-guided simulation is illustrated with respect to existing statistical and analytical methods in a case study.

Related work. For stochastic automata a hierarchy of scheduler classes has been defined in [9], which concludes that history-dependent prophetic schedulers (c.f. [21]) form the most powerful scheduler class for this modeling formalism. The inherent discrete nondeterminism in HPnGs has previously been resolved ana-lytically in [36] for two scheduler classes, namely (i) history-dependent prophetic and (ii) discrete-history non-prophetic. Recently, Q-learning has been proposed to learn optimal memoryless (non-)prophetic schedulers in SHMs [32]. Together with formal guarantees provided by deductive verification, HPnGs have been used to analyze performability for provably safe SHM [2].

Statistical model checking has been proposed for different kinds of (hybrid) stochastic systems. For Hybrid Petri nets, statistical model checking has been proposed for linear evolutions in [35,38] and for non-linear evolutions in [33,38]. While the Modest Toolset's [20] modes simulator [4] supports SHM with linear dynamics as well as lightweight scheduler sampling [30] to approximate optimal schedulers, it provides the latter only for non-hybrid models [8,10]. Addition-ally, the Q-learning approach presented in [32] has also been integrated into the modes simulator. However, it also suffers from high computational costs for large numbers of required training runs.

The term *guided simulation* is also used in rare-event simulation. In importance sampling, the guidance lies in modifying probability distributions to enhance the probability of certain events. In [28] a symbolic analysis is combined with simulation for stochastic priced timed automata in UPPAAL SMC. Importance splitting guides the simulation by stopping and branching simulation runs based on an importance function, e.g. [3,45]. In contrast, our approach modifies neither the distributions, nor the simulation runs, but is guided through a symbolic state-space representation.

Analytical approaches have various limitations: A recently proposed discretization in time and space is for switched diffusions only [29]. Pilch et al. [36] cannot solve for complex prophetic schedulers. HPnGs form a restricted subclass of SHMs, which can be used as a high-level formalism of singular automata with random clocks (c.f. [37]). Nondeterminism has been optimized for the resulting model class via discrete-history non-prophetic and history-dependent prophetic schedulers in [40,44]. prohver [18] provides upper (lower) bounds on maximum (minimum) probabilities only. Delta reachability in ProbReach [42] does not support nondeterminism. Stochastic SMT solving [13,14] effectively works for nondeterministic choices over initial values/parameters only, limiting the types of schedulers that can be considered. All of these techniques hardly scale as the number of abstract/symbolic states or choice combinations explodes.

Learning for SHMs is considered, e.g., in ProbReach, which applies the cross-entropy method for resolving nondeterminism [43]. Also [11] enriches an SMT-based approach with decision trees and AI planning algorithms to handle nondeterminism. Reinforcement learning has also been used on MDPs to improve performance and safety (e.g. [23]), as well as to deal with *unknown* stochastic behavior [5,22], and with linear-time logic specifications (e.g. [5,19,41]).

Outline. The paper is further organized as follows. Section 2 repeats the syntax and semantics of HPnGs. Section 3 explains the computation of the PLT, Sect. 4 introduces the analytically-guided simulation and Sect. 5 illustrates the feasibility of our approach. Section 6 concludes the paper.

2   Hybrid Petri Nets with General Transitions

Hybrid Petri nets with general transitions (HPnG) [17] are a high-level formalism for a restricted class of SHMs. Next to continuous and discrete variables, HPnGs include arbitrarily distributed random variables. In the following, HPnGs are defined as in [27,39] including multiple firings of general transitions.

A HPnG consists of places, transitions and arcs which are gathered in a tuple $\mathcal{H} = (\mathcal{P}, \mathcal{T}, \mathcal{A}, \mathbf{M_0}, \varPhi)$ together with the initial marking and a tuple of parameter functions specifying the components of the HPnG.

The set of places $\mathcal{P} = \mathcal{P}^d \uplus \mathcal{P}^c$ contains the disjoint finite sets of discrete and continuous places. Continuous places $P_i^c \in \mathcal{P}^c$ contain a continuous marking

$x_i \in \mathbb{R}_0^+$. The parameter function $\Phi_b^P : \mathcal{P}^c \to \mathbb{R}^+ \cup \infty$ assigns each continuous place a possibly infinite upper boundary. In contrast, discrete places $P_i^d \in \mathcal{P}^d$ contain a discrete marking $m_i \in \mathbb{N}_0$ and can not be bounded. The initial marking for all places is given by $\mathbf{M_0}$. Transitions change the markings of the places as follows: The finite set of transitions $\mathcal{T}$ consists of immediate $\mathcal{T}^I$, deterministic $\mathcal{T}^D$ and general $\mathcal{T}^G$ transitions which change the discrete marking and continuous transitions $\mathcal{T}^C$ which change the continuous marking.

Immediate transitions fire as soon as they are enabled. We refer to [17] for a detailed discussion of *enabling*. Deterministic transitions have a deterministic firing time, specified by the parameter function $\phi_d^{\mathcal{T}} : \mathcal{T}^D \to \mathbb{R}^+$. We assign a random variable which follows a cumulative absolute continuous probability distribution function assigned by $\phi_g^{\mathcal{T}}$ to every general transition. Each deterministic and general transition has an associated clock which runs while the transition is enabled. Upon firing, the clock value equals the firing time and it is reset. Continuous transitions $T \in \mathcal{T}^C$ have a constant nominal flow rate assigned by $\phi_f^{\mathcal{T}} : \mathcal{T}^C \to \mathbb{R}^+$.

Transitions and places are connected via the finite set of arcs $\mathcal{A}$. There are two types of arcs: (i) arcs defining which transitions modify the marking of certain places and (ii) arcs enabling transitions based on the marking of the connected places. Arcs of the first type are discrete $\mathcal{A}^d$ and continuous $\mathcal{A}^f$ arcs. Discrete places and discrete transitions are connected via discrete arcs and continuous transitions and continuous places by continuous arcs, respectively. An *input* place has an arc towards the transition and the marking of the place decreases when the transition fires, an arc from the transition to the *output* place increases the marking. Each arc is assigned a weight $\phi_w^{\mathcal{A}}$ which weights the change of marking when firing the transition. If a continuous place reaches one of its boundaries, rate adaption reduces the actual flow rates of the affected continuous transitions based on the share $\phi_s^{\mathcal{A}}$ and priority $\phi_p^{\mathcal{A}}$ of the corresponding continuous arcs to prevent under- or overflow of that place. The second type of arcs are guard arcs which consist of test $\mathcal{A}^t$ and inhibitor $\mathcal{A}^h$ arcs. Guard arcs enable and disable connected transitions based on the marking of the connected places. Test arcs enable the transition if the marking is larger or equal to the weight of the guard arc. Inhibitor arcs are antithetic as the transition is enabled if the marking is lower than the weight. Note that discrete transitions also require that their input places match the weight of the connecting arcs in order to be enabled.

Definition 1. The state of a HPnG $\Gamma = (\mathbf{m}, \mathbf{x}, \mathbf{c}, \mathbf{d}, \mathbf{g}, \mathbf{e})$ contains all information of the variables in the HPnG. The discrete marking of all discrete places is in the vector $\mathbf{m}$ and the continuous marking of all continuous places in the vector $\mathbf{x}$. The current clock values of the deterministic transitions are in the vector $\mathbf{c}$ and the clock values of the general transitions are in the vector $\mathbf{g}$. The drift of all continuous places $\mathbf{d}$ describes the current change of fluid for each place and the (boolean) enabling status of all transitions is contained in the vector $\mathbf{e}$.

The set of all states is denoted as $\mathcal{S}$. The drift and enabling status are included in the definition of a state to simplify later computations, but can be derived uniquely from the given HPnG and the marking of the state. The initial state of the HPnG is defined as $\Gamma_0 = (\mathbf{m}_0, \mathbf{x}_0, \mathbf{0}, \mathbf{d}_0, \mathbf{0}, \mathbf{e}_0)$, where $\mathbf{m}_0$ and $\mathbf{x}_0$ are given by the initial marking $\mathbf{M}_0$, and $\mathbf{d}_0$ as well as $\mathbf{e}_0$ are derived from it.

Definition 2. (Event). An event $\Upsilon(\Gamma_i, \Gamma_{i+1}) = (\Delta\tau_{i+1}, \epsilon_{i+1})$ changes state Γ_i to state Γ_{i+1}. The model element that caused the event is given by $\epsilon_{i+1} \in \mathcal{P}^c \cup \mathcal{T} \setminus \mathcal{T}^C \cup \mathcal{A}^T$ and $\Delta\tau_{i+1}$ is the relative time from the previous event such that

1. a discrete transition fires and the discrete marking changes ($\epsilon_{i+1} \in \mathcal{T} \setminus \mathcal{T}^C$),
2. a lower or upper boundary is reached by a continuous place ($\epsilon_{i+1} \in \mathcal{P}^c$),
3. the fluid of a continuous place changes, such that a guard arc condition is now fulfilled or stops being fulfilled ($\epsilon_{i+1} \in \mathcal{A}^T$).

The first event type relates to a change of the discrete marking, the second changes the drift. The third type can have different consequences: If the enabling status of a continuous transition changes, the drift of at least one place also changes. If the enabling status of a discrete transition changes, initially only the enabling vector changes. This potentially influences the next event. We denote the set of events from a state $\Gamma_i \in S$ as $\mathcal{E}(\Gamma_i) = \{\Upsilon(\Gamma_i, \Gamma_{i+1})\}$ and its subset containing events with the minimum remaining time as:

$$\mathcal{E}^{min}(\Gamma_i) = \{\Upsilon(\Gamma_i, \Gamma_{i+1}) \in \mathcal{E}(\Gamma_i) \mid \nexists \{\Upsilon(\Gamma_i, \Gamma_j) \in \mathcal{E}(\Gamma_i) \colon \Delta\tau_j < \Delta\tau_{i+1}\}. \quad (1)$$

There may be multiple events with the same remaining time, i.e., $|\mathcal{E}^{min}(\Gamma_i)| > 1$.

Following [36], conflicts of discrete transition firings of the same type are considered as conflict and the existing order of events from [17] is maintained. Hence, we are only interested in conflicts between immediate and deterministic transitions, since the probability of multiple general transitions firings at the same time equals zero since their distributions are absolute continuous. Note that events caused by over- or underflow are not considered a conflict as rate adaption is executed after the firing of the transitions. Conflicts can be resolved, e.g., via weights [17] or using schedulers [32,36]. Events provide a symbolic partitioning of the infinite state-space into a finite number of sets. Within each set, the discrete part of the state and the drift of the continuous variables is constant. One time-bounded execution of the Zeno-free [24] model is represented by a finite path.

Definition 3. (Finite Path). A finite path with length $n \in \mathbb{N}$ is an alternating sequence of states and events

$$\sigma = \Gamma_0 \xrightarrow{(\Delta\tau_0, \epsilon_0)} \cdots \xrightarrow{(\Delta\tau_{n-1}, \epsilon_{n-1})} \Gamma_n,$$

where for every $i \in \{0, \dots, n-1\}$ an event $\Upsilon(\Gamma_i, \Gamma_{i+1}) = (\Delta\tau_i, \epsilon_i) \in \mathcal{E}^{min}(\Gamma_i)$ exists. The set of all finite paths with arbitrary lengths $n \in \mathbb{N}$ starting from the initial state Γ_0 is denoted as $Paths_\mathcal{H}(\Gamma_0)$.

3   Partitioning the State Space

The parametric location tree (PLT) partitions the infinite state-space of the HPnG into a finite subset of parametric locations. The presentation of the PLT is based on [27]. The PLT consists of nodes and transitions, where the nodes are parametric locations which represent a set of uncountably many states of the HPnG and the root node includes the initial state. Each edge represents an event, such that the respective child locations include the entry states after executing the event and all states until the occurrence of the next event. Multiple child locations are possible, due to nondeterministic decisions or due to random variables. The number of parametric locations is finite for Zeno-free models, as only time-bounded properties are considered.

Definition 4. (Parametric Location [27]). A parametric location is a tuple $\Lambda = (ID, t, p, \Gamma, \mathbf{S}, \mathbf{o})$ with identifier $\Lambda.ID$. The possible firing times of previous general transition firings are included in the potential domain of the random variables $\Lambda.\mathbf{S}$ and the firing order of general transitions is stored as vector $\Lambda.\mathbf{o}$, which is unique in a given parametric location. If a conflict is resolved probabilistically, the conflict probability is given by $\Lambda.p$ which is derived from the weights of the conflicting transitions. The entry time $\Lambda.t : \Lambda.\mathbf{S} \to \mathbb{R}_0^+$ is a linear function of the firing times of previous general transition firings and the state of the HPnG $\Lambda.\Gamma : \Lambda.\mathbf{S} \to \mathcal{S}$ is a linear function describing the model state at the entry time in dependence of the previous general transition firings. The valuations of the continuous variables and clocks are, as the entry time, linear functions of the firing times. The discrete markings, the drift and the enabling status is constant.

The PLT orders the parametric locations starting from the root node, which includes the initial state, child nodes are determined via the possible subsequent events of the parent location.

Definition 5. (Parametric Location Tree (PLT) [27]). The PLT $(\mathbf{V}, \mathbf{E}, \Lambda_0)$ is a tree with a finite set of parametric locations $\mathbf{V}$. The finite set of edges $\mathbf{E} \subset \mathbf{V} \times \mathbf{V}$ contains an edge $e_i = (\Lambda_j, \Lambda_k) \in \mathbf{E}$ for each model element that may cause an event $M(\Lambda_j) = \{\epsilon \mid \exists \Delta\tau \in \mathbb{R}_0^+, \exists \mathbf{f}_j \in \Lambda_j.\mathbf{S} : (\Delta\tau, \epsilon) \in \mathcal{E}^{min}(\Lambda_j.\Gamma(\mathbf{f}_j))\}$. The root node of the tree is the initial location $\Lambda_0 = (0, 0, 1, \Gamma_0, \mathbf{S}^\infty, \mathbf{o}_0)$, where Γ_0 is the initial state, $\mathbf{S}^\infty$ is the not yet limited domain of all enabled random transitions in the initial state and $\mathbf{o}_0$ is the empty vector.

We extend the definition of child locations from [27] by the set of entry times.

Definition 6. (Child Locations). Given a PLT $(\mathbf{V}, \mathbf{E}, \Lambda_0)$ with parametric location $\Lambda \in \mathbf{V}$, the child locations of Λ are collected in the set $\mathbf{\Lambda}_c(\Lambda) = \{\Lambda_i | (\Lambda, \Lambda_i) \in \mathbf{E}\}$. The set $\Theta = \{\Lambda_i.t | \Lambda_i \in \mathbf{\Lambda_c}(\Lambda)\}$ contains all entry times of the child locations. The subset $\mathbf{\Lambda}_T(\Lambda) \subseteq \mathbf{\Lambda}_c(\Lambda)$ contains all child locations where the event corresponds to the firing of a non-general transition $\mathbf{\Lambda}_T(\Lambda) = \{\Lambda_i \in \mathbf{\Lambda}_c(\Lambda) | |\Lambda.\mathbf{o}| = |\Lambda_i.\mathbf{o}|\}$.

Conflicts of transitions, as presented in Sect. 2, correspond to conflicts of parametric locations in the PLT. Conflicts have been defined in [37] via non-empty intersections of potential domains. In contrast our definition is based on the entry times of the child locations and is well-suited for simulation.

Definition 7. (Nondeterministic Conflict in PLT). Given a PLT $(\mathbf{V}, \mathbf{E}, \Lambda_0)$ and a parametric location $\Lambda \in \mathbf{V}$ with child locations $\mathbf{\Lambda}_c(\Lambda)$, for each entry time $t_e \in \Theta$, the set $\mathbf{\Lambda}_{t_e} = \{\Lambda_i \in \mathbf{\Lambda}_T(\Lambda) | \Lambda_i.t = t_e\}$ contains all parametric locations possibly reached if an event occurs at t_e. A nondeterministic conflict occurs, if $|\mathbf{\Lambda}_{t_e}| > 1$, and the corresponding conflict set of transitions is $C^{\mathcal{T}}_{t_e}(\Lambda) = \{T \in \mathcal{T} | \exists \Lambda_i \in \mathbf{\Lambda}_{t_e}, \exists \Delta\tau \in \mathbb{R}_0^+, \exists \mathbf{s} \in \Lambda.S, \exists \mathbf{s}_i \in \Lambda_i.S : \Upsilon(\Lambda.\Gamma(\mathbf{s}), \Lambda_i.\Gamma(\mathbf{s}_i)) = (\Delta\tau, T)\}$.

Note that potentially multiple conflict sets exist for one parent location. In addition to [27], we add a definition of paths through the PLT and their properties.

Definition 8. (Path through PLT). A path through a PLT $(\mathbf{V}, \mathbf{E}, \Lambda_0)$ is an alternating sequence of tuples $(\Lambda_i, \mathbf{f_i}) \in V \times (\mathbb{R}_0^+)^{|\Lambda_i.o|}$ for $i \in \{0, \ldots, n\}$ and model elements $\epsilon_j \in \mathcal{P}^c \cup \mathcal{T} \setminus \mathcal{T}^C \cup \mathcal{A}^T$ causing an event, for $j \in \{0, \ldots, n-1\}$. The vector $\mathbf{f_i} \in \Lambda_i.S$ contains the firing times of previous general transition firings according to the order stored in $\Lambda_i.o$. A path is then defined as:

$$\pi = (\Lambda_0, \mathbf{f_0}) \xrightarrow{\epsilon_0} \ldots \xrightarrow{\epsilon_{n-1}} (\Lambda_n, \mathbf{f_n}), \tag{2}$$

where for every $j \in \{0, \ldots, n-1\}$, we require that $\epsilon_j \in M(\Lambda_j)$ leads to Λ_{j+1}. The set of all paths with arbitrary length $n \in \mathbb{N}$ starting from the initial location Λ_0 and the empty firing vector $\mathbf{f_0}$ is denoted as $Paths_{PLT}(\Lambda_0)$. $\pi(i)$ refers to $(\Lambda_i, \mathbf{f_i})$ in path π.

The correspondence between paths through the PLT and paths in the HPnG is discussed in the following theorem.

Theorem 1. *A bijective function* $m : Paths_{\mathcal{H}}(\Gamma_0) \to Paths_{PLT}(\Lambda_0)$ *exists for* $\Gamma_0 = \Lambda_0.\Gamma$. *The following function then maps a path* $\sigma \in Paths_{\mathcal{H}}(\Gamma_0)$ *in the HPnG to the corresponding path* $\pi \in Paths_{PLT}(\Lambda_0)$ *in the PLT:*

$$m(\Gamma_0 \xrightarrow{(\Delta\tau_0, \epsilon_0)} \ldots \xrightarrow{(\Delta\tau_{n-1}, \epsilon_{n-1})} \Gamma_n) = (\Lambda_0, \mathbf{f_0}) \xrightarrow{\epsilon_0} \ldots \xrightarrow{\epsilon_{n-1}} (\Lambda_n, \mathbf{f_n}). \tag{3}$$

Proof. For each $\sigma \in Paths_{\mathcal{H}}(\Gamma_0)$, a unique corresponding path $\pi \in Paths_{PLT}(\Lambda_0)$ is iteratively constructed starting from $\Gamma_0 = \Lambda_0.\Gamma$, which induces an initial location Λ_0 following Definition 5. Note that initially $\mathbf{f_0}$ is an empty vector.

For $i \in \{0, \ldots, n-1\}$ and $\Gamma_i = \Lambda_i.\Gamma(\mathbf{f_i})$, each event $\Upsilon(\Gamma_i, \Gamma_{i+1}) = (\Delta\tau_i, \epsilon_i)$ between states Γ_i and Γ_{i+1} corresponds to an edge from location Λ_i that is caused by model element $\epsilon_i \in M(\Lambda_i)$ and leads to the child location $\Lambda_{i+1} \in \mathbf{\Lambda}_c(\Lambda)$. If $\epsilon_i \in \mathcal{T}^G$, the firing time of the general transition ϵ_i equals $f_{\epsilon_i} = \Gamma_i.\mathbf{g}_{\epsilon_i} + \Delta\tau_i$ which must be included in $\mathbf{f_{i+1}} = [\mathbf{f_i}, f_{\epsilon_i}]$. If the event is not caused by a general transition firing, $\mathbf{f_{i+1}} = \mathbf{f_i}$ holds. Hence, m is a function.

For every path $\pi = (\Lambda_0, \mathbf{f}_0) \xrightarrow{\epsilon_0} \ldots \xrightarrow{\epsilon_{n-1}} (\Lambda_n, \mathbf{f}_n) \in Paths_{PLT}(\Lambda_0)$, there is a path $\sigma \in Paths_{\mathcal{H}}(\Gamma_0)$ which maps to $\pi = m(\sigma)$. σ contains the states of the HPnG $\Gamma_i = \Lambda_i(\mathbf{f}_i)$ for $i \in \{0, \ldots, n\}$. The edges of the path consist of $\Delta\tau_j = \Lambda_{j+1}.t(\mathbf{f}_{j+1}) - \Lambda_j.t(\mathbf{f}_j)$ for $j \in \{0, \ldots, n-1\}$ and the copied model element ϵ_j. Hence, m is surjective.

Given two arbitrary but fixed paths $\sigma_1, \sigma_2 \in Paths_{\mathcal{H}}(\Gamma_0)$ with $\sigma_1 \neq \sigma_2$ and respective length $n_1, n_2 \in \mathbb{N}$, there exists an index $i \in \mathbb{N}$ with $i \leq \min\{n_1, n_2\}$ for which the states of the paths differ, i.e., $\Gamma_i^{\sigma_1} \neq \Gamma_i^{\sigma_2}$. Then, for $\pi_1 = m(\sigma_1)$ and $\pi_2 = m(\sigma_2)$, the tuples $(\Lambda_i^{\pi_1}, \mathbf{f}_i^{\pi_1}) \neq (\Lambda_i^{\pi_2}, \mathbf{f}_i^{\pi_2})$ at index i also differ in the PLT path due to the linearity of $\Lambda_i.t$ and $\Lambda_i.\Gamma$. Hence, m is injective.   □

Theorem 2. *Given a path through the PLT π which ends in state $(\Lambda_i, \mathbf{f}_i)$ with $n \in \mathbb{N}$ conflict sets $C_{t_1}^{\mathcal{T}}(\Lambda_i), \ldots, C_{t_n}^{\mathcal{T}}(\Lambda_i)$. The parametric location Λ of the following state in the path $(\Lambda, \mathbf{f}_i)$ is, regardless of the conflict resolution, always from exactly one conflict set $C_{t_i}^{\mathcal{T}}(\Lambda_i)$, $i \in \{1, \ldots, n\}$.*

Proof. Each conflict set has a different entry time function and the probability that they evaluate to the same value, given a fixed $\mathbf{f}_i$, equals 0, as general transitions fire according to absolute continuous probability distribution.   □

The above theorem ensures, that at any time of a simulation run, as will be explained in Sect. 4, at most one conflict set needs to be resolved.

4   Simulation

Statistical Model Checking executes several simulation runs and checks the validity of a property until a predefined accuracy for the probability estimate of the property is reached. During one run, starting from a given initial state, the successor state is computed iteratively by identifying the corresponding next event. All possible future events are identified by computing their remaining execution times and the next event has the minimum time. Simulation needs to keep track of the global time and the values of all discrete and continuous variables, since they are required for the computation of the next state and event. This process repeats until the predefined time-bound is reached. While discrete-event simulation usually jumps from one explicit state in the model to the next, our analytically-guided simulation works with symbolic states and simulates through the PLT (cf. Definition 8). This considerably simplifies the computation of the next event and its successor state as presented in the following.

4.1   Simulating Through the PLT

In the following we simulate through the PLT, starting in its root location. The simulation run is then determined by two things: (i) the firing times of the general transitions, and (ii) the conflict resolution in case of a nondeterministic conflict. The firing times of the general transitions are sampled from their corresponding probability density functions, as soon as the respective general

---

Algorithm 1 getNextState(simulation state L)

1: minEventTime = t_{max}
2: **for** $\Lambda_i : \mathbf{\Lambda}_c(L.\Lambda)$ **do**
3:    **if** $(\Delta\tau, \epsilon) = \Upsilon(L.\Lambda.\Gamma, \Lambda_i.\Gamma) \in \mathbb{R}_0^+ \times \mathcal{T}^G$ **then**   # *general firing leads to* Λ_i
4:       **if** $L.\mathbf{s}[\epsilon]$.empty() **then**   # *check if sample in sim. state*
5:          sample = sampleValue(ϵ)   # *sample required*
6:          $L.\mathbf{s}[\epsilon]$ = sample   # *save sample in sim. state*
7:       **else**
8:          sample = $L.\mathbf{s}[\epsilon]$ # *sampled in previous location*
9:       **end if**
10:       entryTime = $\Lambda_i.t([L.\mathbf{f}, \text{sample}])$
11:    **else**   # *no general firing*
12:       entryTime = $\Lambda_i.t(L.\mathbf{f})$
13:    **end if**
14:    **if** entryTime ¡ minEventTime **then**
15:       minEventTime = entryTime   # Λ_i *new prospect for next event*
16:       chosenChild = Λ_i
17:       conflictSet.clear()   # *clear prior found conflict set*
18:    **else if** entryTime == minEventTime **then**
19:       conflictSet.add(chosenChild, Λ_i)   # Λ_i *and chosenChild in conflict*
20:    **end if**
21: **end for**
22: **if** !conflictSet.empty() **then**   # *nondeterministic conflict*
23:    chosenChild = resolveConflict(conflictSet) # *one child is chosen*
24: **end if**
25: **if** $(\Delta\tau, \epsilon) = \Upsilon(L.\Lambda.\Gamma, L.\Lambda_i.\Gamma) \in \mathbb{R}_0^+ \times \mathcal{T}^G$ **then** # *general firing event*
26:    $L.\mathbf{f} = [L.\mathbf{f}, L.\mathbf{s}[\epsilon]]$ # *add sample to firings*
27:    removeSample($L.\mathbf{s}[\epsilon]$)   # *remove sample from unexpired samples*
28: **end if**
29: $L.\Lambda$ = chosenChild   # *move to child location*
30: **return** L

---

transitions becomes enabled. Thus, a different sample could have resulted in a different firing order and hence, a different path. For the simulation through the PLT we define a *simulation state*, which tracks the current parametric location Λ and the samples of the random variables. During a simulation run, samples for the general transitions are generated which are sorted in two variables. Vector $\mathbf{f}$ contains the (relative) expired sampling times in order $\Lambda.\mathbf{o}$. These can be used for the computation of the current simulation time and the valuations of continuous variables. Map $\mathbf{s}$ contains the samples which did not expire yet, but is not a list of future events. Instead these are given by the child locations.

Definition 9. (Simulation State). The simulation state consists of the tuple $L = (\Lambda, \mathbf{f}, \mathbf{s})$, with the current parametric location Λ, the vector $\mathbf{f} \in \Lambda.S$ with all expired samples in their firing order $\Lambda.o$. All yet unexpired samples s_i of general transitions $T_i \in \mathcal{T}^G$ are in a map $\mathbf{s}$ with $\mathbf{s}[T_i] = s_i$ for $i \in \{0, \ldots, |\mathcal{T}^G| - 1\}$.

Algorithm 2 simulateOneRun(simulation state L, property Ψ)

1: propertyState = undecided
2: **while** $(L.entryTime \le t_{max})$ **and** (propertyState == undecided) **do**
3:     $L' = \text{getNextState}(L)$
4:     propertyState = checkProperty(L, L', Ψ)
5:     $L = L'$
6: **end while**
7: **return** propertyState

The initial simulation state is defined by the root location, an empty vector $\mathbf{f}$ and without unexpired samples in $\mathbf{s}$. Algorithm 1 sketches how the next event and the next simulation state are determined given a simulation state $L = (\Lambda, \mathbf{f}, \mathbf{s})$. For each child location $\Lambda_i \in \mathbf{\Lambda}_c(\Lambda)$, the entry time is computed by using the linear function $\Lambda.t$ of the previous fired general transitions $L.\mathbf{f}$. In case the event between Λ and child location Λ_i is a general transition firing (line 3), the entry time also depends on the sample of the firing general transition. A sample for a general transition $T_i \in \mathcal{T}^G$ is generated according to its distribution $\phi_g^{\mathcal{T}}(T_i)$ when it is enabled for the first time since the simulation start or the last firing. That is the case, if no sample in $\mathbf{s}$ exists (line 4). The entry times of other events, i.e., no general transition firing, only depend on already fired transitions and thus require the past firings (line 12). The child with the smallest entry time is chosen (lines 14–16) and if entry times are equal, a nondeterministic conflict occurs. In case of a nondeterministic conflict, a conflict set is built while iterating through all child locations (line 19) which is then resolved (line 23). Different types of conflict resolutions are discussed in Sect. 4.3. In case of a general transition firing, the firing vector and the unused samples must be updated (lines 25–28) additionally to the parametric location in the simulation state L (line 29). The computation of the entry time requires $|\mathbf{f}|$ multiplications and $|\mathbf{f}|+1$ additions (in case of a general transition firing event +1 each) per child location. All possible events are already pre-computed and their time of occurrence is given as the entry time function $\Lambda.t$ of respective Λ. More computations are not required, as the state of the HPnG is already contained in the parametric locations. Hence, the model variables and its derivatives are only required for model checking during the simulation which facilitates the simulation.

4.2   Statistical Model Checking

Stochastic Time Logic (STL) is used to express properties regarding the state of the model at a given time point t. We follow the definition from [39] for HPnGs.

Definition 10. (STL formula [39]). A STL formula $\varphi ::= P_{\bowtie\theta}(\Psi)$ with bound $\theta \in [0, 1]$, comparison operator $\bowtie \in \{<, >, \le, \ge\}$ and property

$$\Psi ::= tt \mid AP \mid \neg\Psi \mid \Psi \wedge \Psi \mid \Psi\, U^{[t_1,t_2]}\Psi$$

denotes whether the probability that property Ψ fulfills $\bowtie \theta$. The property consists of true (tt) and atomic properties (AP), which can be negated and combined with and or *until*. A discrete atomic property $d_i \sim a$ compares a discrete marking d_i with a constant $a \in \mathbb{N}$ via $\sim \in \{=, <, >, \leq, \geq\}$. A continuous atomic property $x_i \sim b$ compares a continuous marking x_i with a constant $b \in \mathbb{R}$.

For the definition of the probability space for HPnGs and the satisfaction relation for STL, we refer to [39]. We are specifically interested in property $\Psi = \neg\Phi_1 \mathcal{U}^{[0, t_{max}]} \Phi_2$, where Φ_1 and Φ_2 are potentially nested STL properties, however without the until operator. The property Ψ then translates to reaching a state that fulfills Φ_2 within time $[0, t_{max}]$ along a path of states which avoid Φ_1. For a detailed description of the STL semantic, we refer to [39].

Every simulation starts at the predefined initial state, and traverses through the PLT as illustrated in Algorithm 2. According to line 2, each simulation run is executed until the validity of property Ψ can be decided or the time-bound of the property is reached. During every execution of the while loop, the next simulation state $L' = (\Lambda', \mathbf{f}', \mathbf{s}')$ is obtained in line 3 given simulation state $L = (\Lambda, \mathbf{f}, \mathbf{s})$. Note that the state stored in L' corresponds to the state at the event occurrence time, i.e., the entry time of the parametric location $\Lambda'.t(\mathbf{f}')$, as returned by Algorithm 1. The time spent between simulation states L and L' is denoted residence time and defined as $\Delta\tau = \Lambda.t(\mathbf{f}) - \min\{\Lambda'.t(\mathbf{f}'), t_{max}\}$, i.e., the difference between the entry time of the current simulation state $\Lambda.t(\mathbf{f})$ and the minimum of the entry time $\Lambda'.t(\mathbf{f}')$ of L' and the time-bound t_{max}.

The valuations of discrete variables are constant within a parametric location, hence checking the validity of a discrete atomic property between two simulation states is straight forward. In case of a continuous atomic property, the respective continuous variable x must further be tracked between two consecutive simulations states. The value between the states L and L' evolves according to $x_0(t) = \Lambda.\Gamma.x_0(\mathbf{f}) + \Lambda.\Gamma.d_{x_0} \cdot t$ for $t \in \{0, \ldots, \Delta\tau\}$. Hence, checking the validity of a continuous atomic property (line 4) requires information on the current state and the location residence time. The validity of nested STL formulas without *Until* can then be checked by evaluating the corresponding boolean expressions. The bijection shown in Theorem 1, ensures that the validity of atomic properties is maintained in the analytically-guided simulation.

The probability that property Ψ holds is estimated via multiple simulation runs. The result of each run is a Bernoulli-distributed random variable. Hence, the validity of Ψ corresponds to a sample of a $b \in \{0, 1\}$. For $n \in \mathbb{N}$ simulation runs, a sequence of independent values $b_1, \ldots, b_n$ is computed and the arithmetic mean $\hat{p} = \frac{1}{n} \sum_{i=1}^{n} b_i$ is an estimate of the actual probability.

Instead of the arithmetic mean, confidence intervals with $\hat{p} \in [a, b]$ can be considered for $a, b \in [0, 1]$. Repeating the simulation several times, $100 * \delta\%$ of the computed confidence intervals cover the real probability for a desired level of confidence $\delta \in [0, 1]$. The simulation can be executed, such that for a desired interval width $b - a = w$ with $w \in (0, 1]$ and confidence level δ, the number of simulation runs is adapted. We refer to [39] for a detailed explanation.

4.3   Nondeterminism

Schedulers solve nondeterministic conflicts. Different scheduler classes are discussed in [9] and have been adapted for HPnGs and singular automata with random clocks. This paper presents a unified definition of four different scheduler classes in HPnGs. Different scheduler classes are obtained depending on the information available to the scheduler.

Definition 11. (Scheduler). A scheduler is a measurable function $\mathfrak{s} : \Omega \to Dist(\mathcal{T})$ which maps states $\omega \in \Omega$ to a discrete probability distribution over the set of all transitions in conflict $C^{\mathcal{T}}(\omega)$ with $support(\mathfrak{s}(\omega)) \subseteq C^{\mathcal{T}}(\omega)$. Let $\mathcal{L}_{\mathcal{H}}$ be the set of all simulation states of a HPnG $\mathcal{H}$. The projection on parts of the simulation state r is denoted as $\mathcal{L}_{\mathcal{H}}|_r$, e.g., $\mathcal{L}_{\mathcal{H}}|_\Lambda = \{\Lambda \mid (\Lambda, \mathbf{f}, \mathbf{s}) \in \mathcal{L}_{\mathcal{H}}\}$. The type of scheduler then depends on the choice of Ω, as follows:

$$\Omega = \begin{cases} \mathcal{L}_{\mathcal{H}} & \text{history-dependent prophetic,} \\ \mathcal{L}_{\mathcal{H}}|_\Lambda & \text{discrete-history non-prophetic,} \\ \mathcal{S} & \text{memoryless non-prophetic,} \\ \mathcal{S} \times \mathcal{L}_{\mathcal{H}}|_\mathbf{s} & \text{memoryless prophetic.} \end{cases}$$

If the scheduler is memoryless non-prophetic, it only requires knowledge on the state-space of the HPnG $\mathcal{S}$. History-dependent schedulers require knowledge on the set of simulation states $\mathcal{L}_{\mathcal{H}}$. For $\Omega = \mathcal{L}_{\mathcal{H}}$, this corresponds to history-dependent prophetic schedulers. If the information available to the scheduler is restricted to the parametric location, i.e., the domain is $\Omega = \mathcal{L}_{\mathcal{H}}|_\Lambda$, the scheduler is discrete-history non-prophetic. If the unused samples $\mathbf{s}$ remain part of Ω, the scheduler also has information on the future and is hence prophetic. The learned schedulers which maximize or minimize probabilities in [32] are memoryless prophetic and non-prophetic with knowledge on the current state of the model $\Gamma \in \mathcal{S}$ and $\mathcal{L}_{\mathcal{H}}|_\mathbf{s}$ if prophetic. Q-Learning is used for optimization and requires a finite state-space, which is obtained by discretization with proven convergence to optimal probabilities [32]. While this approach could be extended to history-dependent schedulers in a classical simulation approach, this would lead to a much larger discretized state-space for Q-learning, and hence potentially to longer training times. Instead, we include Q-learning in the analytically-guided simulation as presented in Sect. 4.1. This allows to flexibly learn schedulers from the classes presented in Definition 11. For history-dependent schedulers, the discretized state-space remains small, as the parametric location identifier and the firings already include the whole history. The parametric location identifier suffices for discrete-history schedulers.

Memoryless schedulers require more computations as the valuations of the continuous variables are not evaluated during the simulation. The general transitions firings **f** must not be given to the scheduler, as they include information on the history. Hence, at every nondeterministic conflict the valuations of the continuous variables have to be computed while the markings of the discrete variables can be taken from the parametric location. The necessity of computing the valuations of the continuous variables occurs at nondeterministic conflicts and then reduces the advantage of the analytically-guided simulation.

5 Case Study

The analytically-guided simulation is implemented in hpnmg[1] [26] building on the PLT construction. Samples are generated with a C++ Mersenne Twister pseudo-random generator [31]. Our experiments have been executed single-threaded on a machine with an AMD Ryzen 7 PRO 5850U CPU and 32 GB of RAM (Fig. 1).

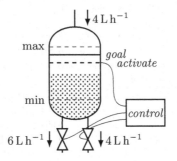

Fig. 1. A water tank with two controllable valves [44].

We reuse the water tank Fig. 1 in [40] to be able to compare our results with existing analytical and statistical results [32]. Initially, the tank of 20 m height is filled 4 m. When the tank reaches 16 m, a draining valve can be chosen nondeterministically. One valve reduces the water level by $6\,\mathrm{m\,h^{-1}}$ for 2 h, the other one by $4\,\mathrm{m\,h^{-1}}$ for 1 h. Every valve is blocked after usage for a uniformly distributed time between 0 and 6 hours. A visual representation of the underlying HPnG model is shown in [32, Fig. 3] and the corresponding hybrid automaton model is shown in [40, Fig. 5] (see Appendix A for convenience). We maximize the probability that the tank reaches a height h of 18 m before t_{max}:
$\Psi = tt\ U^{[0,t_{max}]} h \geq 18$ for different values of $t_{max} \in \{7, \ldots, 11\}$.

---

[1] https://zivgitlab.uni-muenster.de/ag-sks/tools/hpnmg/-/tree/simulation.

Table 1. Comparison of results for different scheduling classes for the tank case study.

		$t_{\max}$	7	8	9	10	11
Discrete-history non-prophetic	HPnG [44]	p_{max}	0	0.5347	0.6264	0.6444	0.7375
		Runtime	0.01 s	32.74 s	55.64 s	62.23 s	141.45 s
	Analytically-guided simulation	Midpoint	0	0.5278	0.6219	0.6447	0.7372
		PLT constr.	0.001 s	0.002 s	0.005 s	0.012 s	0.031 s
		Train. time	0.001 s	0.005 s	0.004 s	0.004 s	0.005 s
		Sim. time	0.004 s	0.076 s	0.074 s	0.072 s	0.065 s
Memoryless non-prophetic	modes ML [32]	Midpoint	0	0.53	0.62	0.64	0.74
		Train. time	1.00 s	1.1 s	1.10 s	1.30 s	1.40 s
		Sim. time	0.20 s	2.70 s	3.10 s	3.30 s	3.00 s
	Analytically-guided simulation	midpoint	0	0.5386	0.6278	0.6397	0.7386
		PLT constr.	0.001 s	0.002 s	0.005 s	0.012 s	0.031 s
		Train. time	0.001 s	0.005 s	0.007 s	0.006 s	0.007 s
		Sim. time	0.005 s	0.086 s	0.084 s	0.083 s	0.070 s
Memoryless prophetic	Modes ML [32]	Midpoint	0	0.60	0.64	0.65	0.74
		Train. time	3.00 s	3.40 s	4.10 s	3.90 s	4.00 s
		Sim. time	0.20 s	2.60 s	2.90 s	2.80 s	2.60 s
	Analytically-guided simulation	Midpoint	0	0.6060	0.6471	0.6493	0.7439
		PLT constr.	0.001 s	0.002 s	0.005 s	0.012 s	0.031 s
		Train. time	0.002 s	0.035 s	0.037 s	0.041 s	0.045 s
		Sim. time	0.004 s	0.080 s	0.077 s	0.078 s	0.068 s
History-dep. prophetic	Flowpipe [44]	p_{max}	0	0.6041	0.6488	0.6514	0.7798
		Runtime	0.25 s	2.17 s	11.68 s	71.53 s	3277.94 s
	Analytically-guided simulation	Midpoint	0	0.6039	0.6467	0.6533	0.7710
		PLT constr.	0.001 s	0.002 s	0.005 s	0.012 s	0.031 s
		Train. time	0.121 s	1.625 s	1.592 s	1.456 s	1.846 s
		Sim. time	0.005 s	0.099 s	0.071 s	0.071 s	0.058 s

We compare previously published results from different tools, which compute optimized probabilities for different scheduler classes. We adapt our used scheduler class to match the corresponding tool. Both analytical approaches, HPnG and Flowpipe, are exact up to a statistically estimated error of at most 10^{-3} which stems from the multidimensional integration. modes ML and our approach compute confidence intervals, here with $\delta = 0.99$ and $w = 0.02$. The number of training runs and the training parameters are adapted from [32].

Table 1 presents the results of our analytically-guided simulation with different scheduler classes and results computed by the above mentioned tools. For modes ML and the analytical-guided simulation, the midpoint of the computed confidence interval is given together with the training time of a scheduler and the simulation time required to obtain a confidence interval with width w. To ensure a fair comparison, the run time of the analytically-guided simulation always indicates the time to generate the PLT. However, note that it would suffice to generate the PLT once for each t_{max}.

HPnG computes optimal probabilities for discrete-history non-prophetic schedulers. Our results match as the confidence intervals include the respective p_{max}. modes ML learns memoryless (non-)prophetic schedulers and in both cases, the results match, as the confidence intervals overlap. With the Flow-pipe approach, discrete-history non-prophetic and history-dependent prophetic schedulers are considered. To keep the table clear, the former are not shown, but match the results of HPnG [44] with run times similar to the prophetic scheduler. To match the history-dependent prophetic scheduler in the Flowpipe, 1 million training runs were required. Note that in [32] 1 million training runs required 68 s, while it only requires 1.846 s in the analytically-guided simulation.

Our approach clearly outperforms both, the analytical approaches and modes ML in all cases. modes ML was executed on a different machine (i5-6600T, 16 GB memory), however the impact on performance should be negligible, as modes ML is single-threaded. While the run times of the analytical approaches increase considerably with t_{max}, simulation scales better. Training and simulation times only increase marginally with the time-bound. The time to build the PLT scales worse than the simulation and training time, but remains small in this model.

6   Conclusion

We presented analytically-guided simulation which has the ability to significantly reduce the computation effort when learning optimal schedulers based on simulating paths in the symbolic state-space representation of a PLT. By leveraging analytical knowledge to guide the simulation process, our approach outperforms existing analytical and statistical approaches for computing reachability probabilities optimized for different scheduler classes. As a consequence of Theorem 1 analytically-guided simulation explores the same state-space as discrete-event simulation over paths of a HPnG. Future work will apply the concept to more expressive model classes, e.g., rectangular automata with random clocks [7]. Further, we will integrate algorithms for rare-event probabilities.

A   Visual Representation of the Tank Model

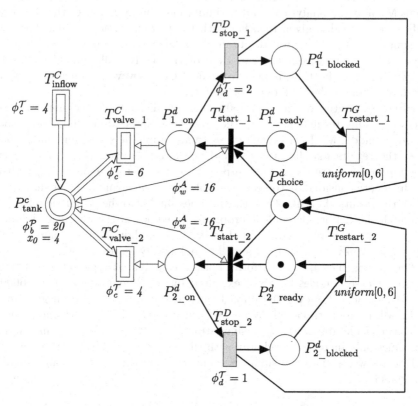

Fig. 2. Tank system modeled as HPnG as in [32]. The continuous place P_{tank}^c models the fluid level of the tank. The two valves are modeled by the continuous transitions $T_{\text{valve\_1}}^C$ and $T_{\text{valve\_2}}^C$, which are enabled while a token is in $P_{1\_\text{on}}^d$ respectively $P_{2\_\text{on}}^d$. The nondeterministic choice is modeled by the conflict of the immediate transitions $T_{\text{start\_1}}^I$ and $T_{\text{start\_2}}^I$ if a token is in P_{choice}^d.

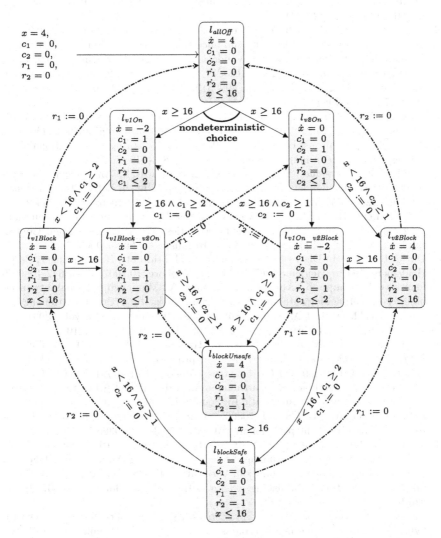

Fig. 3. Tank system modeled as singular automaton with random clocks [40]. The fluid level of the tank is modeled by the variable x. The nondeterministic choice is highlighted. The active time for the two valves is given by the clocks c_1 and c_2. Additionally the random blocking times for the valves are modeled by the random clocks r_1 and r_2.

References

1. Abate, A., Katoen, J.P., Lygeros, J., Prandini, M.: Approximate model checking of stochastic hybrid systems. Eur. J. Control. **16**(6), 624–641 (2010). https://doi.org/10.3166/ejc.16.624-641

2. Adelt, J., Herber, P., Niehage, M., Remke, A.: Towards safe and resilient hybrid systems in the presence of learning and uncertainty. In: Leveraging Applications of Formal Methods, Verification and Validation. Verification Principles—11th International Symposium, ISoLA 2022, Rhodes, Greece, October 22–30, 2022, Proceedings, Part I. LNCS, vol. 13701, pp. 299–319. Springer (2022). https://doi.org/10.1007/978-3-031-19849-6_18

3. Budde, C.E., D'Argenio, P.R., Hartmanns, A.: Better automated importance splitting for transient rare events. In: Dependable Software Engineering. Theories, Tools, and Applications, LNCS, vol. 10606, pp. 42–58. Springer International Publishing, Cham (2017). https://doi.org/10.1007/978-3-319-69483-2_3

4. Budde, C.E., D'Argenio, P.R., Hartmanns, A., Sedwards, S.: An efficient statistical model checker for nondeterminism and rare events. Int. J. Softw. Tools Technol. Transfer **22**(6), 759–780 (2020). https://doi.org/10.1007/s10009-020-00563-2

5. Cai, M., Peng, H., Li, Z., Kan, Z.: Learning-based probabilistic LTL motion planning with environment and motion uncertainties. IEEE Trans. Autom. Control **66**(5), 2386–2392 (2021). https://doi.org/10.1109/TAC.2020.3006967

6. David, R., Alla, H.: Discrete, Continuous, and Hybrid Petri Nets. Springer, Berlin Heidelberg, Berlin, Heidelberg (2010). https://doi.org/10.1007/978-3-642-10669-9

7. Delicaris, J., Schupp, S., Ábrahám, E., Remke, A.: Maximizing reachability probabilities in rectangular automata with random clocks. In: 17th International Symposium on Theoretical Aspects of Software Engineering. LNCS, vol. 13931, pp. 1–19. Springer (2023). https://doi.org/10.1007/978-3-031-35257-7_10

8. D'Argenio, P., Legay, A., Sedwards, S., Traonouez, L.M.: Smart sampling for lightweight verification of Markov decision processes. Int. J. Softw. Tools Technol. Transfer **17**(4), 469–484 (2015). https://doi.org/10.1007/s10009-015-0383-0

9. D'Argenio, P.R., Gerhold, M., Hartmanns, A., Sedwards, S.: A hierarchy of scheduler classes for stochastic automata. In: Foundations of Software Science and Computation Structures, LNCS, vol. 10803, pp. 384–402. Springer International Publishing, Cham (2018). https://doi.org/10.1007/978-3-319-89366-2_21

10. D'Argenio, P.R., Hartmanns, A., Sedwards, S.: Lightweight statistical model checking in nondeterministic continuous time. In: Leveraging Applications of Formal Methods, Verification and Validation. Verification, LNCS, vol. 11245, pp. 336–353. Springer International Publishing, Cham (2018). https://doi.org/10.1007/978-3-030-03421-4_22

11. Ellen, C., Gerwinn, S., Fränzle, M.: Statistical model checking for stochastic hybrid systems involving nondeterminism over continuous domains. Int. J. Softw. Tools Technol. Transfer **17**(4), 485–504 (2015). https://doi.org/10.1007/s10009-014-0329-y

12. Fränzle, M., Hahn, E.M., Hermanns, H., Wolovick, N., Zhang, L.: Measurability and safety verification for stochastic hybrid systems. In: Proceedings of the 14th International Conference on Hybrid Systems: Computation and Control—HSCC '11. p. 43. ACM Press, Chicago, IL, USA (2011). https://doi.org/10.1145/1967701.1967710

13. Fränzle, M., Teige, T., Eggers, A.: Engineering constraint solvers for automatic analysis of probabilistic hybrid automata. J. Logic Algebraic Program. **79**(7), 436–466 (2010). https://doi.org/10.1016/j.jlap.2010.07.003

14. Gao, Y., Fränzle, M.: A solving procedure for stochastic satisfiability modulo theories with continuous domain. In: 12th International Conference on Quantitative Evaluation of Systems (QEST). LNCS, vol. 9259, pp. 295–311. Springer (2015). https://doi.org/10.1007/978-3-319-22264-6_19

15. Ghasemieh, H., Remke, A., Haverkort, B.R.: Survivability evaluation of fluid critical infrastructures using hybrid petri nets. In: IEEE 19th Pacific Rim International Symposium on Dependable Computing, PRDC 2013, Vancouver, BC, Canada, December 2–4, 2013, pp. 152–161. IEEE Computer Society (2013). https://doi.org/10.1109/PRDC.2013.34

16. Ghasemieh, H., Remke, A., Haverkort, B.R.: Survivability analysis of a sewage treatment facility using hybrid petri nets. Perform. Evaluation **97**, 36–56 (2016). https://doi.org/10.1016/j.peva.2015.11.004

17. Gribaudo, M., Remke, A.: Hybrid Petri nets with general one-shot transitions. Perform. Eval. **105**, 22–50 (2016). https://doi.org/10.1016/j.peva.2016.09.002

18. Hahn, E.M., Hartmanns, A., Hermanns, H., Katoen, J.P.: A compositional modelling and analysis framework for stochastic hybrid systems. Formal Methods Syst. Des. **43**(2), 191–232 (2013). https://doi.org/10.1007/s10703-012-0167-z

19. Hahn, E.M., Perez, M., Schewe, S., Somenzi, F., Trivedi, A., Wojtczak, D.: Faithful and effective reward schemes for model-free reinforcement learning of omega-regular objectives. In: Automated Technology for Verification and Analysis, LNCS, vol. 12302, pp. 108–124. Springer International Publishing, Cham (2020). https://doi.org/10.1007/978-3-030-59152-6_6

20. Hartmanns, A., Hermanns, H.: The modest toolset: an integrated environment for quantitative modelling and verification. In: Tools and Algorithms for the Construction and Analysis of Systems, LNCS, vol. 8413, pp. 593–598. Springer, Berlin Heidelberg, Berlin, Heidelberg (2014). https://doi.org/10.1007/978-3-642-54862-8_51

21. Hartmanns, A., Hermanns, H., Krčál, J.: Schedulers are no Prophets. In: Semantics, Logics, and Calculi, LNCS, vol. 9560, pp. 214–235. Springer International Publishing, Cham (2016). https://doi.org/10.1007/978-3-319-27810-0_11

22. Hasanbeig, M., Kantaros, Y., Abate, A., Kroening, D., Pappas, G.J., Lee, I.: Reinforcement learning for temporal logic control synthesis with probabilistic satisfaction guarantees. In: 2019 IEEE 58th Conference on Decision and Control (CDC), pp. 5338–5343. IEEE, Nice, France (2019). https://doi.org/10.1109/CDC40024.2019.9028919

23. Hasanbeig, M., Abate, A., Kroening, D.: Cautious reinforcement learning with logical constraints. In: Proceedings of the 19th International Conference on Autonomous Agents and Multiagent Systems, pp. 483–491 (2020)

24. Heymann, M., Feng Lin, Meyer, G., Resmerita, S.: Analysis of Zeno behaviors in a class of hybrid systems. IEEE Trans. Autom. Control **50**(3), 376–383 (2005). https://doi.org/10.1109/TAC.2005.843874

25. Hüls, J., Remke, A.: Model checking hpngs in multiple dimensions: Representing state sets as convex polytopes. In: Formal Techniques for Distributed Objects, Components, and Systems—39th IFIP WG 6.1 International Conference, FORTE 2019, Held as Part of the 14th International Federated Conference on Distributed Computing Techniques, DisCoTec 2019, Kongens Lyngby, Denmark, June 17–21, 2019, Proceedings. LNCS, vol. 11535, pp. 148–166. Springer (2019). https://doi.org/10.1007/978-3-030-21759-4_9

26. Hüls, J., Niehaus, H., Remke, A.: hpnmg: AC++ tool for model checking hybrid Petri nets with general transitions. In: NASA Formal Methods, LNCS, vol. 12229,

pp. 369–378. Springer International Publishing, Cham (2020). https://doi.org/10. 1007/978-3-030-55754-6_22

27. Hüls, J., Pilch, C., Schinke, P., Niehaus, H., Delicaris, J., Remke, A.: State-space construction of hybrid Petri nets with multiple stochastic firings. ACM Trans. Model. Comput. Simul. **31**(3), 1–37 (2021). https://doi.org/10.1145/3449353

28. Jegourel, C., Larsen, K.G., Legay, A., Mikučionis, M., Poulsen, D.B., Sedwards, S.: Importance sampling for stochastic timed automata. In: Dependable Software Engineering: Theories, Tools, and Applications, LNCS, vol. 9984, pp. 163–178. Springer International Publishing, Cham (2016). https://doi.org/10.1007/978-3-319-47677-3_11

29. Laurenti, L., Lahijanian, M., Abate, A., Cardelli, L., Kwiatkowska, M.: Formal and efficient synthesis for continuous-time linear stochastic hybrid processes. IEEE Trans. Autom. Control **66**(1), 17–32 (2021). https://doi.org/10.1109/TAC.2020. 2975028. Jan

30. Legay, A., Sedwards, S., Traonouez, L.M.: Scalable verification of Markov decision processes. In: Software Engineering and Formal Methods, LNCS, vol. 8938, pp. 350–362. Springer International Publishing, Cham (2015). https://doi.org/10. 1007/978-3-319-15201-1_23

31. Matsumoto, M., Nishimura, T.: Mersenne twister: a 623-dimensionally equidistributed uniform pseudo-random number generator. ACM Trans. Model. Comput. Simul. **8**(1), 3–30 (1998). https://doi.org/10.1145/272991.272995

32. Niehage, M., Hartmanns, A., Remke, A.: Learning optimal decisions for stochastic hybrid systems. In: Proceedings of the 19th ACM-IEEE International Conference on Formal Methods and Models for System Design, pp. 44–55. ACM, Virtual Event China (2021). https://doi.org/10.1145/3487212.3487339

33. Niehage, M., Pilch, C., Remke, A.: Simulating Hybrid Petri nets with general transitions and non-linear differential equations. In: Proceedings of the 13th EAI International Conference on Performance Evaluation Methodologies and Tools, pp. 88–95. ACM, Tsukuba Japan (2020). https://doi.org/10.1145/3388831.3388842

34. Niehage, M., Remke, A.: Learning that grid-convenience does not hurt resilience in the presence of uncertainty. In: Formal Modeling and Analysis of Timed Systems—20th International Conference, FORMATS 2022, Warsaw, Poland, September 13–15, 2022, Proceedings. LNCS, vol. 13465, pp. 298–306. Springer (2022). https:// doi.org/10.1007/978-3-031-15839-1_17

35. Pilch, C., Edenfeld, F., Remke, A.: HYPEG: Statistical model checking for hybrid Petri nets: tool paper. In: Proceedings of the 11th EAI International Conference on Performance Evaluation Methodologies and Tools—VALUETOOLS 2017, pp. 186–191. ACM Press, Venice, Italy (2017). https://doi.org/10.1145/3150928.3150956

36. Pilch, C., Hartmanns, A., Remke, A.: Classic and non-prophetic model checking for Hybrid Petri nets with stochastic firings. In: Proceedings of the 23rd International Conference on Hybrid Systems: Computation and Control, pp. 1–11. ACM, Sydney New South Wales Australia (2020). https://doi.org/10.1145/3365365.3382198

37. Pilch, C., Krause, M., Remke, A., Ábrahám, E.: A transformation of Hybrid Petri nets with stochastic firings into a subclass of stochastic hybrid automata. In: NASA Formal Methods, LNCS, vol. 12229, pp. 381–400. Springer International Publishing, Cham (2020). https://doi.org/10.1007/978-3-030-55754-6_23

38. Pilch, C., Niehage, M., Remke, A.: HPnGs go non-linear: statistical dependability evaluation of battery-powered systems. In: 2018 IEEE 26th International Symposium on Modeling, Analysis, and Simulation of Computer and Telecommunication Systems (MASCOTS), pp. 157–169. IEEE, Milwaukee, WI (2018). https://doi. org/10.1109/MASCOTS.2018.00024

39. Pilch, C., Remke, A.: Statistical model checking for Hybrid Petri nets with multiple general transitions. In: 2017 47th Annual IEEE/IFIP International Conference on Dependable Systems and Networks (DSN), pp. 475–486. IEEE, Denver, CO, USA (2017). https://doi.org/10.1109/DSN.2017.41

40. Pilch, C., Schupp, S., Remke, A.: Optimizing reachability probabilities for a restricted class of stochastic hybrid automata via Flowpipe-construction. In: Quantitative Evaluation of Systems, LNCS, vol. 12846, pp. 435–456. Springer International Publishing, Cham (2021). https://doi.org/10.1007/978-3-030-85172-9_23

41. Sadigh, D., Kim, E.S., Coogan, S., Sastry, S.S., Seshia, S.A.: A learning based approach to control synthesis of Markov decision processes for linear temporal logic specifications. In: 53rd IEEE Conference on Decision and Control, pp. 1091–1096. IEEE, Los Angeles, CA, USA (2014). https://doi.org/10.1109/CDC.2014.7039527

42. Shmarov, F., Zuliani, P.: ProbReach: verified probabilistic delta-reachability for stochastic hybrid systems. In: Proceedings of the 18th International Conference on Hybrid Systems: Computation and Control, pp. 134–139. ACM, Seattle Washington (Apr 2015). https://doi.org/10.1145/2728606.2728625

43. Shmarov, F., Zuliani, P.: Probabilistic hybrid systems verification via SMT and Monte Carlo techniques. In: Hardware and Software: Verification and Testing, LNCS, vol. 10028, pp. 152–168. Springer International Publishing, Cham (2016). https://doi.org/10.1007/978-3-319-49052-6_10

44. da Silva, C., Schupp, S., Remke, A.: Optimizing reachability probabilities for a restricted class of stochastic hybrid automata via flowpipe-construction. ACM Trans. Model. Comput. Simul. (2023). https://doi.org/10.1145/3607197

45. Zimmermann, A., Maciel, P.: Importance function derivation for RESTART simulations of Petri nets. In: 9th International Workshop on Rare Event Simulation (2012)

Kubernetes-in-the-Loop: Enriching Microservice Simulation Through Authentic Container Orchestration

Martin Straesser[1]([✉]), Patrick Haas[1], Sebastian Frank[2], Alireza Hakamian[3], André van Hoorn[2], and Samuel Kounev[1]

[1] University of Würzburg, Würzburg, Germany
{martin.straesser,samuel.kounev}@uni-wuerzburg.de,
patrick.haas@informatik.uni-wuerzburg.de
[2] University of Hamburg, Hamburg, Germany
{sebastian.frank,andre.van.hoorn}@uni-hamburg.de
[3] University of Stuttgart, Stuttgart, Germany
mir-alireza.hakamian@iste.uni-stuttgart.de

Abstract. Microservices deployed and managed by container orchestration frameworks like Kubernetes are the bases of modern cloud applications. In microservice performance modeling and prediction, simulations provide a lightweight alternative to experimental analysis, which requires dedicated infrastructure and a laborious setup. However, existing simulators cannot run realistic scenarios, as performance-critical orchestration mechanisms (like scheduling or autoscaling) are manually modeled and can consequently not be represented in their full complexity and configuration space. This work combines a state-of-the-art simulation for microservice performance with Kubernetes container orchestration. Hereby, we include the original implementation of Kubernetes artifacts enabling realistic scenarios and testing of orchestration policies with low overhead. In two experiments with Kubernetes' *kube-scheduler* and *cluster-autoscaler*, we demonstrate that our framework can correctly handle different configurations of these orchestration mechanisms boosting both the simulation's use cases and authenticity.

Keywords: Kubernetes · Microservices · Container orchestration · Discrete event simulation · Cloud computing · Software performance

1 Introduction

Microservices are a modern architectural style for developing complex software systems with a steadily increasing adoption in practice [20]. Containers are the most popular deployment technology for microservices enabling improved elasticity and faster start times compared to virtual machines [38,39,43,49]. As manual management of hundreds to thousands of containers is impractical, container

E. Kalyvianaki and M. Paolieri (Eds.): VALUETOOLS 2023, LNICST 539, pp. 82–98, 2024.
https://doi.org/10.1007/978-3-031-48885-6_6

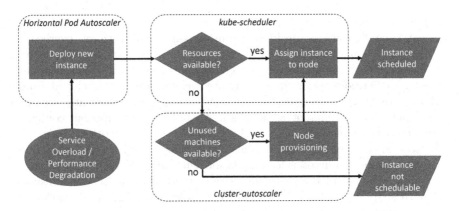

Fig. 1. Interactions between Kubernetes components.

orchestration (CO) frameworks are widely used, with Kubernetes being the most popular platform [13]. CO frameworks must maintain an acceptable quality of service of the managed applications, fulfilling many performance-relevant tasks, such as autoscaling, scheduling, or container networking [41]. As previous studies have shown, CO frameworks can significantly influence performance metrics of deployed applications, like response times or CPU usage [35,37,44,45].

Consequently, microservice performance models have to consider the CO frameworks' behavior for accurate performance prediction. However, several challenges arise here. First, the orchestration mechanisms to be simulated are highly complex. For example, the Kubernetes scheduling algorithm has nine extension points that can be individually configured for specific use cases [28]. Second, there are dependencies between single orchestration mechanisms or application-level patterns [40]. Figure 1 shows how Kubernetes' Horizontal Pod Autoscaler, *kube-scheduler* and *cluster-autoscaler* work together when new service instances need to be deployed reacting to a performance degradation. Third, CO frameworks are regularly updated, leading to a change in behavior and quickly causing performance models to be outdated. Previous work in microservice performance modeling and simulation integrates either no or only self-implemented, simplified runtime orchestration mechanisms [8,17,22,46].

This work aims to establish a link between microservice performance simulation and modern CO frameworks. We present an approach that enables connecting a discrete event simulation and an event-based system. We use this approach to extend the microservice simulator MiSim [17] with Kubernetes orchestration mechanisms using their original code artifacts. By this, orchestration mechanisms can be integrated with simulation in their full complexity without requiring abstract models, making the simulation more authentic. Our implementation uses an adapter that translates events from the simulation to Kubernetes events and vice versa. Actions of the Kubernetes components directly modify simulated entities. We validate our approach in experiments with Kubernetes' kube-scheduler and cluster-autoscaler. We show that different complex scheduling and autoscaling configurations can be tested in the simulation with low overhead.

Microservice application designers can use our framework to evaluate realistic scenarios with impact factors present at runtime early in the development process. Furthermore, performance engineers could use the developed framework to study the performance of a microservice application in what-if scenarios in conjunction with different workloads and Kubernetes component configurations. Container orchestration researchers can use the framework to design new orchestration mechanisms and evaluate their behavior with different applications. Combining a microservice simulation with original Kubernetes components allows the use of the full complexity of the orchestration mechanisms in each of these use cases, leading to a more expressive and realistic simulation. All in all, the contribution of this paper is twofold:

- We present an approach to connect a discrete-event simulation with the event-based system of Kubernetes and use it to extend the state-of-the-art microservice performance simulator MiSim [17].
- We analyze the usability and overhead of our approach in two detailed case studies on (i) container scheduling and (ii) cluster autoscaling.

The remainder of this paper is structured as follows. In the next section, we present the foundations of this work: the microservice simulator MiSim, as well as information about the architecture of Kubernetes. Section 3 discusses related works and the differences to this paper. Section 4 explains our approach in detail, while Sect. 5 presents our case studies with the kube-scheduler and cluster-autoscaler as examples of integrated Kubernetes components. Section 6 discusses the advantages, disadvantages, and limitations of our approach, while Sect. 7 concludes the work.

2   Foundations

2.1   MiSim: A Discrete Event Simulator for Microservice Performance and Resilience

Frank et al. [17] propose MiSim, a simulator for microservice performance and resilience. Technically, MiSim utilizes a discrete-event simulation (DES) realized through the DES framework DESMO-J [32]. As an input, a lightweight architectural description with microservice descriptions and active resilience mechanisms is required. Microservice properties include instance numbers, available operations and their dependencies, CPU demands, and more. These elements are simulated together with dynamic aspects, like user requests. Notably, MiSim supports the simulation of common mechanisms relevant to request behavior and thus performance, i.e., circuit breakers, connection limiters, retries, load balancers, and autoscalers. MiSim can process time-varying workloads and outputs several performance metrics, such as response times and CPU utilization. MiSim is conceptually and technically developed to be extensible. In particular, it uses the Strategy design pattern for many components, allowing to substitute their behavior easily. For example, four CPU scheduling policies are implemented. By default, MiSim uses Multi-Level Feedback Queues and the SARR algorithm proposed by Matarneh [34] that schedules computation time based on the median of the remaining burst time of all scheduled processes.

2.2 Kubernetes Architecture and Communication Patterns

In this work, we exploit the internal architecture and communication of Kubernetes [27] to connect to MiSim. The Kubernetes control plane consists of four essential components: an *etcd database*, the *kube-controller-manager*, the *kube-scheduler*, and the *kube-apiserver*. The etcd database persists the states of the cluster resources. The controller manager runs a series of processes that, for example, monitor nodes or jobs. The scheduler assigns containers, organized in so-called pods, to worker nodes for execution. The central component is the kube-apiserver, which handles every communication between the control plane and worker nodes. It is based on the Kubernetes API [25] and serves endpoints for every resource type in the cluster (e.g., nodes, pods). When a consumer (e.g., the kube-scheduler) requests information about a resource type in the cluster (e.g., nodes), it queries the corresponding endpoint. Kubernetes uses a "list-then-watch" principle to distribute information to all interested consumers. After starting a Kubernetes component, it requests the latest list of selected resources with a list request. This list contains a resource version, which is later used as a reference to this list. The consumer stores this list in an internal cache. Then the consumer sends a watch request with the resource version of its cached list as a query parameter. This request sets up an HTTP streaming connection between the kube-apiserver and the consumer. If a change to subscribed resources happens (e.g., a new node is added to the cluster), a watch event is emitted. The watch event has a type (*added, modified,* or *deleted*) and a representation of the affected resource. The consumer receives this event, modifies its cache, and performs an action if necessary. We refer to the official documentation for more information about the Kubernetes API [25].

3 Related Work

There are different ways to evaluate the performance of container orchestration (CO) frameworks. COFFEE [41] is a benchmarking framework for CO frameworks that allows the characterization of the performance of an orchestrator (configuration) with different metrics. Other works use benchmarking approaches, primarily focusing on Kubernetes [11,21,37,47]. While benchmarking can provide the most accurate results and realistic scenarios, it requires an extensive infrastructure. Simulations usually give less precise results but are much more cost-efficient. There are several simulations for component-based systems that cover models of selected CO mechanisms, e.g., load balancing [9,50], autoscaling [7] or networking [46]. In contrast to these works, we aim to combine microservice simulation with multiple CO tasks and mechanisms using their original implementation, i.e., without hand-crafted models.

Previous works have already dealt with the connection between simulations and real code. *Software-in-the-Loop* [14] is a term in this area that describes this connection, inspired by Hardware-in-the-Loop simulations. Such approaches focus primarily on testing control software in autonomous systems [10,19]. Erb and Kargl [16] note general analogies between discrete-event simulations and event-driven architectures. In the area of software performance simulations, a similar concept has been used by Von Massow et al. [33], combining a simulation and an adaptation controller. In this work, we apply a similar concept to microservice simulation and Kubernetes using scheduling and cluster autoscaling as exemplary CO mechanisms. In general, both Kubernetes scheduling and cluster autoscaling are active research areas, as confirmed by recent articles [12,42,48]. For Kubernetes scheduling, there is a community project called kube-scheduler-simulator [30] where different scheduling policies can be tested similarly to our experiment in Sect. 5.1 but without evaluating their impact on the performance of deployed services.

4   Approach

In this section, we explain our concept to integrate Kubernetes orchestration mechanisms in the microservice simulation MiSim. First, some entities and basic CO models need to be integrated into MiSim. Section 4.2 presents our approach to combine discrete event simulation and event-based systems, while Sect. 4.3 shows how we handle incompatible models and events. We conclude this section with a detailed look at Kubernetes scheduling and cluster autoscaling. Our implementation [1] is to be seen as a wrapper that is 100% compatible with the MiSim core and builds on its extension points.

4.1   Integration of Basic Container Orchestration Models

The MiSim core does not have any deployment models but only models for microservice architectures and resilience patterns. CPU resources are considered independently from nodes. For this reason, we add some basic entities and associated events relevant at deployment time in the simulation: A *node* is modeled as a bunch of resources. A *cluster* is a graph with a set of nodes connected with edges indicating network latencies between individual nodes. A *container* has a 1:1 relationship to a microservice instance from the MiSim core and is deployed on exactly one node. Next, we need to define which aspects of container orchestration should be considered in our simulation. We build on the work of Straesser et al. [41] in which eight performance-relevant tasks of container orchestration frameworks are identified: container deployment, scheduling, resource allocation, availability, health monitoring, scaling, load balancing, and networking. We add support for all of these tasks in the simulation and implement simple orchestration mechanisms directly.

Performance overheads due to the deployment of containers are taken into account in the simulation by startup times. Each container has a certain resource requirement, which has to be considered during scheduling. When the scheduler assigns a container to a node, a certain amount of resources are reserved and unavailable for other containers on the same node. The scheduler has to check if enough resources are available on the node. We implement two standard scheduling algorithms: random and round-robin. Health monitoring is represented in the simulation by periodic events that check the status of all deployed containers. Restarts can be simulated if a container has been crashed (e.g., by MiSim's chaos monkey function). Networking is determined by the cluster network graph indicating the mean latency and standard deviation between nodes. Furthermore, we have adapted one autoscaling and several load balancing strategies already available in MiSim to work with the new container and node models.

4.2 Connecting a Discrete Event Simulation and an Event-Driven System

General Concept. This section presents our abstract concept for combining a discrete event simulation (DES) with an event-driven system (EDS). Our goal is to extend the authenticity and use cases of the DES by including mechanisms/algorithms used in the EDS. A discrete-event simulation [31] is a sequence of events where each event $e \in E$ is associated with a time point t in the simulation time. Here, E denotes the set of all possible types of events. Each event e is associated with a function $F(e)$, which is executed as soon as e occurs. This function can, for example, change modeled entities in the simulation. An event-driven system [36] is a popular architectural style for developing component-based software. Two components communicate with each other by the sender (producer) emitting an event e' and sending it via a proxy and middleware (channel) to the receiver (consumer). In the following, we denote the set of defined event types in the EDS as E'.

Consider a set of special event types $\Theta \subseteq E$ in the DES. We modify all functions $F(e)$ for all events $e \in \Theta$ such that these events are passed to the EDS. If such an event e occurs at simulation time t in the simulation, two more steps are needed to make the event processable by the EDS. First, we need a transformation τ that maps the event e to an event or a sequence of events $e' \in E'$, as usually not all events in the DES are represented in the EDS and vice versa. Second, passing a representation of the simulation state $S(t)$ at time t may be necessary. This is especially necessary if not all events $e \in E$ are passed to the EDS. $S(t)$ should contain the states of all simulated entities relevant to the EDS. If the interface of the EDS allows only event-based communication, the simulation state $S(t)$ must be transformed into a sequence of events from E'. When sending e' and $S(t)$, the DES acts as an event producer from the EDS' point of view. The EDS forwards all received events to consuming components. The consumers now execute a black-box logic and generate responses $r \in E'$

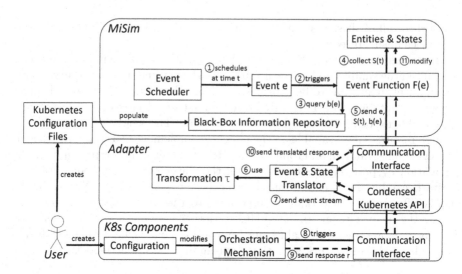

Fig. 2. Overview of our approach and component interactions.

as reactions to received events. The responses are passed back to the DES and processed by $F(e)$. As a consequence, entities or states in the simulation might be modified.

Application to MiSim and Kubernetes. In our use case, we connect the DES MiSim with event-based orchestration mechanisms of Kubernetes. Figure 2 shows an overview of our developed framework. To bridge the gap between MiSim and Kubernetes, we decided to use an adapter [2]. This has the advantage that the simulation remains slim, and if no Kubernetes components are to be used, no unnecessary code must be loaded and executed. We select a set of events Θ from MiSim, that are relevant for Kubernetes components. Θ includes all events affecting containers and nodes, while several other MiSim events, e.g., related to CPUs or logging, are excluded. The simulation sends selected events and the state of the simulated entities to the adapter. The adapter is responsible for the event transformation τ and the processing and transformation of the components' responses r. It implements relevant parts of the Kubernetes API, especially endpoints for pods and nodes. Hence, it acts like the kube-apiserver from the Kubernetes components' point of view. Because the kube-apiserver handles all communication in the Kubernetes control plane, we only need this one adapter for different components. The adapter and Kubernetes components are started prior to the simulation. We initialize the component caches with empty lists for all resource types. When the simulation is started, events for modeled resource types (like pods or nodes) are forwarded to the Kubernetes components.

4.3 Handling Incompatible Events and Models

General Concept. In the following, we consider cases where the DES and the EDS use different models or entities that cannot be transformed into each other. In the following, let M_D be the set of models and entities which appear in the DES but have no equivalent in the EDS. Similarly, let M_E be the set of models and entities that exist in EDS but have no equivalent in the DES. Let M_{D+E} be the set of models and entities with equivalences in DES and EDS. First, we consider elements from M_D. Since, in our case, we are only interested in the results of the DES, these do not pose a problem. We simply exclude all events concerning entities M_D from the set Θ. We just have to ensure that we correctly model interactions between entities from M_D and entities from M_{D+E}.

We can divide elements from M_E into two groups. We ignore the group of models or entities from M_E that have no interaction with elements from M_{D+E} or whose interactions should not be considered in the DES. The second group of elements from M_E that have relevant interactions with elements from M_{D+E} has to be considered in our approach. These can, for example, influence the response r to an event e from the DES and thus influence the simulation run. To solve this problem, we propose to use a black-box information repository (BIR). The DES receives a set of additional EDS-specific information B before starting a run, as well as information about which events $e \in \Theta$ should use which information $b \in B$. The simulation does not interpret or change elements in B but stores them in the repository. The function $F(e)$ passes them to the EDS for specific events e together with the simulation state $S(t)$. This way, entities not modeled in the DES can still be considered in simulation runs and in the black-box logic of the EDS components.

Application to MiSim and Kubernetes. In this paper, we choose scheduling and cluster autoscaling as two Kubernetes orchestration mechanisms to integrate into MiSim. The scheduling algorithm comprises nine extension points where user-defined plugins can be attached [28]. As these plugins contain arbitrary logic, it is impossible to integrate this configuration space in the simulation using traditional models. Similarly, the *cluster-autoscaler* has more than 30 configuration options [18]. Simulative evaluation is especially beneficial since cluster autoscaling can only be performed with special infrastructure where nodes can be added or deleted on demand. Both mechanisms use entities that are not present in MiSim (like node affinities, labels, or machine set definitions). Kubernetes uses YAML files to define these entities. Our framework stores these user-created files in the BIR and forwards the contents on specific events. In the following, we look deeper into how the kube-scheduler and cluster-autoscaler are integrated into MiSim using the aforementioned concepts.

4.4 A Detailed Look at Scheduling and Cluster Autoscaling

The kube-scheduler receives a request from the adapter whenever an event in MiSim is triggered that creates a new container. This request contains information about the container to be deployed (e.g., its resource requirements) and all other currently deployed containers (the simulation state). The selected node or an error (e.g., if all resources in the cluster are reserved) is expected as a response. The adapter converts this request into a series of Kubernetes watch events and sends them to the scheduler. The kube-scheduler determines nodes with enough resources and selects a node for the container according to its scheduling policy. This policy is set as a configuration [28] at the start, like in a real cluster. If no node is available, the kube-scheduler returns an error to the adapter, which passes it on to the simulation.

Scheduling policies in Kubernetes can also be influenced by other factors (e.g., pod affinities [24]). These are examples of critical elements from the set M_E, i.e., entities that exist in Kubernetes but do not exist in the simulation and yet affect relevant tasks in the simulation. For the example mentioned above, we create node definitions with labels and pod definitions with affinities in the form of Kubernetes YAML files that populate the BIR at the simulation start. The simulation and adapter forward them on events concerning nodes or pods, respectively. The kube-scheduler uses this information for scheduling. With this approach, we can cover the scheduling policies' maximum complexity without implementing new logic ourselves. We demonstrate the different usage of scheduling policies in Sect. 5.1.

As a second Kubernetes component, we integrate the cluster-autoscaler (CA) into the simulation. It becomes active whenever the kube-scheduler cannot deploy a pod (upscaling, see Fig. 1) or when the utilization of a node falls below a certain threshold (downscaling). Hence, the CA subscribes events for pods and nodes; our adapter forwards all decisions of the kube-scheduler directly to the CA. Furthermore, the CA needs endpoints to manage node groups. Here, different implementations for cloud providers exist [26]. We use the generic open-source Kubernetes Cluster API [29]. Note that the chosen cloud provider implementation does not influence the autoscaling logic. By now, we support the integration of *MachineSets* from the Cluster API. A MachineSet is a set of machines with equal resources that can be scaled from a specified minimum value (≥ 0) to a maximum value. The user can specify definitions of MachineSets as part of the BIR at the simulation start. We compare two different upscaling policies for the CA in Sect. 5.2.

5   Evaluation

In the following, we provide empirical evidence on the usefulness of our approach for evaluating orchestration policies and validate the behavior of the included Kubernetes components by conducting two experiments. First, we consider a microservice application whose services are deployed in a global cluster. We examine the interactions between different scheduling policies, the application, and the cluster architecture. In the second experiment, we deploy an increasing number of service instances in a heterogeneous cluster with two machine types. We look at different expansion policies of the CA and show that our framework can correctly capture the interactions between the CA and the kube-scheduler. We provide a CodeOcean capsule [3] where all experiments can be reproduced.

5.1   Scheduling Policies in a Global Cluster

Overview. In this experiment, we model a cluster with nodes in different geographic regions. A microservice reference application is deployed in this cluster. We simulate a constant load and analyze the response time of different user operations. Three different scheduling policies are tested, causing services to be deployed on different nodes and experiencing different network latencies. We show that our framework can use the kube-scheduler in a way that it behaves the same as in the real cluster and that the simulation can reflect the effects of different scheduling policies on the simulated test application.

Cluster Environment. We use a cluster with five workers and one master in the Google Cloud, as shown in Fig. 3a. All machines are of type e2-standard-4 with four CPU cores. Two workers (eu1 and eu2) and the master are deployed in Germany. The remaining workers run in Singapore, Brazil, and Iowa (USA). Every node has its compute zone as a Kubernetes node label. Before the experiment, we measure the network latency between all nodes using 100 ping packets. The network latencies are given to the simulation as means and standard deviations. We use Kubernetes YAML files to specify the five workers for the simulation. At the simulation start, this information is forwarded to the kube-scheduler, which extracts available resource capacities, node labels, and more. The master node is not considered in the simulation.

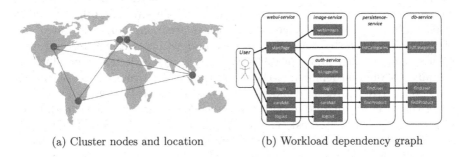

(a) Cluster nodes and location   (b) Workload dependency graph

Fig. 3. Modeled cluster environment and test application workload.

Microservice Test Application and Workload. We use the popular benchmarking application TeaStore [23] with seven microservices in our experiments. All microservices request 0.8 CPU cores per instance. In the real cluster, we use the HTTP load generator [4] to generate a constant load of 20 requests per second for five minutes. A user behavior consisting of four steps is simulated. First, a user accesses the start page and then logs in with his account data. Afterward, the user adds a random product from the store to his cart and then logs out again. In the simulation, we build on the architecture model of the TeaStore used by Frank et al. [17] and extend it with the database service. The defined workload stimulates a total of five services and 15 endpoints. The dependency graph of the operations for our workload is shown in Fig. 3b.

Scheduling Policies. We deploy one instance of each TeaStore service in our cluster. Hence, the total CPU core requirement is 5.6 cores, meaning that at least two nodes are needed for the deployment. We evaluate three scheduling policies: *default, most-allocated,* and *europe-only.* The default scheduling policy deploys the pod to the node where the least resources have been reserved so far. This results in the services being distributed to all nodes. Kubernetes offers two general options to influence scheduling. First, different configurations of the kube-scheduler can be used, resulting in a different algorithm being used for all pods. The most-allocated policy is an example of this. We use a profile of the kube-scheduler [28], which causes the next pod to be deployed to the node with the most resources reserved but still enough resources to run the pod. This policy requires two nodes to run the services. The scheduling policy is set at the start of the kube-scheduler. The second option to influence the scheduling in Kubernetes is to set special properties of the pods. These will influence the scheduling only for selected pods. For our europe-only policy, we use node affinities. Precisely, we specify that our services can only be deployed on nodes with a label indicating that they belong to the compute zone Europe. This causes the services to be distributed to the nodes eu1 and eu2. Both in the simulation and the real cluster, we use Kubernetes deployment files to specify the affinities.

Start State. Before deploying the services, all nodes have no reserved resources. Therefore, the nodes are equally suitable for selection. Furthermore, the order in which the containers are to be deployed plays a role in the scheduling since the kube-scheduler processes the pods one after the other. In initial tests, both factors led to different placements occurring during repeated simulation and real cluster runs. We made two adjustments to ensure the experiment's comparability and repeatability. First, we fixed the order in which the containers should be deployed to the recommended deployment order of the TeaStore [5]. Furthermore, we deployed other containers on four of the five worker nodes that occupy different resources at the nodes: Singapore (0.05 cores), Brazil (0.1 cores), eu2 (0.15 cores), and USA (0.2 cores). This setup leads to the scheduling decisions not being random and the experiment being repeatable.

Results. Fig. 4a gives an overview of the scheduling for different policies. These scheduling decisions are the same in the real cluster and the simulation. This shows that our approach can correctly represent different scheduling policies in the simulation without implementing them. The second question to be answered is whether the effects of different scheduling policies on the performance of the modeled microservice application can be simulated. Figure 4b shows the simulated and measured response times with the standard deviation for all four considered request types. We see that the scheduling policies significantly impact the response times. The default policy that distributes the services worldwide has the highest response times, while the europe-only policy has the lowest. This is visible in both the measured and simulated results. Furthermore, using the logout operation as an example, we see an interaction between application architecture and scheduling. As shown in Fig. 3b, the logout operation depends only on one operation of the auth service. According to Fig. 4a, the default policy causes webui and auth to be deployed in Europe. In contrast, in the most-allocated policy, the auth service is deployed in the USA, and the webui service is in Europe. This explains the higher response time for this operation in the most-allocated policy compared to the default policy.

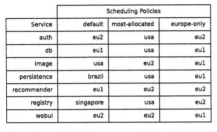

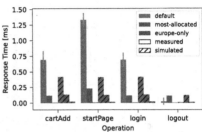

(a) Selected nodes for services   (b) Measured and simulated response times

Fig. 4. Effects of different scheduling policies in a global cluster.

Overall, the effects of different scheduling policies on microservice performance can be qualitatively modeled. However, some operations also have significant errors in the response time prediction. These are caused by inaccuracies in the MiSim performance model. For example, the large deviation for the startPage operation in the default policy is caused by large payloads with variable sizes (here: images) sent over the network. MiSim lacks support for modeling different payload sizes and parametric dependencies. Hence, the real network overhead cannot be predicted accurately in this case. However, this is a limitation of MiSim's performance model rather than a weakness of our approach for including orchestration mechanisms, as further discussed in Sect. 6. We also analyzed the overhead of our adapter and the integration in total. In this experiment, we measure only a tiny overhead. The simulation runs take, on average, about 9.2 s, of which only about ten milliseconds are spent on the communication with the adapter and kube-scheduler. This shows that our approach has a reasonable overhead and can enrich MiSim with authentic Kubernetes container orchestration mechanisms.

5.2 Expansion Policies for Cluster Autoscaling

Overview. In this section, we demonstrate our simulation with the CA and show its ability to capture the interactions between the cluster-autoscaler and the kube-scheduler (see Fig. 1). We model a heterogeneous cluster with two different node groups. The CA offers the possibility to define *expansion policies*, i.e., to configure which node groups should be prioritized during upscaling. We compare two expansion policies and prove they work as expected in our framework.

Simulated Cluster Environment. We define a cluster with two machine sets. Machines in the *small-set* have 4 CPU cores and in the *large-set* 8 cores. Both machine sets can be scaled from one to ten nodes. One node from each machine set is deployed at the start. The analogy in a real cluster would be to deploy different instance groups with different resources and pricing models. Unfortunately, we cannot directly compare this experiment to a Google Kubernetes cluster where a proprietary, not freely configurable version of the CA is used.

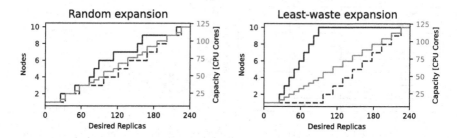

Fig. 5. Cluster scaling with nodes from small-set (solid) and large-set (dashed).

Expansion Policies and Test Application. The expansion policies of the CA can be adjusted via a command line flag. The CA triggers upscaling whenever the kube-scheduler cannot assign a pod to a node due to a lack of resources. We consider two expansion policies. The *random* policy randomly selects a node group for upscaling. In contrast, the *least-waste* policy prefers the node group, where as few resources as possible (here: CPU cores) are wasted after the deployment of the new pods. In this case, the machine set with four cores is always preferred. We use a Kubernetes deployment file of the TeaStore registry service as a test application, with each replica requesting 0.5 cores. For demonstration purposes, we use an autoscaler that requests a new instance every 15 s.

Results. Fig. 5 shows the two expansion policies in comparison. Since the random policy returns different results with repeated runs, Fig. 5 shows only a selected test run. Both expansion policies behave as expected: The random expander deploys alternating instances with 4 and 8 CPU cores on average (both blue lines increase early). The least-waste expander first scales the machine set with 4 CPU cores up to the maximum number of 10 (only the solid blue line rises first). This leads to a slow increase in the number of provided CPU cores (red line) and many upscaling decisions being necessary initially. The random policy makes capacity increase more stable, making it a policy that can be used when nothing is known about workload changes. The least-waste policy is a cost-optimized policy that can be used when slowly increasing loads and few upscaling are expected. Both policies stop the expansion when the maximum size of the machine sets is reached. Overall, we show that different CA configurations can be correctly executed in our simulation. The basis for this is the interaction of the CA with the kube-scheduler, as shown in Fig. 1. Hence, we show that multiple Kubernetes components can be used in parallel in our framework.

6 Discussion

This section summarizes our approach's strengths, weaknesses, and limitations. As already mentioned, there are different user groups of our framework. We enable designers of microservice architectures to simulate realistic scenarios with authentic container orchestration. We provide a new lightweight test platform for Kubernetes or container orchestration developers, where real code and new configurations can be tested without requiring a cluster. A significant advantage is that orchestration mechanisms can be included in the simulation in their full complexity without having to model them. The drawback is that expert knowledge of the orchestrator interfaces is required to integrate its code. This could be an obstacle for microservice designers, less for developers of CO frameworks.

To include new orchestration mechanisms in our framework, the interfaces required by the mechanism must be identified and implemented in the adapter. In a concrete use case, the question of whether integration in this form is worthwhile or whether a simple model of the mechanism is sufficient must be answered. The integration is worthwhile if the mechanism has a complex configuration and logic. If it is a relatively simple algorithm without regular updates, a simple model should be preferred. Generally, we assume that the integrated components are independently deployable and work event-based. A current limitation of our approach is that component responses are always executed immediately in the simulation. While this is a good approximation for the kube-scheduler, cluster autoscaling includes non-negligible node start times. Extensions in our framework for these purposes are planned. Since we do not change the performance models in MiSim, the challenge for accurate predictions for response times and similar metrics remains the correct calibration of the performance models as well as a correct modeling of parametric dependencies [15]. However, these weaknesses concern the MiSim core rather than the extension presented in this paper, which in theory, would also support other performance models.

7 Conclusion

This paper presented a new approach for connecting a microservice simulation with Kubernetes components based on a general concept for combining discrete-event simulation and event-driven systems. We validated our approach in experiments with the kube-scheduler and cluster-autoscaler. We have shown that different component configurations can be represented in the simulation by using the actual Kubernetes components and without abstract models or manual re-implementation. Our framework can be used, for example, by microservice application developers to simulate real-world scenarios and by CO framework developers to test new orchestration policies. Future work will focus on evaluating complex scenarios, simulation-based optimization of CO mechanisms, and increasing the simulation accuracy, e.g., by considering startup times.

Acknowledgements. This work was funded by the Deutsche Forschungsgemeinschaft (DFG, German Research Foundation) - 510552229. We thank the German Federal Ministry of Education and Research (dqualizer FKZ: 01IS22007B and Software Campus 2.0 — Microproject: DiSpel, FKZ: 01IS17051), the Google Cloud Research Credits program (GCP213506809) and our student researchers Lion Wagner and Lukas Mönch for supporting this work. The work was conducted in the context of the SPEC RG DevOps Performance Working Group [6].

References

1. https://github.com/DescartesResearch/misim-orchestration
2. https://github.com/DescartesResearch/misim-k8s-adapter
3. https://doi.org/10.24433/CO.4913288.v1
4. https://github.com/joakimkistowski/HTTP-Load-Generator
5. https://github.com/DescartesResearch/TeaStore
6. https://research.spec.org/devopswg
7. Aslanpour, M.S., Toosi, A.N., Taheri, J., Gaire, R.: Autoscalesim: A simulation toolkit for auto-scaling web applications in clouds. Simul. Modelling Pract. Theory (2021)
8. Bao, L., Wu, C., Bu, X., Ren, N., Shen, M.: Performance modeling and workflow scheduling of microservice-based applications in clouds. IEEE Trans. Parallel Distrib. Syst. (2019)
9. Becker, M., Becker, S., Meyer, J.: Simulizar: design-time modeling and performance analysis of self-adaptive systems. Softw. Eng. (2013)
10. Ben Ayed, M., Zouari, L., Abid, M.: Software in the loop simulation for robot manipulators. Eng., Technol. Appl. Sci. Res. (2017)
11. Bozóki, S., Szalontai, J., Pethő, D., Kocsis, I., Pataricza, A., Suskovics, P., Kovács, B.: Application of extreme value analysis for characterizing the execution time of resilience supporting mechanisms in Kubernetes. In: Dependable Computing—EDCC 2020 Workshops (2020)
12. Carrión, C.: Kubernetes Scheduling: Taxonomy, Ongoing Issues and Challenges. ACM Comput, Surv. (2022)
13. Cloud Native Computing Foundation: Cncf annual survey 2022 (2023). https://www.cncf.io/reports/cncf-annual-report-2022/
14. Demers, S., Gopalakrishnan, P., Kant, L.: A generic solution to software-in-the-loop. In: MILCOM 2007—IEEE Military Communications Conference (2007)
15. Eismann, S., Walter, J., von Kistowski, J., Kounev, S.: Modeling of parametric dependencies for performance prediction of component-based software systems at run-time. In: IEEE International Conference on Software Architecture (ICSA) (2018)
16. Erb, B., Kargl, F.: Combining discrete event simulations and event sourcing. In: Proceedings of the 7th International ICST Conference on Simulation Tools and Techniques. SIMUTools **14** (2014)
17. Frank, S., Wagner, L., Hakamian, A., Straesser, M., van Hoorn, A.: Misim: a simulator for resilience assessment of microservice-based architectures. In: IEEE 22nd International Conference on Software Quality, Reliability and Security (QRS) (2022)
18. Friedman, N.: Kubernetes cluster autoscaler command line options (2023). https://gist.github.com/neerfri/4bd7477920cb33a2a229807ed10c29c2
19. Hellerer, M., Schuster, M.J., Lichtenheldt, R.: Software-in-the-loop simulation of a planetary rover. In: The International Symposium on Artificial Intelligence, Robotics and Automation in Space (2016)

20. IBM Market Development & Insights: Microservices in the enterprise (2021). https://www.ibm.com/downloads/cas/OQG4AJAM
21. Jawarneh, I.M.A., Bellavista, P., Bosi, F., Foschini, L., Martuscelli, G., Montanari, R., Palopoli, A.: Container orchestration engines: a thorough functional and performance comparison. In: IEEE International Conference on Communications (ICC) (2019)
22. Jindal, A., Podolskiy, V., Gerndt, M.: Performance modeling for cloud microservice applications. In: Proceedings of the ACM/SPEC International Conference on Performance Engineering (2019)
23. von Kistowski, J., Eismann, S., Schmitt, N., Bauer, A., Grohmann, J., Kounev, S.: Teastore: a micro-service reference application for benchmarking, modeling and resource management research. In: IEEE 26th International Symposium on Modeling, Analysis, and Simulation of Computer and Telecommunication Systems (MASCOTS) (2018)
24. Kubernetes Documentation: Assign pods to nodes using node affinity (2023). https://kubernetes.io/docs/tasks/configure-pod-container/assign-pods-nodes-using-node-affinity/
25. Kubernetes Documentation: Kubernetes API concepts (2023). https://kubernetes.io/docs/reference/using-api/api-concepts/
26. Kubernetes Documentation: The kubernetes cluster autoscaler (2023). https://github.com/kubernetes/autoscaler/blob/master/cluster-autoscaler/README.md
27. Kubernetes Documentation: Kubernetes components (2023). https://kubernetes.io/docs/concepts/overview/components/
28. Kubernetes Documentation: Scheduling framework (2023). https://kubernetes.io/docs/concepts/scheduling-eviction/scheduling-framework/
29. Kubernetes SIG Cluster API: Kubernetes cluster API (2023). https://cluster-api.sigs.k8s.io/
30. Kubernetes SIG Scheduling: Kube-scheduler-simulator (2023). https://github.com/kubernetes-sigs/kube-scheduler-simulator
31. Law, A.M., Kelton, W.D.: Simulation modeling and analysis, vol. 3. Mcgraw-hill New York (2007)
32. Lechler, T., Page, B.: Desmo-j: An object oriented discrete simulation framework in java. In: Proceedings of the 11th European Simulation Symposium (ESS) (1999)
33. von Massow, R., van Hoorn, A., Hasselbring, W.: Performance simulation of runtime reconfigurable component-based software architectures. In: 5th European Conference on Software Architecture (ECSA) (2011)
34. Matarneh, R.J.: Self-adjustment time quantum in round robin algorithm depending on burst time of the now running processes. Am. J. Appl. Sci. (2009)
35. Mekki, M., Toumi, N., Ksentini, A.: Microservices configurations and the impact on the performance in cloud native environments. In: IEEE 47th Conference on Local Computer Networks (LCN) (2022)
36. Michelson, B.M.: Event-driven architecture overview. Patricia Seybold Group (2006)
37. Pan, Y., Chen, I., Brasileiro, F., Jayaputera, G., Sinnott, R.: A performance comparison of cloud-based container orchestration tools. In: IEEE International Conference on Big Knowledge (ICBK) (2019)
38. Schmoll, R., Fischer, T., Salah, H., Fitzek, F.H.P.: Comparing and evaluating application-specific boot times of virtualized instances. In: 2nd IEEE 5G World Forum (2019)

39. Straesser, M., Bauer, A., Leppich, R., Herbst, N., Chard, K., Foster, I., Kounev, S.: An empirical study of container image configurations and their impact on start times. In: 23rd IEEE International Symposium on Cluster, Cloud and Internet Computing (CCGrid) (2023)
40. Straesser, M., Grohmann, J., von Kistowski, J., Eismann, S., Bauer, A., Kounev, S.: Why is it not solved yet? challenges for production-ready autoscaling. In: Proceedings of the ACM/SPEC on International Conference on Performance Engineering (2022)
41. Straesser, M., Mathiasch, J., Bauer, A., Kounev, S.: A systematic approach for benchmarking of container orchestration frameworks. In: Proceedings of the ACM/SPEC International Conference on Performance Engineering (2023)
42. Tamiru, M.A., Tordsson, J., Elmroth, E., Pierre, G.: An experimental evaluation of the Kubernetes cluster autoscaler in the cloud. In: IEEE International Conference on Cloud Computing Technology and Science (CloudCom) (2020)
43. Tesfatsion, S.K., Klein, C., Tordsson, J.: Virtualization techniques compared: Performance, resource, and power usage overheads in clouds. In: ACM/SPEC International Conference on Performance Engineering (2018)
44. Truyen, E., Bruzek, M., Van Landuyt, D., Lagaisse, B., Joosen, W.: Evaluation of container orchestration systems for deploying and managing nosql database clusters. In: IEEE 11th International Conference on Cloud Computing (CLOUD) (2018)
45. Truyen, E., Van Landuyt, D., Lagaisse, B., Joosen, W.: Performance overhead of container orchestration frameworks for management of multi-tenant database deployments. In: Proceedings of the 34th ACM/SIGAPP Symposium on Applied Computing. SAC 19 (2019)
46. Valera, H.H.A., Dalmau, M., Roose, P., Larracoechea, J., Herzog, C.: Draceo: a smart simulator to deploy energy saving methods in microservices based networks. In: IEEE 29th International Conference on Enabling Technologies: Infrastructure for Collaborative Enterprises (WETICE) (2020)
47. VMware: K-bench (2023). https://github.com/vmware-tanzu/k-bench
48. Wang, M., Zhang, D., Wu, B.: A cluster autoscaler based on multiple node types in Kubernetes. In: IEEE 4th Information Technology, Networking, Electronic and Automation Control Conference (ITNEC) (2020)
49. Xavier, B., Ferreto, T., Jersak, L.: Time provisioning evaluation of KVM, Docker and Unikernels in a cloud platform. In: 16th IEEE/ACM International Symposium on Cluster, Cloud and Grid Computing (2016)
50. Zhang, Y., Gan, Y., Delimitrou, C.: μqsim: enabling accurate and scalable simulation for interactive microservices. In: IEEE International Symposium on Performance Analysis of Systems and Software (ISPASS) (2019)

Quantum-Enhanced Control of a Tandem Queue System

George T. Stamatiou[1]([envelope])[ORCID] and Kostas Magoutis[1,2][ORCID]

[1] Institute of Computer Science, Foundation for Research and Technology - Hellas (FORTH), Heraklion, Greece
stamatiou@ics.forth.gr, magoutis@csd.uoc.gr
[2] Computer Science Department, University of Crete, Heraklion, Greece

Abstract. Controlling computer systems in an optimal way using quantum devices is an important step towards next generation infrastructures that will be able to harness the advantages of quantum computing. While the implications are promising, there is a need for evaluating new such approaches and tools in comparison with prevalent classical alternatives. In this work we contribute in this direction by studying the stabilization and control of a tandem queue system, an exemplary model of a computer system, using model predictive control and quantum annealing. The control inputs are obtained from the minimization of an appropriately constructed cost function and the optimal control problem is converted into a quadratic unconstrained binary optimization problem to be solved by the quantum annealer. We find that as the prediction horizon increases and the core optimization problem becomes complicated, the quantum-enhanced solution is preferable over classical simulated annealing. Moreover, there is a trade-off one should consider in terms of variations in the obtained results, quantum computation times and end-to-end communication times. This work shows a way for further experimentation and exploration of new directions and challenges and underscores the experience gained through utilization of the state-of-the-art quantum devices.

Keywords: Model predictive control · Quantum annealing · Tandem queue system

1 Introduction

Adaptive computing systems, such as robots that plan their motion [30] and data-center management systems that enforce end-to-end quality-of-service [8,15,22], operate in a real-time feedback loop setting with appropriate control inputs to achieve their goals optimally, requiring the repeated solution of an optimization problem within a specific time interval to take appropriate action in time. A prevalent method for optimal control is Model Predictive Control

© ICST Institute for Computer Sciences, Social Informatics and Telecommunications Engineering 2024
Published by Springer Nature Switzerland AG 2024. All Rights Reserved
E. Kalyvianaki and M. Paolieri (Eds.): VALUETOOLS 2023, LNICST 539, pp. 99–114, 2024.
https://doi.org/10.1007/978-3-031-48885-6_7

(MPC)[5,25,27,30], an advanced control strategy widely used in engineering and industrial processes. MPC involves creating a mathematical model that describes the system's behavior and formulating an optimization problem to determine optimal control actions. The aim is to minimize an objective function that captures both tracking performance (deviation from desired reference points) and control effort (penalizing excessive control actions or changes). MPC is also designed to handle constraints effectively. Constraints can represent physical limitations or operational requirements of the system. These constraints can be imposed on inputs, outputs, or states and can be hard or soft. Hard constraints must be strictly satisfied, while soft constraints can be violated within certain bounds. By incorporating constraints into the optimization problem, MPC ensures that the control actions respect these limitations, ensuring feasibility and safety in real-time control. A main appeal of MPC is that rather than optimizing the whole process it operates over a finite time horizon, usually called prediction horizon N_s, which specifies how far into the future the system behavior is predicted. By applying only the first control action of the optimal sequence, MPC allows for adjustments at each time step, creating a receding horizon effect and the process is re-initialized for the next time window. This enables MPC to react to changes in the system and adapt the control actions based on updated predictions and measurements. A key challenge with MPC feedback loops is that the computational effort involved in the MPC optimization problem increases dramatically as the control period becomes shorter and/or the optimization problem increases in complexity by considering longer task horizon for example. Consequently, adaptive behavior for large distributed systems aiming for short sample times, in the order of tens of milliseconds, currently resort to using overly simple models, short prediction horizons, and often an explicit solution of the optimization problem by solving the problem in an offline fashion, in advance. Although approximations to the MPC optimization problem are commonly used, they are still inadequate for large configuration search spaces.

Quantum computers available today, known as Noisy - Intermediate - Scale Quantum (NISQ) devices [24], though not a commodity yet, are in the direction of solving real-world problems. A quantum computer is a device that exploits properties of quantum physics, such as superposition and entanglement, to perform computations. The main building block of a quantum device is the qubit, which is the quantum analog of a classical bit. While a classical bit can be in either state 0 or 1, a qubit can exist in a superposition of both states, allowing it to represent and process multiple possibilities simultaneously. The main approaches towards utility quantum computing currently include but not limited to *gate-based* models and *quantum annealers*. Gate-based quantum computing is based on the concept of a quantum circuit, a sequence of quantum gates which manipulate and transform the qubits. The combinations of gates perform operations on the qubits, such as rotations, entanglement, and measurements, allowing for complex computations and the development of quantum algorithms. Quantum annealers, used in our work, are based on the concept of quantum annealing, a computational optimization technique that utilizes principles of quantum mechanics to solve optimization problems where one needs to search over a large space of possible solutions and find an optimal one [14,28,35]. Thus, it is a specialized application of quantum computing that focuses on finding the global minimum (or maximum) of a given objective function. Classical simulated annealing [17,31] is inspired by the annealing process in metallurgy, where a material is heated and then slowly cooled to obtain a desired structure with minimal defects. Similarly, in optimization the process involves starting with a high-energy state and gradually cooling the system to reach a low-energy state corresponding to the optimal solution. In quantum annealing this concept is evolved by leveraging quantum mechanical effects, such as quantum tunneling, to explore the solution space in a more efficient way than classical optimization algorithms. Examples of quantum annealers include the D-Wave 2000Q and its next-generation successor, the Advantage System. To work with a quantum annealer, the problem to be optimized is mapped onto the configuration of qubits. The objective function of an optimization problem, which is typically expressed as an Ising model, defines the problem's energy landscape [20]. The Ising model is a mathematical model used to describe the interactions between spins in a physical system, where spins can take values of either $+1$ or -1. The energy landscape of the problem is encoded in the system's Hamiltonian, which is a mathematical operator representing the total energy of the system. The Hamiltonian consists of two components: initial Hamiltonian (H_0) and the problem Hamiltonian (H_p),

$$H = \left(1 - \frac{t}{T}\right) H_0 + \frac{t}{T} H_p$$

$$= \left(1 - \frac{t}{T}\right) \sum_i \hat{\sigma}_i^x + \frac{t}{T} \left(\sum_i h_i \hat{\sigma}_i^z + \sum_{i>j} J_{ij} \hat{\sigma}_i^z \hat{\sigma}_j^z \right). \tag{1}$$

where $\hat{\sigma}_i$ are the Pauli matrices operating on qubit i, h_i is the on-site energy (local field) of qubit i and J_{ij} represents the pairwise interaction strength between qubits i and j determining how strongly the states of two qubits influence each other in the objective function being optimized. Quantum annealing relies on the adiabatic theorem of quantum mechanics which states that if we start in the ground state (the state with the lowest energy) of the initial Hamiltonian H_0, by slowly modifying time t transforming H_0 into H_p, the system remains in its ground state, providing us with the solution for our problem by measuring the quantum state at a future time $t = T$. To solve an optimization problem using quantum annealing, we first need to formulate the objective function as a quadratic unconstrained binary optimization (QUBO) problem equivalent to (1) where the optimization variables are translated into binary variables resulting to the expression

$$f(b_1, \ldots, b_n) = \sum_i C_i b_i + \sum_{i,j} J_{ij} b_i b_j. \tag{2}$$

where $b_i \in \{0,1\}$ and C_i, J_{ij} are parameters. In this form the problem can be mapped onto the graph structure of the quantum processor chip (QPU).

The evolution of quantum devices gives rise to new possibilities for solving hard computational problems with higher accuracy and speed compared to existing classical solutions. In this work, we investigate the *quantum-enhanced* solution of an MPC problem using quantum annealers designed and built by D-Wave Systems. We choose the *tandem queue system* as a simple performance model of a computer system network. The choice is also made as to provide insight into expressing a complex MPC problem and its respective cost function into forms amenable for quantum annealing. Accelerating optimization tasks at the core of MPC feedback loops via quantum annealing opens up new avenues for adaptive computing systems to become more intelligent, by virtue of being able to solve difficult optimization problems as their environment and external inputs change rapidly.

The remainder of this paper proceeds as follows. In Sect. 2 we review previous work related to the current research. In Sect. 3 we present the model of the tandem queue system expressed as a control problem in a state-space representation, the construction of the cost function and a way to transform the optimal control problem to a QUBO expression which is used as input for the quantum annealer. Section 4 presents our analysis and evaluation results for the D-Wave 2000Q and Advantage System. Finally, in Sect. 5 we discuss implications of our work, future directions and conclude the paper.

2   Related Work

Performance modeling and analysis of computer systems based on queueing models has been thoroughly studied through the years [1,3,18]. A tandem queue system is used to model systems in which customers must pass through a connected series of service stations (or queues) in order to complete a transaction or process. In a tandem queue system, the output of one queue becomes the input to the next queue, forming a sequence or chain of queues. Tandem queue systems have been considered appropriate performance models for many applications ranging from call centers, healthcare systems, manufacturing processes to packet-switched computer networks, stream-processing systems, and multi-tier computer systems in general [1,4,18,19]. Previous research efforts have studied performance properties of tandem queues, such as throughput and total queueing delay, under various assumptions for the distributions of arrivals and service times at all servers, fixed buffers (blocking) vs. infinite buffers at each queue, number of servers at each stage, etc. Another area of interest around tandem queues and multi-stage pipelines concerns their controllability, namely the ability to affect system outputs such as end-to-end response time via control inputs such as buffer size. Optimal control of computer systems, a key capability to achieving adaptive, self-managing systems has also received attention in recent years [6,11,12]. Linear quadratic regulators (LQR) are a classical approach to optimal control embodying an optimization problem with an appropriately crafted cost function [2,12,16]. Mathematical aspects concerning the optimal control of finite queues and tandem queues can be found in older works

[21, 26, 32]. There have also been recent works that investigate MPC in queueing networks [10, 29, 34], and others that explore the benefits of QDs comparing quantum annealing over simulated annealing for network optimization tasks [33]. A recent work [13] proposes an MPC algorithm for using the D-Wave 2000Q quantum annealer tested on mechanical-oriented system models for a fixed prediction horizon. Another, promising direction combining MPC and quantum annealing is the efficient control of HVAC systems in buildings [9]. However, there is no prior work on investigating the advantages of combining MPC and the utilization of quantum devices for the control of queueing-network models, experimenting with different prediction horizons, or with more recent quantum-annealing devices such as the D-Wave Advantage. In this paper we design, implement, and experimentally evaluate quantum-enhanced MPC control of a tandem queue system, improving over previous research in this space by means of tackling a system model with significant practical relevance, and carry out a broad experimental evaluation (various prediction horizons and number of samples per quantum device invocation) exhibiting key trade-offs in state-of-the-art quantum devices.

The main contributions in this paper are:

- Implementation of a MPC approach to stabilize and control an unstable tandem queue system by minimizing a designed cost function using both quantum-enhanced (quantum annealing) and classical (exact, simulated annealing) methodologies.
- Evaluation of quantum-enhanced MPC solution on state-of-the-art D-Wave Advantage System and 2000Q QDs investigating different predictions horizons and number of states (output solutions) to read from the QD solver.
- Highlighting the efficiency of quantum-enhanced MPC vs. classical simulation approximations for longer MPC horizons.

3   Methodology

3.1   Mathematical Model

The tandem queue system, as shown in Fig. 1, consists of two M/M/1/K queues Q_1, Q_2 where the inter-arrival times of the incoming requests are exponentially distributed with mean $\frac{1}{\lambda_i}, (i = 1, 2)$, the service times are exponentially distributed with mean $\frac{1}{\mu_i}, (i = 1, 2)$. There is 1 server in each queue and $K_i, (i = 1, 2)$ is the finite buffer size. The incoming requests arrive at Q_1 and the service begins immediately. In the case that the server is not available, the requests wait in the buffer of Q_1 until the server is available again. If the incoming request finds that the buffer is full, then the request is discarded. The departures from the Q_1 become arrivals at Q_2 which handles the requests on the same manner. Finally, the departures from the queueing system Q_2 are outgoing requests. For the matter of simplicity, we assume that the buffer size of Q_2 is sufficiently large ($K_2 >> K_1 \equiv K$) so that arrivals in Q_2 are never discarded. We focus on the average response times for the requests entering-leaving Q_1 and Q_2 denoted

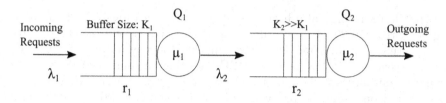

Fig. 1. Architecture diagram of a tandem queue system.

by R_1 and R_2, respectively. The main objective is to control the end-to-end response time defined as $R = R_1 + R_2$ by optimally tuning the buffer size K of the first queue Q_1. The control input of the system is the buffer size K for system Q_1 and the measured system output is the total response time R.

The dynamics of each one of the queueing systems Q_1, Q_2 can be represented using a first-order difference equation model

$$r_1(k+1) = a_{11}r_1(k) + bu(k)$$
$$r_2(k+1) = a_{21}r_1(k) + a_{22}r_2(k) \tag{3}$$

where $a_{11}, a_{21}, a_{22}, b$ are parameters to be determined through system identification and $k \in \mathbb{N}$ denotes the discrete time. For the dynamics we use the lowercase $r_1(k), r_2(k), u(k)$ denoting the offset values for the response times and the buffer size defined as

$$\mathbf{r}(k) = \begin{bmatrix} r_1(k) \\ r_2(k) \end{bmatrix} = \begin{bmatrix} R_1(k) - \langle R_1 \rangle \\ R_2(k) - \langle R_2 \rangle \end{bmatrix}, \quad u(k) = K(k) - \langle K \rangle \tag{4}$$

where $\langle R_1 \rangle, \langle R_2 \rangle, \langle K \rangle$ are the respective mean values we define as the operating points -or the reference values- of the system. The state-space dynamics of the tandem queue system as a linear time-invariant (LTI) system is

$$\mathbf{r}(k+1) = A\mathbf{r}(k) + B\mathbf{u}(k)$$
$$\mathbf{R}(k) = C\mathbf{r}(k) \tag{5}$$

where $\mathbf{r}(k) \in \mathbb{R}^n$ is the vector of state variables (the response times for each queue), $\mathbf{u}(k) \in \mathbb{R}^m$ is the vector of inputs (the buffer size), $\mathbf{R}(k) \in \mathbb{R}^l$ is the vector of outputs (the end-to-end response time). $A \in \mathbb{R}^{n \times n}$, $B \in \mathbb{R}^{n \times m}$, $C \in \mathbb{R}^{l \times n}$ are constant matrices that encompass the system dynamics.

3.2 Model Predictive Control

The state and output predictions can be derived from (5) in a recursive manner up to the prediction horizon $N_s \in \mathbb{N}$ of future steps [27]. Thus, we obtain

$$
\begin{bmatrix}
R(k) \\
R(k+1) \\
R(k+2) \\
R(k+3) \\
\vdots \\
R(k+N_s-1)
\end{bmatrix}
=
\begin{bmatrix}
C \\
CA \\
CA^2 \\
CA^3 \\
\vdots \\
CA^{N_s-1}
\end{bmatrix}
\mathbf{r}(k)
+
\begin{bmatrix}
0 & 0 & 0 & \dots \\
CB & 0 & 0 & \dots \\
CAB & CB & 0 & \dots \\
CA^2B & CAB & CB & \dots \\
\vdots & \vdots & \vdots & \vdots \\
CA^{N_s-2}B & CA^{N_s-3}B & CA^{N_s-4}B & \dots
\end{bmatrix}
\mathbf{u}(k),
$$

and (5) becomes in vectorized form

$$
\mathbf{R}(k) = \mathbb{A}\mathbf{r}(k) + \mathbb{B}\mathbf{u}(k) \tag{6}
$$

where $\mathbf{R}(k) = [R(k), R(k+1), \dots, R(k+N_s-1)]^T \in \mathbb{R}^{lN_s}$ are the system outputs, $\mathbf{u}(k) = [u(k), u(k+1), \dots, u(k+N_s-1)]^T \in \mathbb{R}^{mN_s}$ are the control inputs and $\mathbb{A} \in \mathbb{R}^{lN_s \times n}$, $\mathbb{B} \in \mathbb{R}^{lN_s \times mN_s}$. In order to implement the MPC optimization strategy to control the tandem queue system we first introduce a cost function (or objective function) that we aim to minimize

$$
\mathcal{J} = \mathbf{R}(k)^T \mathcal{Q}\mathbf{R}(k) + \mathbf{u}(k)^T \mathcal{R}\mathbf{u}(k), \tag{7}
$$

where $\mathcal{Q} \in \mathbb{R}^{lN_s \times lN_s}$, $\mathcal{R} \in \mathbb{R}^{mN_s \times mN_s}$ are symmetric diagonal positive definite weighting matrices which tune the trade-off between tracking performance and control effort. The optimal control problem aims to to find the appropriate control input sequence $u^*(k)$ which minimizes the cost function J. By substituting (6) to (7) we obtain after some matrix algebraic operations that

$$
\mathcal{J} = \mathbf{u}(k)^T \Big[\mathbb{B}\mathcal{Q}\mathbb{B} + \mathcal{R} \Big] \mathbf{u}(k) + 2\mathbf{r}(k)^T \mathbb{A}^T \mathcal{Q}\mathbb{B}\mathbf{u}(k) + \mathbf{r}(k)^T \mathbb{A}^T \mathcal{Q}\mathbb{A}\mathbf{r}(k), \tag{8}
$$

which is the cost function expressed in terms of states and control inputs.

3.3 QUBO Form of the Cost Function

In order to utilize quantum annealing (8) should be translated to a QUBO form. Given a finite ordered set $\mathcal{U}_m = \{u_1, u_2, u_3, \dots, u_M\}$ of fixed and equally spaced elements representing the control inputs that our system can receive, we want to express every element in terms of binary variables. It is convenient that the length of $\mathcal{U}_m$ is $M = 2^L$, where $L \in \mathbb{N}$ is the number of binary variables[13]. First, we normalize the elements according to the rule: $u_i \longrightarrow u_i - u_{\frac{M}{2}+1}$. In general, for m-inputs in our system one may write each element u_i as a function of L binary variables in vector form as

$$
\mathbf{u_i} =
\begin{bmatrix}
p_1(-2^{L-1}b_{1,L} + \sum_{j=1}^{L-1} 2^{j-1}b_{1,j}) \\
\vdots \\
p_m(-2^{L-1}b_{m,L} + \sum_{j=1}^{L-1} 2^{j-1}b_{m,j})
\end{bmatrix},
\tag{9}
$$

where $b_{i,j} \in \{0,1\}(i = 1, \ldots, m$ and $j = 1, \ldots, L)$ is a binary variable and $p_i \in \mathbb{R}$ is a scaling parameter. We provide an example to better illustrate the procedure. Let a system with $m = 2$ control inputs and given values $\mathcal{U}_1 = \{-2, 1, 4, 7\}$ and $\mathcal{U}_2 = \{150, 200, 250, 300\}$, where $L_1 = L_2 = L = 2$ so that $M_1 = M_2 = M = 2^L = 4$. The normalization of $\mathcal{U}_1, \mathcal{U}_2$ according to the aforementioned rule, results in $\mathcal{U}_1 = \{-6, -3, 0, 3\}$ and $\mathcal{U}_2 = \{-100, -50, 0, 50\}$. From (9) we obtain

$$\mathbf{u_i} = \begin{bmatrix} p_1(-2b_{1,2} + b_{1,1}) \\ p_2(-2b_{2,2} + b_{2,1}) \end{bmatrix} = \begin{bmatrix} 3b_{1,1} - 6b_{1,2} \\ 50b_{2,1} - 100b_{2,2} \end{bmatrix} \longrightarrow \begin{bmatrix} \{-6, -3, 0, 3\} \\ \{-100, -50, 0, 50\} \end{bmatrix}$$

where we set $p_1 = 3$, $p_2 = 50$ and take all the combinations of zeros and ones. Now, we can write (9) in matrix form as

$$\mathbf{u_i} = \begin{bmatrix} W_1 & \cdots & 0 \\ & W_2 & \vdots \\ \vdots & & \ddots \\ 0 & \cdots & W_m \end{bmatrix} \begin{bmatrix} b_{1,1} \\ \vdots \\ b_{1,L} \\ \vdots \\ b_{m,1} \\ \vdots \\ b_{m,L} \end{bmatrix} = Wb \qquad (10)$$

where $W \in \mathbb{R}^{m \times mL}$, $W_i \in \mathbb{R}^{1 \times L}$ and $b \in \{0,1\}^{mL}$. In terms of the previous example we have

$$\mathbf{u_i} = \begin{bmatrix} 3 & -6 & 0 & 0 \\ 0 & 0 & 50 & -100 \end{bmatrix} \begin{bmatrix} b_{1,1} \\ b_{1,2} \\ b_{2,1} \\ b_{2,2} \end{bmatrix}$$

Now, we proceed by incorporating the predictions for the control inputs for prediction horizon N_s as

$$\begin{bmatrix} u(k) \\ u(k+1) \\ \vdots \\ u(k + N_s - 1) \end{bmatrix} = \begin{bmatrix} W & & \\ & W & \\ & & \ddots \\ & & & W \end{bmatrix} \begin{bmatrix} b(k) \\ b(k+1) \\ \vdots \\ b(k + N_s - 1) \end{bmatrix} \Leftrightarrow \mathbf{u}(k) = \mathbb{W}\mathbf{b}(k), \quad (11)$$

where $\mathbb{W} \in \mathbb{R}^{mN_s \times mLN_s}$ and $\mathbf{b}(k) \in \{0,1\}^{mLN_s}$. The substitution of (11) to (8) reads

$$\mathcal{J} = \mathbf{b}(k)^T \left[\mathbb{W}^T \mathbb{B}^T \mathcal{Q} \mathbb{B} \mathbb{W} + \mathbb{W}^T \mathcal{R} \mathbb{W} \right] \mathbf{b}(k) + 2\mathbf{r}(k)^T \mathbb{A}^T \mathcal{Q} \mathbb{B} \mathbb{W} \mathbf{b}(k)$$
$$+ \mathbf{r}(k)^T \mathbb{A}^T \mathcal{Q} \mathbb{A} \mathbf{r}(k), \qquad (12)$$

which is the cost function expressed in terms of states and binary control inputs. Equation (12) is minimized by the quantum annealer with respect to vector $\mathbf{b}(k)$ of binary variables. Notice that the last relation encompasses the dynamics of the initial system we aim to control along with the future predictions required for the MPC strategy.

4   Evaluation and Results

The tandem queue system simulation involves the utilization of *ciw* [23], a discrete event simulation Python library for queueing networks. The arrival rate for Q_1 is set to $\lambda_1 = 3.8$ reqs/sec and the service rate for both Q_1 and Q_2 is $\mu_1 = \mu_2 = 4.0$ reqs/sec. The steady-state response time for an M/M/1/K queue using Little's law ([3,12]) is given by

$$R_1 = \frac{\mathcal{N}_1}{\lambda_1} = \frac{\rho_1}{\lambda_1(1-\rho_1)} \cdot \frac{1 - (K+1)\rho_1^K + K\rho_1^{K+1}}{1 - \rho_1^{K+1}}, \tag{13}$$

where $\rho_1 = \lambda_1/\mu_1$ is the utilization and $\mathcal{N}_1$ is the expected number in the system Q_1. Our work is focused on small buffer sizes $K \in [0,15]$ where the relation between response time and buffer size is closer to linear [12]. In this region the average response times of the system are calculated performing 50 different experiments for each K. The main objective is to examine how the change in the buffer size K affects the total response time R of the tandem queue system. In other words what are the optimal values for the control input K in order for the R to reach a desired value.

The dynamics of the tandem queue system is given by (3) and because this is a simple model, we choose to study a rather non-trivial case in which the system is unstable, in order to examine whether the MPC along with quantum annealing will manage to stabilize and control it showing how this procedure works in this case. From the state-space form of (5), our system has $n = 2$ state variables (average response times of the two queues), $m = 1$ control input (buffer size K) and $l = 1$ output (end-to-end average response time) and the constant matrices for the considered model parameters are

$$A = \begin{bmatrix} 1.00076975 & 0 \\ 0.78485803 & 0.33908979 \end{bmatrix}, \quad B = \begin{bmatrix} -0.00283586 \\ 0 \end{bmatrix}, \quad C = \begin{bmatrix} 1 & 1 \end{bmatrix}. \tag{14}$$

The system is unstable as the eigenvalues of matrix A are outside the unit circle. From the simulation and data analysis the obtained mean values are $\langle R_1 \rangle = 1.25$, $\langle R_2 \rangle = 1.83$ and $\langle K \rangle = 8$ which we assume to be the reference values of the system (see Sect. 3.1). In order for the system to operate near the reference points we aim for the offset values $r_i(k) = R_i(k) - \langle R_i \rangle, i = 1, 2$ and $u(k) = K(k) - \langle K \rangle$ to be near 0. The set of available control inputs is $\mathcal{U} = \{0, 1, 2, \ldots, 14, 15\}$. Based on methodology in Sect. 3.3 the set becomes $\mathcal{U} = \{-8, -7, -6, -5, -4, -3, -2, -1, 0, 1, 2, 3, 4, 5, 6, 7\}$. The set $\mathcal{U}$ consists of values with constant intervals, its length is $M = 2^4 = 16$ and each element is expressed using $L = 4$ binary variables. In our case, the control input is $m = 1$ so (9) reads

$$u_i = \begin{bmatrix} b_{1,1} + 2b_{1,2} + 4b_{1,3} - 8b_{1,4} \end{bmatrix}.$$

where we set $p_1 = 1$. From (10) we obtain $W = W_1 = \begin{bmatrix} 1 & 2 & 4 & -8 \end{bmatrix}$ and $b = \begin{bmatrix} b_{1,1} & b_{1,2} & b_{1,3} & b_{1,4} \end{bmatrix}^T$. The last step completes the necessary ingredients needed for the cost function in (12) to be implemented to the quantum annealer.

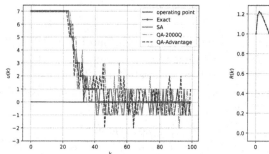 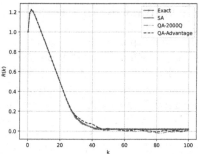

Fig. 2. (Left) Control inputs u as a function of time steps k and (Right) System output $R(k)$ using for prediction horizon $N_s = 6$ and initial conditions $(r_1(0), r_2(0)) = (0.6, 0.4)$. The *num-reads* parameter for all methods is set to default.

To perform the minimization of J we employ and compare different approaches. First, the exact solution which searches all the available space of possible solutions, second, the classical optimization method of simulated annealing and third, quantum annealing. The quantum annealers that are used in the present study are the D-Wave Advantage System as well as the previous generation D-Wave 2000Q. The Advantage_System5.3 we used is located in Germany whereas the D-Wave 2000Q machine is physically located in British Columbia, Canada. Our analysis is mostly focused on the Advantage System, the closest D-Wave infrastructure to our environment resulting in the lowest HTTP communication times between our MPC loop and the quantum device. To communicate with and execute our programs at the available devices we utilize the LEAP cloud-based service along with Ocean software [7] supporting Python provided by D-Wave. More specifically, for the exact solution we used the exact solver from *dimod* API for samplers, for the simulated annealing the *neal* library and for the quantum annealing the *dwave-system* tool. An important tuning parameter is the *num-reads* which indicates the number of states (output solutions) to read from the solver before the selection of the one with the minimum energy. The value of *num-reads* improves the solution profile at the cost of an increase in the QPU access times.

The experiment runs for 100 time steps and each time step is denoted by k. Initially, for quantum and simulated annealing all parameters (including *num-reads*) are set set to default values and the prediction horizon is set to $N_s = 6$. For all experiments, the diagonal elements of the weighting matrices $\mathcal{Q}$, $\mathcal{R}$ (see (7)) are set to $Q = 10^7$ and $R = 1$, respectively. Increasing the order of magnitude of values between the weight matrices may benefit performance and in that case the stabilization and control may be achievable even earlier. The specific values used in this evaluation were empirically chosen to yield satisfying convergence. To demonstrate our simulation results we choose the initial conditions $r_1(0) = 0.6$ and $r_2(0) = 0.4$ denoting a positive offset of the response times from the system's operating point. In Fig. 2 (left), we observe that the $u(k)$ values are discrete and

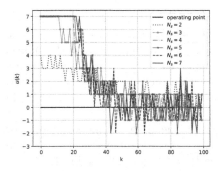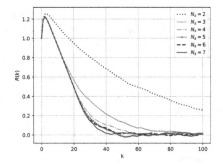

Fig. 3. Scaling of the solution with the MPC prediction horizons $N_s = 2, 3, 4, 5, 6, 7$ using the D-Wave Advantage System. (Left) Control inputs u as a function of time step k and (Right) System output $R(k)$. The initial conditions are $r_1(0) = 0.6$ and $r_2(0) = 0.4$ and the *num-reads* parameter is set to default.

Table 1. Elapsed times for MPC optimization *per time step* (*in ms*)

Methods	$N_s = 3$	$N_s = 4$	$N_s = 5$	$N_s = 6$	$N_s = 7$
Exact	6.88	77.80	1390.42	25210.21	timed out
SA	10.28	12.44	15.61	19.82	24.51
QA *sampler-call*	62.33	129.08	288.41	610.55	1061.57
QA *qpu-access*	15.94	15.96	15.98	16.02	16.36

equally spaced with respect to the previously defined control input set $\mathcal{U}$. In all cases, the control inputs are gradually decreasing and the unstable tandem queue system is stabilized reaching the desired operating point. However, although the solutions for the different methodologies are close with each other, the classical simulated annealing is found to perform better than the quantum counterparts in terms of fluctuations and proximity to the exact solution. Moreover, between the two quantum annealers, we found that 2000Q performs a little better than the Advantage System as can be seen in Fig. 2 (right) showing the resulted system output of end-to-end system response time.

Next, we examine in more detail different prediction horizons for the stabilization and control of the tandem queue system which is an aspect not studied in previous works. Figure 3 shows the scaling of the solution with MPC prediction horizon values $N_s = 2, 3, 4, 5, 6, 7$. The initial conditions are the same $r_1(0) = 0.6, r_2(0) = 0.4$ and the *num-reads* parameter is set to default. In Fig. 3 (left) we observe that an increasing prediction horizon leads to an improvement in the performance of the system. Indeed, during the first few tens of time steps, the obtained control inputs show a shifting to the right and the system is stabilized and controlled before the end of the experiment at time step 100. Specifically, there is quite a difference between the solution $N_s = 2$ which cannot converge during the simulation time and the solution with $N_s = 7$ which reaches the operating point in half the simulation time. The total response time shown in Fig. 3 (right) is also improving showing a saturation as $N_s \rightarrow 7$. This indicates that for this particular case of the unstable tandem queue system a prediction horizon of $N_s = 5$ or 6 would suffice for an acceptable performance. On the other hand, a prediction horizon as small as $N_s = 2$ is found to return a response times far from the operating point within the time step limit. However, this improvement in performance comes with a cost which we try to address in the following.

In Table 1 the elapsed times measured for the different methods and for different prediction horizons N_s per time step are presented. All times are in milliseconds. For the exact solution, we see that for $N_s \geq 5$ solving the MPC optimization problem at each time step k can be very costly; for $N_s = 7$ the calculation does not terminate in our local system. For the quantum annealing method we examine two metrics: the *sampler-call* time and *qpu-access* time. The *sampler-call* metric indicates the time taken by each call to the D-Wave sampler (implemented in the SDK), which starts executing in our local system and interacts over REST-based remote calls with the quantum device, at each time step. The *qpu-access* metric is the QPU time spent at each invocation of the quantum device including programming and sample time. The latter depends on the number of samples requested. We note that *qpu-access* time is a sub-component of *sampler-call* time.[1] The time needed for the quantum-annealing process *per sample* is reported to be 20 μs independent of problem size [7]. This indicates that the evolution time of the quantum annealing process for each sample does not depend on N_s at least for the range considered in this work ($N_s \in [2, 7]$). From Table 1 we also see that the classical simulated annealing (SA) results in lower elapsed times than the QA *sampler-call* for all N_s. This is due to the fact that the former is executed locally whereas the latter includes communication overhead. The reason to show the *sampler-call* times is to have a sense for the timing of all involving parts (computation and communication) which is important to know if we aim to control a system in real-time. Another observation is that while for prediction horizons $N_s \leq 5$, SA is faster than the purely quantum part (*qpu-access*), the latter takes advantage as the MPC optimization problem gets harder ($N_s > 5$). This result is promising as it shows the quantum advantage compared to the classical case.

In Fig. 4 we show a visualization of the results from Table 1 focusing on the relation between QA *sampler-call* and QA *qpu-access* times as the *num-reads* parameter increases from 1 (default) to 100. We observe that the time spent in the quantum device (*qpu-access* time) is a small fraction of the overall *sampler-call* time (e.g. < 3% for $N_s = 6$). This fraction is seen to increase as *num-reads* varies from 1 to 100. The remaining percentage is classical end-to-end communication time between the D-Wave machine and our infrastructure. We attribute this overhead to progressively larger message sizes, as problems (and thus QUBO expressions) that are communicated to the quantum device become more complex with increasing N_s. Another aspect we study is the effect of a varying *num-reads* parameter. In Fig. 5 we show the impact of the *num-reads*

---

[1] https://docs.dwavesys.com/docs/latest/c_qpu_timing.html.

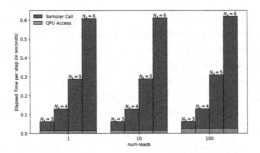

Fig. 4. Histogram showing *sampler-call* and *qpu-access* times for *num-reads* = 1, 10, 100 and $N_s = 3, 4, 5, 6$.

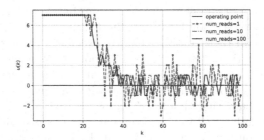

Fig. 5. The effect of *num-reads* parameter to the control input values for prediction horizon $N_s = 6$ using the Advantage System.

parameter on the quality of the obtained control inputs for the tandem queue system with *num-reads* = 1, 10, 100 for $N_s = 6$ using the Advantage System. We observe that the fluctuations are significantly reduced as *num-reads* increases. A comparison with the times presented in Fig. 4 shows first that a careful tuning of the parameters is required and second that in this case one may choose *num-reads* = 10 with a negligible difference concerning the time cost but a significant difference in the variance of the control input values. However, increasing *num-reads* leads into more expensive QPU access (Fig. 4), highlighting an important trade-off further discussed in the next section.

5   Conclusions

This work describes the construction and simulation of a tandem queue system, which we aim to stabilize and control using MPC in a quantum-enhanced manner. For this optimization problem a designed cost function is minimized leveraging the quantum annealing approach using state-of-the-art quantum devices, as well as classical methodologies such as the exact solution and simulated annealing. Specifically, we evaluate solutions from the D-Wave Advantage System and 2000Q machines investigating variations and providing insights for the significance of the prediction horizon N_s. A long prediction horizon improves the overall model performance at the cost of an increase in computation resources. In our case, we show that a prediction horizon as long as $N_s = 6$ yields acceptable results and could be sufficient to control the system. Another aspect is the significance of the *num-reads* parameter. An important result from Table 1 is that with *num-reads* fixed, QPU access time is found to increase with increasing prediction horizons but at a much slower pace compared to classical simulated annealing. This highlights the efficiency of quantum-enhanced MPC compared to classical simulation approximations for longer prediction horizons. However, simulated annealing is found to result into less variance in control inputs compared to those obtained with any of the two D-Wave quantum annealers. This indicates that in some cases existent classical solutions perform well but this is case-dependent and further experimentation is needed. Tuning the *num-reads* parameter results in a trade-off of lower variations but higher QPU access times. Adaptive applications striving for a very short control period may want to settle for higher noise in their control inputs in exchange for shorter QPU access execution times per time step. Other applications may opt for more accurate control inputs but also more expensive quantum device invocations. The network communication part of the interaction with the quantum device is a key aspect affecting latency that should not be overlooked. This leads to an interesting question, whether real-time control is in fact possible with this approach of using quantum computing for optimization. This is important for the general functionality and faster response of complex adaptive computing systems or even mechanical/robotic systems. Our results indicate that the simulated annealing and the quantum-annealing methods for the tandem-queue system with $N_s = 6$ are able to return a solution every 19.82 ms and 16.02 ms, respectively (see Table 1) which is within 100ms, sampling time that highly-responsive adaptive systems may aim for.

As part of ongoing and future work, the current problem can be extended to a more complex generalized queueing network with multiple servers. In addition, one could experiment with other distributions for the arrival and service times as well as systems that exhibit non-linear behavior. From the perspective of quantum computing, a promising direction suitable for large problems instances is further experimentation with the available D-Wave's LEAP solvers. Our work in this paper evaluates the methodology and tooling needed to explore this promising new direction for adaptive computing systems.

Acknowledgements. We thankfully acknowledge funding by the Hellenic Foundation for Research and Innovation through the STREAMSTORE faculty grant (GrantID HFRI-FM17-1998)

References

1. Balsamo, S., De Nitto Personè, V., Inverardi, P.: A review on queueing network models with finite capacity queues for software architectures performance prediction. Perform. Eval. **51**(2), 269–288 (2003). https://doi.org/10.1016/S0166-5316(02)00099-8
2. Bertsekas, D.P.: Dynamic Programming and Optimal Control: Volumes I-II. Athena Scientific, Belmont, MA (1995)
3. Bhat, U.: An Introduction to Queueing Theory: Modeling and Analysis in Applications. Statistics for Industry and Technology, Birkhäuser Boston (2015)
4. Boxma, O., Resing, J.: Tandem queues with deterministic service times. Ann. Oper. Res. **49**, 221–239 (1994). https://doi.org/10.1007/BF02031599
5. Camacho, E., Bordons, C.: Model Predictive Control. Springer, London, UK (2004)
6. Cerf, S., Berekmeri, M., Robu, B., Marchand, N., Bouchenak, S.: Cost function based event triggered model predictive controllers application to big data cloud services. In: 2016 IEEE 55th Conference on Decision and Control (CDC), pp. 1657–1662 (2016). https://doi.org/10.1109/CDC.2016.7798503
7. D-Wave: Ocean SDK Documentation (2023). https://docs.ocean.dwavesys.com
8. De Matteis, T., Mencagli, G.: Proactive elasticity and energy awareness in data stream processing. J. Syst. Softw. **127**, 302–319 (2017). https://doi.org/10.1016/j.jss.2016.08.037
9. Deng, Z., Wang, X., Dong, B.: Quantum computing for future real-time building hvac controls. Appl. Energy **334**, 120621 (2023). https://doi.org/10.1016/j.apenergy.2022.120621
10. Fang, Q., Wang, J., Gong, Q.: Qos-driven power management of data centers via model predictive control. IEEE Trans. Autom. Sci. Eng. **13**(4), 1557–1566 (2016). https://doi.org/10.1109/TASE.2016.2582501
11. Filieri, A., Maggio, M., Angelopoulos, K., D'Ippolito, N., Gerostathopoulos, I., Hempel, A.B., Hoffmann, H., Jamshidi, P., Kalyvianaki, E., Klein, C., Krikava, F., Misailovic, S., Papadopoulos, A.V., Ray, S., Shariﬂoo, A.M., Shevtsov, S., Ujma, M., Vogel, T.: Software engineering meets control theory. In: 2015 IEEE/ACM 10th International Symposium on Software Engineering for Adaptive and Self-Managing Systems, pp. 71–82 (2015). https://doi.org/10.1109/SEAMS.2015.12
12. Hellerstein, J., Diao, Y., Parekh, S., Tilbury, D.M.: Feedback Control of Computing Systems. Wiley Interscience Press (2004)
13. Inoue, D., Yoshida, H.: Model predictive control for finite input systems using the d-wave quantum annealer. Sci. Rep. 10(1591) (2020). https://doi.org/10.1038/s41598-020-58081-9
14. Kadowaki, T., Nishimori, H.: Quantum annealing in the transverse ising model. Phys. Rev. E **58**, 5355–5363 (1998). https://doi.org/10.1103/PhysRevE.58.5355
15. Karniavoura, F., Magoutis, K.: Decision-making approaches for performance QOS in distributed storage systems: a survey. IEEE Trans. Parallel Distrib. Syst. (TPDS) **30**(8), 1906–1919 (2019). https://doi.org/10.1109/TPDS.2019.2893940. August
16. Kirk, D.E.: Optimal Control Theory: An Introduction. Prentice-Hall, Englewood Cliffs, N.J. (2004)
17. Kirkpatrick, S., Gelatt, C.D., Vecchi, M.P.: Optimization by simulated annealing. Science **220**(4598), 671–680 (1983) https://doi.org/10.1126/science.220.4598.671, https://www.science.org/doi/abs/10.1126/science.220.4598.671

18. Kobayashi, H., Konheim, A.: Queueing models for computer communications system analysis. IEEE Trans. Commun. **25**(1), 2–29 (1977). https://doi.org/10.1109/TCOM.1977.1093702

19. Le Gall, P.: The theory of networks of single-server queues and the tandem queue model. J. Appl. Math. Stoch. Anal. **10**(4), 363–381 (1997)

20. Lucas, A.: Ising formulations of many np problems. Front. Phys. **2** (2014). https://doi.org/10.3389/fphy.2014.00005

21. Neuts, F.M.: Two queues in series with a finite, intermediate waitingroom. J. Appl. Prob. **5**(1), 123–142 (1968). http://www.jstor.org/stable/3212081

22. Padala, P., Hou, K.Y., Shin, K.G., Zhu, X., Uysal, M., Wang, Z., Singhal, S., Merchant, A.: Automated control of multiple virtualized resources. In: Proceedings of the 4th ACM European Conference on Computer Systems (EuroSys). Nuremberg, Germany (2009)

23. Palmer, G.I., Knight, V.A., Harper, P.R., Hawa, A.L.: CIW: An open-source discrete event simulation library. J. Simul. **13**(1), 68–82 (2019). https://doi.org/10.1080/17477778.2018.1473909

24. Preskill, J.: Quantum computing in the NISQ era and beyond. Quantum **2**(79) (2018)

25. Qin, S., Badgwell, T.: A survey of industrial model predictive control technology. Control. Eng. Pract. **93**(316), 733–764 (2003)

26. Rosberg, Z., Varaiya, P., Walrand, J.: Optimal control of service in tandem queues. IEEE Trans. Autom. Control **27**(3), 600–610 (1982). https://doi.org/10.1109/TAC.1982.1102957

27. Rossiter, J.A.: A First Course in Predictive Control. CRC Press (2018)

28. Santoro, G.E., Tosatti, E.: Optimization using quantum mechanics: quantum annealing through adiabatic evolution. J. Phys. A: Math. General **39**(36), R393 (2006). https://doi.org/10.1088/0305-4470/39/36/R01, https://dx.doi.org/10.1088/0305-4470/39/36/R01

29. Schoeffauer, R., Wunder, G.: Model-predictive control for discrete-time queueing networks with varying topology. IEEE Trans. Control Netw. Syst. **8**(3), 1528–1539 (2021). https://doi.org/10.1109/TCNS.2021.3074250

30. Schwenzer, M., Ay, M., Bergs, T., Abel, D.: Review on model predictive control: An engineering perspective. Int. J. Adv. Manuf. Technol. **117**, 1327–1349 (2021). https://doi.org/10.1007/s00170-021-07682-3

31. Suman, B., Kumar, P.: A survey of simulated annealing as a tool for single and multiobjective optimization. J. Oper. Res. Soc. **57**, 1143–1160 (2006). https://doi.org/10.1057/palgrave.jors.2602068

32. de Waal, P.R.: Performance analysis and optimal control of an mm1k queueing system with impatient customers, pp. 28–40. Springer, Berlin Heidelberg (1987). https://doi.org/10.1007/978-3-642-73016-0_3

33. Wang, C., Chen, H., Jonckheere, E.: Quantum versus simulated annealing in wireless interference network optimization. Sci. Rep. **6**(25797) (2016). https://doi.org/10.1038/srep25797

34. Xu, Q., Ma, G., Ding, K., Xu, B.: An adaptive active queue management based on model predictive control. IEEE Access **8**, 174489–174494 (2020). https://doi.org/10.1109/ACCESS.2020.3025377

35. Yarkoni, S., Raponi, E., Bäck, T., Schmitt, S.: Quantum annealing for industry applications: Introduction and review. Rep. Progr. Phys. **85**(10), 104001 (2022). https://doi.org/10.1088/1361-6633/ac8c54

Networking and Queues

Combining Static and Dynamic Traffic with Delay Guarantees in Time-Sensitive Networking

Lisa Maile[✉][iD], Kai-Steffen Hielscher, and Reinhard German

Computer Networks and Communication Systems, Friedrich-Alexander-Universität
Erlangen-Nürnberg, Erlangen, Germany
{lisa.maile,kai-steffen.hielscher,reinhard.german}@fau.de

Abstract. To support reliable and low-latency communication, Time-Sensitive Networking introduced protocols and interfaces for resource allocation in Ethernet. However, the implementation of these allocation algorithms has not yet been covered by the standards. Our work focuses on deadline-guaranteeing resource allocation for networks with static and dynamic traffic. To achieve this, we combine offline network optimization heuristics with online admission control and, thus, allow for new flow registrations while the network is running. We demonstrate our solution on Credit-Based Shaper networks by using the delay analysis framework Network Calculus. We compare our approach with an intuitive and a brute-force algorithm, where we can achieve significant improvements, both, in terms of quality and runtime. Thereby, our results show that we can guarantee maximum end-to-end delays and also increase the flexibility of the network while requiring only minimal user input.

Keywords: Performance modeling · Network optimization · Latency guarantees · Auto-configuration · Resource allocation · Time-sensitive networking

1 Introduction

With the increasing need for ultra-reliable and low latency communication, there has been a growing demand for more advanced transmission mediums to support them. As a response, the IEEE Time-Sensitive Networking (TSN) task group developed new standards that, i.a., allow for resource allocation in Ethernet with the introduction of central configuration units and decentralized reservation protocols. However, the current standards do not provide guidance on the configuration of TSN networks. Therefore, several works have addressed this by proposing either offline (e.g., [6,10]) or online (e.g., [11,18]) configuration approaches. However, offline solutions do not allow for variable traffic and dynamic flows during the runtime of the network, while online solutions require the a-priori definition

© ICST Institute for Computer Sciences, Social Informatics and Telecommunications Engineering 2024
Published by Springer Nature Switzerland AG 2024. All Rights Reserved
E. Kalyvianaki and M. Paolieri (Eds.): VALUETOOLS 2023, LNICST 539, pp. 117–132, 2024.
https://doi.org/10.1007/978-3-031-48885-6_8

of non-trivial delay bounds by a user. To this end, we introduce a novel tool that combines offline and online configuration to support static and dynamic traffic while providing delay guarantees for time-sensitive flows. Thereby, offline configuration optimizes network setup in advance, while online configuration enables flow reservation and de-reservation while the network is running.

Combining both offline and online resource reservation with delay constraints is crucial in the design and operation of Industry 4.0 networking systems. Firstly, offline optimization allows for the creation of an optimal plan for resource allocation and scheduling. This ensures that the network is designed to operate at peak efficiency and that resources are allocated effectively. However, network conditions are rarely static and can change over time due to varying traffic patterns, new applications, devices, or other factors. Online admission control allows the network to respond quickly to changing conditions while maintaining its performance.

In this paper, we present a new approach that combines offline and online resource reservation for time-sensitive communication. The goal is to offer an auto-configuration framework which eliminates the need for manual intervention while still offering reliable flow delays. To the best of our knowledge, we are the first to propose a combined solution for offline and online configuration for TSN with safe delay guarantees.

The remainder of this paper is structured as follows. Section 2 introduces related work and motivates the problem. Section 3 presents an overview of our framework and its relation to the TSN standards. We explain our heuristic optimization in Sect. 4. Afterwards, we extensively evaluate our approach in Sect. 5. Finally, Sect. 6 concludes this paper.

2   Problem Definition and Related Work

Traditional deadline-constrained optimization approaches take a set of flows as input and determine the optimal configuration of network resources, such as bandwidth or time-slots, as output. For example, when using time-triggered gates, individual time-slots are assigned for each flow, e.g., [4,6]. For other schedulers, such as the Credit-Based Shaper (CBS), optimization approaches optimize the reserved bandwidth per traffic class, called idleSlope, so that all flows keep their deadline constraints, e.g., in [10,16]. However, all of these approaches have in common that, when additional time-sensitive flows are added to the network later, the reserved resources, such as time-slots or bandwidth, need to be adapted. This affects existing flow reservations, which evokes the necessity to re-validate all reservations, making these approaches inapplicable for dynamic networks.

To avoid this, flexible online solutions have been proposed in the last years, such as [11,13,18,19]. They offer the opportunity to add and remove flow reservations while the network is running and still provide safe deadline guarantees. The underlying idea is that, instead of configuring resources such as time-slots or bandwidth, each hop is configured with priority-dependent maximum delay

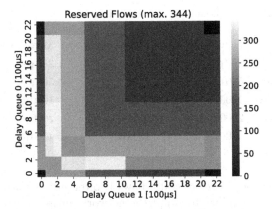

Fig. 1. Impact of delay bounds for individual priority queues on the number of successful flow reservations.

bounds. When the network changes, each hop is allowed to change its configuration, e.g., adapting the reserved bandwidth. Thereby, for each hop, it is validated that the new configuration does not violate the pre-configured delay bounds. This validation can either be done in a central controller instance, such as in [13,18], or with a decentralized reservation protocol, as proposed by [11,19].

While online solutions offer high flexibility, we showed in [18] that the choice of pre-configured delay bounds highly influences the possibility of reserving flows. We illustrate this in Fig. 1, where we used the approach in [18] to reserve flows. We assume a single-hop with two priority queues and a maximum of 344 flows[1] for this example. Figure 1 varies the delay bounds for the two priority queues. We can observe that their choice is of uttermost importance and non-trivial. High delay bounds would lead to a violation of the flows' deadlines, whereas low delay bounds require the reservation of more resources (e.g., more bandwidth to ensure a faster transmission) and, thus, allow for fewer flow reservations in total. Thus, the optimal delay bound values have to be chosen carefully and must neither be too strict nor too loose. Deriving the best delay bounds gets even more complex when more than two priority queues and/or more hops have to be configured.

Grigorjew et al. [12] highlight the fact that brute-forcing the optimal values does not scale for industrial use-cases. Therefore, they employ different machine-learning techniques and show that they can determine fitting delay bounds in the network. However, they assume that the flows' characteristics at each hop are known in advance, which removes the flexibility of online admission control schemes. Besides, in their evaluation, each hop in the network is configured identically, which may lead to potentially sub-optimal results.

---

[1] We defined the flows according to the traffic profiles 1, 2, 3, and 4 as defined in Table 1, with 86 flows per profile and a bandwidth of 1 Gbit/s.

Table 1. Traffic profiles for industrial scenarios [12]

	Sending Interval	Max. Frame Size	Max. Latency
Profile 1	250 µs	64B	250 µs
Profile 2	500 µs	128B	500 µs
Profile 3	1000 µs	256B	1000 µs
Profile 4	2000 µs	512B	2000 µs
Profile 5	4000 µs	1024B	4000 µs

In real applications, a set of static flows is often given, but operators might also wish for some flexibility to adapt the network during runtime. To this end, we propose our combined approach, where an offline optimization derives delay bounds for the online admission control. For our proof-of-concept, we use [18] to demonstrate the applicability of our solution to be used with online admission control. However, it should also be mentioned that this concept can be applied to any admission control scheme which requires delay bounds as input, such as [11,13,18,19]. We use Network Calculus (NC)—as it is a well-established delay analysis framework—to validate the delay bounds when flows are added to the network. NC models complex communication systems to derive performance guarantees, e.g., maximum per hop and end-to-end delays. To achieve this, worst-case maximum arrival and minimum departures of traffic are modeled using cumulative functions and combined using expressions from the min-plus algebra [15]. For an introduction to NC, see [15]. We provide an overview of NC models for TSN in [17].

3   Network Configuration Framework for TSN

We present a framework for the configuration of TSN networks, which provides safe delay guarantees in networks which combine static and dynamic traffic flows. We refer to *offline configuration* as the configuration of bridge parameters, e.g., the number of priority queues and the worst-case per-hop delay bounds. With *online configuration* (or admission control), we refer to the registration and deregistration of flows while the network is running, after checking the flow's path for sufficient resources. Our goal is to offer delay-guaranteeing networks with only minimal required manual input. Therefore, we defined five traffic profiles for flows in Table 1 [12]. The profiles are derived from PROFINET use-cases for industrial sensor-controller networks. We use the term stream and flow interchangeably.

Input: The only input that we require is 1) the network topology, 2) the maximum number of priority queues, and 3) the percentage of bandwidth that shall remain free for future flow reservations. The latter is provided per link and per traffic profile. In addition, our approach can be optionally supplied with a set of static flows.

Offline Network Optimization: We then run a meta-heuristic optimization which determines the number of required priority queues per hop, as well as the

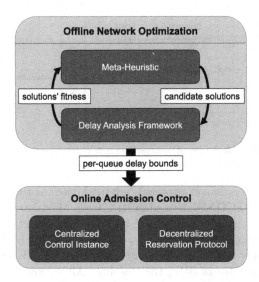

Fig. 2. Framework overview. We use network optimization to derive delay bounds which improve the performance of online admission control.

delay bounds for each priority queue in the network. This is illustrated in Fig. 2. Our heuristic generates potential candidate solutions, which define the delay bounds per priority queue. Each candidate solution is then evaluated according to its potential to provide real-time latency guarantees for the defined traffic profiles. This is expressed as a fitness value, which is defined by the objective function in Sect. 4.2. The latency guarantees are validated using a delay analysis framework. For our tool, we implemented the delay analysis framework using NC, as NC allows for the efficient analysis of large and complex networks. The details of our delay analysis using NC can be found in [18]. The heuristic then iteratively aims at maximizing the fitness value returned by the objective function. We compare two meta-heuristic algorithms, Particle Swarm Optimization (PSO) [14] and Genetic Algorithm (GA) [9], as they have been widely used in various fields.

Online Admission Control: The best candidate solution then defines the delay bounds for each bridge, which are used to configure the network. These bounds remain static, while the actual flow reservations can change adaptively to the network setup, with no re-configuration of the network required. To add new flows to or remove existing flows from the network, existing online admission control algorithms are used, as proposed in [11,13,18,19].

Our framework is suitable for centralized and decentralized network architectures, utilizing protocols specified in the respective standards. In a centralized network, the configuration is done in a so-called Central Network Controller (CNC), as defined by the IEEE 802.1Qcc-2018 standard [1]. The CNC is a separate instance responsible for the reservation and configuration of all flows and nodes in the network. It is aware of the complete network topology, similar to a Software-Defined Networking controller. To communicate with the TSN network

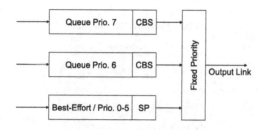

Fig. 3. Example output port with CBS queues.

devices, network management protocols are used, such as the Network Configuration Protocol (NETCONF) defined in RFC 6241.[2] For decentralized networks, the Stream Reservation Protocol (SRP) has been proposed for online admission control in CBS networks. However, as we proved in [19], the delay values proposed for SRP do not cover the worst-case. In 2018, the IEEE TSN group started working on the successor of SRP, the Resource Allocation Protocol (RAP) [2]. Currently, RAP is still undergoing active development and is available in draft version 0.6. RAP considers introducing a pre-configuration phase of the network prior to online admission. This aligns perfectly with the requirements of our framework. Although the existing standards define the necessary protocols, they currently lack a solution for implementing resource allocation with guaranteed delays. Our framework fills this gap, and we hope that our research will help future standardization processes.

4   Meta-Heuristic Optimization

To derive the per-hop delay bounds for the network, we compare two meta-heuristic optimization approaches, PSO and GA. Initially, both algorithms start with a population of random solutions, which we call candidate solutions. The heuristics then successively update their solutions to improve their fitness. Eventually, the heuristics converge to a (near-optimal) solution.

TSN networks allow for up to eight queues in each output port of a bridge. Each queue is configured with a transmission selection algorithm. If multiple queues have eligible packets at the same time, the transmission is defined by the queues' priority. Figure 3 illustrates this for an example output port with two CBS queues. We define a subset of these queues as *priority queues*, meaning that our framework optimizes them for time-critical traffic with deadline guarantees using CBS. All other queues can then be used by non-time-critical traffic without admission control and are not included in our optimization.

4.1   Design Decisions

Our framework includes the following considerations, to ensure that a user only has to provide a minimum of input.

---

[2] https://datatracker.ietf.org/doc/html/rfc6241.

Routing: We use a k-shortest delay-constrained routing algorithm [22], with the links' bandwidth utilization as weight-function. We chose to weight the bandwidth utilization as this balances the network load, and thus, prevents bottlenecks which would decrease the possibility of online flow reservations.

Flow to Priority Assignment: We do not require any kind of flow-to-priority mapping. Instead, our frameworks assign the priority to each flow automatically, by using the k-shortest paths and checking the priorities on each path with an end-to-end delay that is closest to a flow's deadline successively. If no path allows for a reservation, the fitness of the solution decreases. To increase flexibility, we allow for individual per-hop priorities for each flow, instead of mapping a flow to a single priority on its whole path.

Number of Priority Queues: The required number of priorities in a network is an optimization itself. We only require the definition of a maximum number of priority queues instead. Our heuristic will try to find a schedule with no high-priority queue unused, but potentially without using low priorities. Then, unused queues can be left out or used for other purposes, such as non-time-critical traffic.

Discussion: The above considerations do not have any claim on optimality. E.g., instead of balancing the network, we could add the routing decision as part of the solution, thereby offering it as a variable for the optimization. All of these problems have been covered in heuristics themselves (e.g., [5,8,16,21]), and including them increases the solution space and the runtime significantly. Our results show that with the above decision, already highly practical networks can be built.

Note that we also allow for more detailed modeling, e.g., on the path of flows that arrive during online reservation. The more information is available, the better our approach can configure the network. However, to be appealing for real-life scenarios, we wanted to reduce the minimum required input as much as possible.

4.2 Multi-objective Function

Each candidate solution is evaluated based on its capability of reserving all static flows and on the flexibility it offers for future reservations. The heuristics aim at maximizing the following fitness function, defined for each candidate solution s as

$$f(s) = \omega_1 \cdot f_R(s) + \omega_2 \cdot f_A(s) + \omega_3 \cdot f_D(s), \tag{1}$$

where $\omega_i (i = 1, 2, 3)$ define the weight for each of the objectives. We normalized the fitness value, so f and $f_x(x = \{R, A, D\})$ are between 0 and 1.

Thereby, $f_R(s) = 1$, if all flows from the (optional) set of static offline flows can be reserved with the solution s. $f_R(s)$ can be derived by checking for each static flow whether a path can be found which will meet their end-to-end delay requirement. The ratio of successful reservations then defines $f_R(s)$. Even with a suboptimal solution, the flows' deadlines are still safe. We only reduce the maximum number of reservable flows in the network.

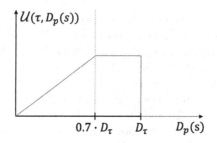

Fig. 4. Utility function for flow τ with delay requirement D_τ and path delay D_p

$f_A(s) = 1$, if it is possible to reserve the required percentage of bandwidth for the online flows. We determine f_A by artificially increasing the arrival function at each link for which the user assigned additional bandwidth for a traffic profile. This is done by dividing the end-to-end delay requirement of each profile into smaller per-hop delays, using the maximum path length of the network. We then check up to which arrival rate we can still guarantee the specified per-hop delay. As we are not aware of the path of the future flows and, thus, do not know the links from which they will arrive at each hop, we use the maximum rate that is possible for each link. f_A then reflects the maximum ratio of available bandwidth when compared to the user's input.

Finally, $f_D(s) = 1$, if the end-to-end delay for the set of offline flows matches their deadline (within a 30% flexibility interval). For each flow τ, we define a utility function $\mathcal{U}(\tau, D_p(s))$ [10] to ensure that its end-to-end delay requirement, D_τ, matches the path delay $D_p(s)$ for the solution s. This is illustrated in Fig. 4. $f_D(s)$ is then defined as

$$f_D(s) = \frac{\sum_{\tau \in \mathcal{F}} \mathcal{U}(\tau, D_p(s))}{|\mathcal{F}|}, \tag{2}$$

where $\mathcal{F}$ is the set of static flows. The reason for f_D is that, if flows are scheduled faster than required, more bandwidth than necessary is reserved, which reduces the performance of best-effort traffic. We define a candidate solution to be invalid, if some bridges in the network only utilize their low-priority queues, whereas the high-priority queues cannot be used for time-sensitive traffic. In these solutions, the high-priority queues would be configured unnecessarily. Therefore, these invalid solutions will be rewarded with a fitness value of 0.

We prioritize the individual objectives in our fitness function as follows: We assume that the successful reservation of the static offline flows is of the most importance. Afterwards, we optimize the bandwidth for future reservations of time-sensitive flows. Only if the above two goals are not hindered, the solution might be improved for best-effort and lower priority traffic. As a result, we chose the weight functions to reflect this prioritization as defined in Table 2.

Table 2. Parameter selection for meta-heuristics

	Values
PSO parameters	
w, c_1, c_2	0.5, 2, 2.4
GA parameters	
Crossover operation	blend crossover, $P_c = 0.45, \alpha = 0.15$
Mutation operation	NSGA-II, $P_m = 0.45, \eta = 70, P_{ind} = 0.3$
Selection algorithm	NSGA-II, $P_s = 0.5$
Shared parameters	
ω_1, ω_2, ω_3	0.9, 0.09, 0.01
Population size, convergence	Uniform config.: 100, 15; Individual config.: 200, 20

4.3   Individual Per-Hop Delays

The offline optimizations introduced in Sect. 2, [10,12], configured each hop in the network identically. We evaluate whether individual configurations for each network device can improve the networks' performance. As individual per-hop delays significantly increase the solution space, the heuristics potentially have a higher chance to remain in local optima, instead of finding the global best solution. Therefore, we propose a new approach, where we initialize the solution for individual delays with the results from the uniform network configuration. With this approach, the individual heuristic is guaranteed to perform equally or better than the uniform approach. We will show that this initialization can significantly improve the performance of the algorithms.

4.4   Parameter Choice

We have implemented both, PSO and GA, using Python3. For the GA implementation, we used the evolutionary computation framework DEAP [7]. To determine generic and efficient parameters for both approaches, we used the hyperparameter optimization framework Optuna [3]. To prevent overfitting, we created an evaluation set with highly variable network topologies, different numbers of priorities, and changing flow characteristics. The topologies are presented in Sect. 5.

GAs are inspired by the principles of biological evolution and natural selection. The candidate solutions are updated using selection, crossover, and mutation operators. Selection involves choosing a percentage of P_s individuals from the current population based on their fitness values. Crossover and mutation then adapt a certain percentage of individuals (P_c and P_m, respectively) to explore the solution space. We evaluated all available GA mutation, crossover, and selection algorithms in DEAP, along with their parameter values.

Similarly, PSO iteratively updates the candidate solutions based on the solution's own experience and the collective knowledge of the population. The update uses an inertia w, a cognitive component c_1, and a social component c_2 as parameters. The inertia term allows particles to maintain their momentum, while the cognitive component focuses on the particle's personal best position, and the social component emphasizes the global best position.

The best set of parameters is provided in Table 2. We also use them for our evaluation.

5   Evaluation

We have defined three different topologies which are typical for sensor-controller networks in the industry. Controllers refer to Programmable Logical Controllers (PLCs) and represent end-stations which control industrial machines, e.g., in manufacturing processes. We assume 1 Gbit/s links in all topologies and test cases. We used the following topologies, as they are typical for industrial use-cases: 1) a *line* topology with four bridges, an end-station connected to each of them, and a PLC at the end of the line, 2) a *star-of-stars* topology with one central bridge connected to four bridges, which are again connected to four end-stations, 3) a ring topology with five bridges and each bridge connected to two end-stations. For topologies 2) and 3), we randomly assign one end-device to be the PLC. In all scenarios, flows are addressing the PLC in the network to create a bottleneck for our evaluation. We defined a discrete search space S with steps of $10\,\mu s$ between 0 and 4 ms, for all algorithms, as 4 ms is the maximum possible deadline for our flows.

5.1   Benchmark Algorithms

We have implemented two approaches as benchmark algorithms for our evaluation. Thereby, we want to evaluate both, the increase in optimality when compared to an intuitive configuration and the gain of performance when compared to an exhaustive search. We evaluate our solution in both categories by using the following two approaches. For comparison, all code is executed without parallelization on an Intel Xeon Silver 4215R processor with 3.20 GHz.

Exhaustive Search (ES): The exhaustive search will iteratively evaluate all possible solutions, and thus, can determine the optimum within the search space. With this approach, we can evaluate how close our results are to the optimal value. However, the exhaustive search suffers from a high runtime. Thus, it cannot cover individual per-hop delays, but will only investigate settings with identical delays for all hops. We will show in our evaluation that, due to this limitation, our solution is able to achieve even better configurations than the exhaustive search.

Intuitive Approach (IA): Our intuitive approach reflects the configuration of a user. It will serve as a benchmark to evaluate whether our heuristics are actually needed to configure high-performance networks. Simply spoken, the intuitive approach will uniformly distribute the end-to-end delays of each flow over its number of hops on the path. The resulting values represent the per-hop delays which each flow requires to meet its deadline requirement. We then configure the network by deriving the quantiles from this set of delays in a way that each flow can be covered by one of the queues. E.g., for four queues, we use the minimum per-hop value, plus the 25, 50, and 75% quantile of the resulting delays to configure the four queues. When compared to our solution, this approach has only minimum runtime, but it does not consider the effect that traffic load has on the queuing delays in the network. As a result, our solution is evaluated against the intuitive approach, i.e., to check for improved fitness values alias more successful flow reservations and evaluate the overhead of performing offline optimization.

5.2   Convergence

Figure 5 illustrates the behavior of the GA and PSO algorithm when compared to the ES in the star-of-stars network, with 150 flows randomly assigned to traffic profiles and end-stations. We assumed a maximum of two CBS queues and a uniform configuration for all network devices. With these settings, the ES can obtain the optimum in 119 min, and we can see how the heuristics perform in comparison. Figure 5 shows the result after each iteration for 30 independent replications, where we consider the algorithms as converged if their results remain constant for 10 iterations.   The final result after the algorithms have converged

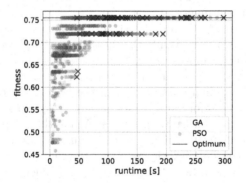

Fig. 5. Results of GA and PSO after each iteration, with results at termination marked as X. The optimum is derived using ES.

is marked with an X. As we can see, both heuristics achieve good results, but GA is faster in reaching high fitness values than PSO. GA performs faster as it only updates solutions with a specific probability (P_c and P_m of Table 2).

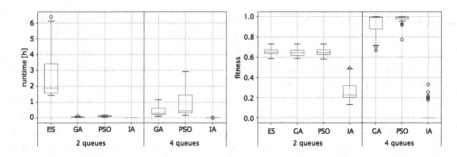

Fig. 6. Runtime and fitness results in networks with uniform bridge configuration.

However, GA is twice as likely to converge in a local rather than global optima when compared to PSO.

5.3 Comparison

To compare our heuristics, we conduct experiments by uniformly choosing one of the three topologies. We randomly generated 200 flows uniformly distributed with the profiles defined in Table 1, originating from random sources and heading to the PLC of the network. We repeat the experiments 30 times for each algorithm. We first assume that all hops are configured with the same delay values.

Figure 6 shows the runtime and resulting fitness values for the experiments, respectively. With the given search space and two priorities, the ES has to evaluate $|S|^2 \approx 160 \cdot 10^3$ possible solutions. Increasing the number of priorities to four would result in $|S|^4 \approx 25 \cdot 10^9$ solutions, which cannot be accomplished by the ES due to its performance.

As we can see in Fig. 6, both heuristics can achieve similar fitness values as the ES for two priorities. While the intuitive approach does allow for some reservations, it cannot compete with the results from our heuristics. For two priorities, the heuristics perform 2.4 times better on average. Additionally, the heuristics can evaluate more priorities than the ES, which results in more successful reservations. E.g., for four priority queues, GA performed 41.4% and PSO 49.3% better than the ES with two priorities. Again, the GA provides better performance in terms of runtime than the PSO, but is more likely to converge in local optima. For the four priority settings, the intuitive approach frequently results in invalid configurations, where high-priority queues remained unused.

5.4 Individual Per-Hop Delays

Individual per-hop delays allow for a better distribution of the network resources when the traffic load is not evenly distributed. For this, we defined the network shown in Fig. 7, based on the PROFINET design guidelines [20] with one priority per flow. Each line is connected to an end-station with an individual traffic

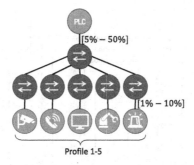

Fig. 7. PROFINET network with given link utlizations.

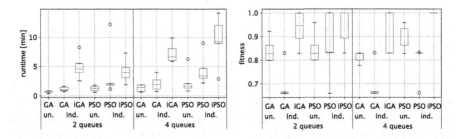

Fig. 8. Runtime and fitness results in a network with individual per-hop configuration.

profile. We randomly generated flows to simulate a link utilization between 5% and 50% on the link to the PLC.

While neither the ES nor the intuitive approach allow for individual per-hop delays, both of our heuristics can evaluate such configurations. Figure 8 shows the result for the GA and PSO algorithms. We compared the uniform network configuration ('un.') with the individual configuration ('ind.'). In addition, we show the results for our initialized solutions ('iGA' and 'iPSO'), which we initialize with the results from the uniform configuration to determine individual delay bounds. We can see that simply allowing for individual queue delays can reduce the performance of the heuristics when compared to the uniform configuration results. This is due to the vast increase of the solution space, which makes it more likely for the heuristics to converge in local optima. However, our initialized algorithms iGA and iPSO can improve the results from the uniform configuration by 10–11% on average and, at the same time, are guaranteed to not provide lower results.

5.5   Flows During Runtime

Finally, to evaluate the benefit for future flow reservations, we again use the star-of-stars topology and define 10 offline flows for each of the profiles 1, 3, and 5. We run different scenarios, where in each scenario, we reserved 50% of the bandwidth for one of the five traffic profiles for future flows. For each sce-

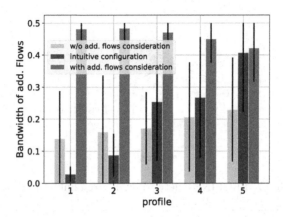

Fig. 9. Successful flow reservations with online admission and one standard deviation. In separate networks, each profile should receive 50% bandwidth.

nario, we repeated the experiment 10 times, resulting in 50 repetitions in total. Figure 9 compares the number of successful reservations during online admission, when the offline optimization considers the bandwidth for the future flows, in comparison to when they are not considered. Additionally, we also compared our heuristics to the intuitive configuration. For these scenarios, we improved the intuitive approach by artificially adding every possible future flow. As we can see, all configurations have some potential to add additional flows during the runtime of the network. However, our combined solution which considers the required bandwidth for future flows can increase the number of successful reservations when compared to the intuitive approach and a configuration without future flow considerations significantly, illustrating our framework's flexibility to support dynamic traffic during runtime. Figure 9 also shows that flows with tight deadline guarantees (e.g., profile 1) profit most from our optimization, while higher latency requirements (e.g. profile 5) are easier to integrate even without specific considerations.

6   Conclusion

We have presented our framework for offline and online configuration of TSN networks with delay guarantees. Thereby, the offline configuration allows for efficient usage of the network resources, while the online configuration allows for the registration and deregistration of flows while the network is running. By considering future flows in the offline configuration phase, we ensure that the network can easily react to changing network conditions while still offering guarantees for the end-to-end delays of time-critical flows. Our framework requires only minimal user input, making it highly relevant for practical application and providing a first step towards the auto-configuration of TSN networks.

We have evaluated two meta-heuristics for our framework and showed that a particle swarm optimization provides better results when compared to a genetic algorithm, with slightly higher runtimes. We also implemented two benchmark algorithms, one exhaustive search to evaluate the optimum for simple configurations, and one intuitive approach to reflect the behavior of a user. We could show that our heuristics reached similar results as the exhaustive search in just a fraction of the time. Due to the high flexibility and the low runtime, our framework can provide even better results than the exhaustive search and significantly better results than an intuitive solution. We demonstrated that allowing individual delay bounds on each hop improves the network's performance. Finally, we also showed the effect on the success of new flow reservations while the network is running. Thereby, considering the required bandwidth of future flows during the offline configuration highly increases the chance for future flow reservations.

As future work, we want to extend the delay-guaranteeing admission approaches as proposed by [11,13,18,19] to more schedulers. Specifically, we would like to cover solutions for the Asynchronous Traffic Shaper and Cyclic Queuing and Forwarding networks, to ensure that our framework is applicable for a wide range of TSN scenarios.

References

1. IEEE standard for local and metropolitan area networks-bridges and bridged networks—amendment 31: stream reservation protocol (SRP) enhancements and performance improvements. IEEE Std 802.1Qcc-2018 (Amendment to IEEE Std 802.1Q-2018) (2018). https://doi.org/10.1109/IEEESTD.2018.8514112
2. P802.1Qdd—resource allocation protocol (2019). https://1.ieee802.org/TSN/802-1qdd/
3. Akiba, T., Sano, S., Yanase, T., Ohta, T., Koyama, M.: Optuna: a next-generation hyperparameter optimization framework. In: Proceedings of the 25th ACM SIGKDD International Conference on Knowledge Discovery and Data Mining (2019)
4. Arestova, A., Hielscher, K.S.J., German, R.: Design of a hybrid genetic algorithm for time-sensitive networking. In: Hermanns, H. (ed.) Measurement, Modelling and Evaluation of Computing Systems, pp. 99–117. Springer International Publishing, Cham (2020)
5. Chuang, C.C., Yu, T.H., Lin, C.W., Pang, A.C., Hsieh, T.J.: Online stream-aware routing for TSN-based industrial control systems. In: 2020 25th IEEE International Conference on Emerging Technologies and Factory Automation (ETFA), vol. 1, pp. 254–261 (2020). https://doi.org/10.1109/ETFA46521.2020.9211969
6. Craciunas, S.S., Oliver, R.S., Chmelík, M., Steiner, W.: Scheduling real-time communication in IEEE 802.1Qbv time sensitive networks. In: Proceedings of the International Conference on Real-Time Networks and Systems, pp. 183–192. ACM Press (2016). https://doi.org/10.1145/2997465.2997470
7. Fortin, F.A., De Rainville, F.M., Gardner, M.A., Parizeau, M., Gagné, C.: DEAP: evolutionary algorithms made easy. J. Machine Learn. Res. **13**, 2171–2175 (2012)
8. Francés, F., Fraboul, C., Grieu, J.: Using Network Calculus to optimize the AFDX network, p. 9 (2006)
9. Fraser, A., Burnell, D.: Computer Models in Genetics. McGraw-Hill, New York (1970)

10. Gavriluţ, V., Pop, P.: Traffic-type Assignment for TSN-based Mixed-criticality cyber-physical systems. ACM Trans. Cyber-Phys. Syst. **4**(2), 1–27 (2020). https://doi.org/10.1145/3371708, https://dl.acm.org/doi/10.1145/3371708

11. Grigorjew, A., Metzger, F., Hoßfeld, T., Specht, J., Götz, F.J., Chen, F., Schmitt, J.: Bounded latency with bridge-local stream reservation and strict priority queuing. In: 11th International Conference on Network of the Future, pp. 55–63 (2020). https://doi.org/10.1109/NoF50125.2020.9249224

12. Grigorjew, A., Seufert, M., Wehner, N., Hofmann, J., Hoßfeld, T.: Ml-assisted latency assignments in time-sensitive networking. In: IFIP/IEEE International Symposium on Integrated Network Management (IM), pp. 116–124 (2021)

13. Guck, J.W., Van Bemten, A., Kellerer, W.: Detserv: network models for real-time QOS provisioning in SDN-based industrial environments. IEEE Trans. Netw. Serv. Manage. **14**(4), 1003–1017 (2017). https://doi.org/10.1109/TNSM.2017.2755769. Dec

14. Kennedy, J., Eberhart, R.: Particle swarm optimization. In: Proceedings of ICNN'95—International Conference on Neural Networks, vol. 4, pp. 1942–1948 (1995). https://doi.org/10.1109/ICNN.1995.488968

15. Le Boudec, J.Y., Thiran, P.: Network calculus: a theory of deterministic queuing systems for the Internet. Springer, Berlin, Heidelberg (2001). https://doi.org/10.1007/3-540-45318-0

16. Li, E., He, F., Zhao, L., Zhou, X.: A SDN-based traffic bandwidth allocation method for time sensitive networking in Avionics. In: 2019 IEEE/AIAA 38th Digital Avionics Systems Conference (DASC), pp. 1–7 (2019). https://doi.org/10.1109/DASC43569.2019.9081700

17. Maile, L., Hielscher, K.S., German, R.: Network calculus results for TSN: an introduction. In: 2020 Information Communication Technologies Conference (ICTC), pp. 131–140. IEEE, Nanjing, China (2020). https://doi.org/10.1109/ICTC49638.2020.9123308

18. Maile, L., Hielscher, K.S.J., German, R.: Delay-guaranteeing admission control for time-sensitive networking using the credit-based shaper. IEEE Open J. Commun. Soc. **3**, 1834–1852 (2022). https://doi.org/10.1109/OJCOMS.2022.3212939

19. Maile, L., Voitlein, D., Grigorjew, A., Hielscher, K.S., German, R.: On the validity of credit-based shaper delay guarantees in decentralized reservation protocols. In: Proceedings of the 31st International Conference on Real-Time Networks and Systems. RTNS 2023, Association for Computing Machinery, New York, NY, USA (2023). https://doi.org/10.1145/3575757.3593644, forthcoming

20. Niemann, K.H.: PROFINET Design Guideline Version 1.53. Tech. Rep. 8.062, PROFIBUS Nutzerorganisation e.V., Karlsruhe, Germany (2022)

21. Soni, A., Scharbarg, J.L., Ermont, J.: Efficient configuration of a QoS-aware AFDX network with deficit round robin. In: 2020 IEEE 18th International Conference on Industrial Informatics (INDIN). vol. 1, pp. 251–258 (2020). https://doi.org/10.1109/INDIN45582.2020.9442115, iSSN: 2378-363X

22. Yen, J.Y.: Finding the K shortest loopless paths in a network. Manage. Sci. **17**(11), 712–716 (1971)

Caching Contents with Varying Popularity Using Restless Bandits

K. J. Pavamana$^{(\boxtimes)}$ and Chandramani Singh

Department of Electronic Systems Engineering, Indian Institute of Science,
Bengaluru, India
{pavamanak,chandra}@iisc.ac.in

Abstract. We study content caching in a wireless network in which the users are connected through a base station that is equipped with a finite capacity cache. We assume a fixed set of contents whose popularity vary with time. Users' requests for the contents depend on their instantaneous popularity levels. Proactively caching contents at the base station incurs a cost but not having requested contents at the base station also incurs a cost. We propose to proactively cache contents at the base station so as to minimize content missing and caching costs. We formulate the problem as a discounted cost Markov decision problem that is a restless multi-armed bandit problem. We provide conditions under which the problem is indexable and also propose a novel approach to manoeuvre a few parameters to render the problem indexable. We demonstrate efficacy of the Whittle index policy via numerical evaluation.

Keywords: Caching · Restless bandits · Threshold policy · Whittle index

1 Introduction

The exponential growth of intelligent devices and mobile applications poses a significant challenge to Internet backhaul, as it struggles to cope with the surge in traffic. According to Cisco's annual Internet report 2023 [1], approximately two-thirds of the world's population will have access to Internet by 2023, and the number of devices connected to IP networks will exceed three times the global population. This extensive user base will generate a high demand for multimedia content, such as videos and music. However, this increased traffic is often due to repeated transmissions of popular content, leading to an unnecessary burden on the network. The resulting influx of content requests has adverse effects on latency, power consumption, and service quality.

To address these challenges, proactive content caching at the periphery of mobile networks has emerged as a promising solution. By implementing caches

This work was supported by Centre for Network Intelligence, Indian Institute of Science (IISc), a CISCO CSR initiative.

E. Kalyvianaki and M. Paolieri (Eds.): VALUETOOLS 2023, LNICST 539, pp. 133–150, 2024.
https://doi.org/10.1007/978-3-031-48885-6_9

at base stations, it becomes possible to pre-store requested content in advance. As a result, content requests can be efficiently served from these local caches instead of remote servers, benefiting both users and network operators. Users experience reduced latency and improved quality of experience when accessing content from intermediary base stations. For network operators, caching content at the network edge significantly reduces network overhead, particularly in cases where multiple users request the same content, such as popular videos and live sports streams.

Notwithstanding the widespread benefits of including content caching abilities in the networks, there are also several challenges in deploying the caching nodes. First of all, the size of a cache is constrained and caching contents incurs a cost as well. So, it is not viable to store each and every content that can possibly be requested by the user in the cache. This calls for efficient strategies to determine the contents that should be stored in the cache.

In this work, we aim at minimizing the discounted total cost incurred in delivering contents to end users, which consists of content missing and caching costs. We consider a fixed set of contents with varying popularity and a single cache, and design policies that decide which contents should be cached so as to minimize the discounted total cost while simultaneously satisfying caching capacity constraint of the base station.

The problem at hand is framed as a Markov decision process (MDP) [2], resembling a restless multiarmed bandit (RMAB) scenario [3]. Although value iteration [2,4] theoretically solves RMAB, it is plagued by the curse of dimensionality and provides limited solution insights. Therefore, it is advantageous to explore less intricate approaches and assess their efficacy. An esteemed strategy for RMAB problems is the Whittle index policy [3]. This Whittle index policy has been widely employed in the literature and has proven highly effective in practical applications [5–7]. Whittle [3] demonstrated the optimality of index-based policies for the Lagrangian relaxation of the restless bandit problem, introducing the concept of the Whittle index as a useful heuristic for restless bandit problems. Hence, we suggest employing this policy to address the task of optimizing caching efficiently.

1.1   Related Work

Content Caching There are two types of caching policies, proactive or reactive. Under a reactive policy, a content can be cached upon the user's request. When a user requests a specific content, the system first checks if the content is available in the local cache. If the content is found in the cache, it is delivered to the user directly from the cache. However, if the content is not present in the cache, the system initiates a process to fetch the content progressively from the server. Li et al. [8] proposed a reactive caching algorithm PopCaching that uses popularity evolution of the contents in determining which contents to cache.

In proactive caching, popularity prediction algorithms are used to predict user demand and to decide which contents are cached and which are evicted. Sadeghi et al. [9] proposed an intelligent proactive caching scheme to cache fixed collection of contents in an online social network to reduce the energy expenditure in downloading the contents. Gao et al. [10] proposed a dynamic probabilistic caching for a scenario where contents popularity vary with time. Abani et al. [11] designed a proactive caching policy that relies on predictability of the mobility patterns of mobiles to predict a mobile device's next location and to decide which caching nodes should cache which contents. Traverso et al. [12] introduced a novel traffic model known as the Shot Noise Model (SNM). This parsimonious model effectively captures the dynamics of content popularity while also accounting for the observed temporal locality present in actual traffic patterns. ElAzzouni et al. [13] studied the impact of predictive caching on content delivery latency in wireless networks. They establish a predictive multicast and caching concept in which base stations (BSs) in wireless cells proactively multicast popular content for caching and local access by end users.

Restless Multi-armed Bandit Problems In a restless multi-armed bandit (RMAB) problem, a decision maker must select a subset of M arms from K total arms to activate at any given time. The controller has knowledge of the states and costs associated with each arm and aims to minimize the discounted or time-average cost. The state of an arm evolves stochastically based on transition probabilities that depend on whether the bandit is active. Solving an RMAB problem through dynamic programming is computationally challenging, even for moderately sized problems. Whittle [3] proposed a heuristic solution known as the Whittle index policy, which addresses a relaxed version of the RMAB problem where M arms are only activated on average. This policy calculates the Whittle indices for each arm and activates the M arms with the highest indices at each decision epoch. However, determining the Whittle indices for an arm requires satisfying a certain indexability condition, which can be generally difficult to verify.

Xiong et al. [14] have formulated a content caching problem as a RMAB problem with the objective being minimizing the average content serving latency. They established the indexability of the problem and used the Whittle index policy to minimize the average latency.

There are very few works on RMABs with switching costs, e.g., costs associated with switching active arms. Ny et al. [15] considered a RMAB problem with switching costs, but they allow only one bandit to be active at any time. Incorporating switching costs in RMAB problems makes the states of the bandits multidimensional. This renders calculation of the Whittle indices much more complex. The literature on multidimensional RMAB is scarce. The main difficulty lies in establishing indexability, i.e., in ordering the states in a multidimensional space. Notable instances are [16–18] in which the authors have derived Whittle indices. But none of them have considered switching cost. We pose the content caching problem as a RMAB problem with switching costs (it is called as caching cost in the context of caching problem) and develop the simple Whittle index policy.

Organisation The rest of the paper is organised as follows. In Sect. 2, we present the system model for the proactive content caching problem and formulate the problem as a RMAB. In Sect. 3, we show that each single arm MDP has a threshold policy as the optimal policy and is indexable. In Sect. 4, we manoeuvre a few cost parameters to render the modified MDP indexable in a few special cases in which the original MDP is nonindexable. In Sect. 6, we show efficacy of the Whittle index policy via numerical evaluation. Finally, we outline future directions in Sect. 7.

2   System Model and Caching Problem

In this section, we first present the system model and then pose the optimal caching problem as a discounted cost Markov decision problem.

2.1   System Model

We consider a wireless network where the users are connected to a single base station (BS) which in turn is connected to content servers via the core network. The content providers have a set of K contents, $\mathcal{C} = \{1, 2, \ldots, K\}$ which are of equal size, at the servers. The BS has a *cache* where it can store up to M contents. We assume a slotted system. Caching decisions are taken at the slot boundaries. We use $a(t) = (a_i(t), i \in \mathcal{C})$ to denote the caching status of various contents at the beginning of slot t; $a_i(t) = 1$ if Content i is cached and $a_i(t) = 0$ otherwise. We let $\mathcal{A}$ denote the set of feasible status vectors;

$$\mathcal{A} = \left\{ a \in \{0, 1\}^K : \sum_{i \in \mathcal{C}} a_i \leq M \right\}.$$

Content Popularity We assume that the contents' popularity is reflected in the numbers of requests in a slot and varies over time. For any content, its popularity evolution may depend on whether it is stored in the BS' cache or not. We assume that for any content, say for Content i, given its caching status a_i, the numbers of requests in successive slots evolve as a discrete time Markov chain as shown in Fig. 1.[1]

In Fig. 1, numbers of requests $\phi_r^i \in \mathbb{Z}_+$ for $r = 1, 2, \ldots$ and it is an increasing sequence. We do not show self loops for clarity. We also make the following assumption.

Assumption 1. For all $i \in \mathcal{C}$, $p_i^{(1)} \geq p_i^{(0)}$ and $q_i^{(1)} \leq q_i^{(0)}$.

Assumption 1 suggests that, statistically, a content's popularity grows more if it is cached. We need this assumption to establish that optimal caching policy is a *threshold policy*.

---

[1] There are several instances of content popularity being modelled as Markov chains, e.g., see [9, 19, 20].

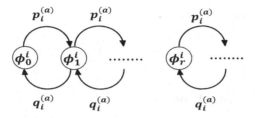

Fig. 1. Popularity evolution of a content. Given its caching status $a \in \{0,1\}$, the average number of requests per slot vary in accordance with these transition probabilities. For clarity, self-loops are not shown.

Costs We consider the following costs.

Content missing cost If a content, say Content i, is not cached at the beginning of a slot and is requested ϕ_r times in that slot, a cost $C_i(\phi_r)$ is incurred. For brevity we write this cost as $C_i(r)$ with a slight abuse of notation. Naturally, the functions $C_i : \mathbb{Z}_+ \to \mathbb{R}_+$ are non-decreasing. We also make the following assumption.

Assumption 2. For all $i \in \mathcal{C}$,

1. $C_i : \mathbb{Z}_+ \to \mathbb{R}_+$ are non-decreasing,
2. $C_i : \mathbb{Z}_+ \to \mathbb{R}_+$ are concave, i.e.,

$$C_i(r+1) - C_i(r) \leq C_i(r) - C_i(r-1) \ \forall r \geq 1. \tag{1}$$

Caching cost At the start of each slot, we have the ability to adjust the caching status of the contents based on their requests in the previous slot. Specifically, we can *proactively* cache contents that are currently not cached, while removing other contents to ensure compliance with the cache capacity restrictions. Let's use d to represent the cost associated with fetching content from its server and caching it.

We can express the total expected cost in a slot as a function of the cache status in this and the previous slots, say a and $\bar{a}$, respectively, and the request vector in the previous slot, say $\bar{r}$. Let $c(\bar{a}, \bar{r}, a)$ denote this cost. Clearly, $c(\bar{a}, \bar{r}, a) = \sum_{i \in \mathcal{C}} c_i(\bar{a}_i, \bar{r}_i, a_i)$ where

$$c_i(\bar{a}_i, \bar{r}_i, a_i) = da_i(1 - \bar{a}_i) + (1 - a_i)\left(p^{a_i} C_i(\bar{r}_i + 1) + \right.$$

$$\left. q^{a_i} C_i((\bar{r}_i - 1)^+) + (1 - p^{a_i} - q^{a_i})C_i(\bar{r}_i) \right). \tag{2}$$

We define operators $T^u, u \in \{0,1\}$ for parsimonious presentation. For any function $g : \mathbb{Z}_+ \to \mathbb{R}_+$, for all $r \in \mathbb{Z}_+$,

$$T^u g(r) = p^u g(r+1) + q^u g((r-1)^+) + (1 - p^u - q^u)g(r).$$

We can rewrite (2) in terms of T^us;

$$c_i(\bar{a}_i, \bar{r}_i, a_i) = da_i(1 - \bar{a}_i) + (1 - a_i)\left(T^{a_i}C_i(\bar{r}_i)\right).$$ (3)

2.2 Optimal Caching Problem

Our goal is to determine caching decisions that minimize the long-term expected discount cost. To be more precise, when provided with the initial request vector r and cache state a, we aim to solve the following problem:

$$\text{Minimize } \mathbb{E}\left[\sum_{t=1}^{\infty} \beta^t c(a(t-1), r(t-1), a(t))\Big|_{r(0)=r}^{a(0)=a,}\right]$$ (4)

$$\text{subject to } a(t) \in \mathcal{A} \ \forall \ t \geq 1.$$

The performance measure (4) is meaningful when the future costs are less important.[2]

Markov Decision Problem We formulate the optimal caching problem as a discounted cost Markov decision problem. The slot boundaries are the decision epochs. The state of the system at decision epoch t is given by the tuple $x(t) :=$ $(a(t-1), r(t-1))$. We consider $a(t)$ to be the action at decision epoch t. Clearly, the state space is $\mathcal{A} \times \mathbb{Z}_+^K$, and the action space is $\mathcal{A}$. From the description of the system in Sect. 2.1, given state $x(t) = (\bar{a}, \bar{r})$ and action $a(t) = a$, the state at decision epoch $t+1$ is $x(t+1) = (a, r)$ where

$$r_i = \begin{cases} \bar{r}_i + 1 & \text{w.p. } p^{\bar{a}_i}, \\ \bar{r}_i - 1 & \text{w.p. } q^{\bar{a}_i}, \\ \bar{r}_i & \text{w.p. } 1 - p^{\bar{a}_i} - q^{\bar{a}_i}. \end{cases}$$ (5)

For a state action pair $((\bar{a}, \bar{r}), a)$, the expected single state cost is given by $c((\bar{a}, \bar{r}), a)$ defined in the previous section (see (3)). A policy π is a sequence of mappings $\{u_t^{\pi}, t = 1, 2, \cdots\}$ where $u_t^{\pi} : \mathcal{A} \times \mathbb{Z}_+^K \to \mathcal{A}$. The cost of a policy π for an initial state (r, a) is

$$V^{\pi}(a, r) := \mathbb{E}\left[\sum_{t=1}^{\infty} \beta^t c(x(t), u_t^{\pi}(x(t)))\Big| x(0) = (a, r)\right]$$

Let Π be the set of all policies. Then the optimal caching problem is $\min_{\pi \in \Pi} V^{\pi}(a, r)$.

---

[2] One can as well consider minimizing expected value of $\sum_{t=1}^{\infty}\sum_{i \in \mathcal{C}} \beta_i^t c_i(a_i(t-1), r_i(t-1), a_i(t))$. This would model the scenario where the contents have geometrically distributed lifetimes with parameters β_is. Our RMAB-based solution continues to apply in this case.

Definition 1. (*Stationary Policies*) A policy $\pi = \{u_t^\pi, t = 1, 2, \cdots\}$ is called stationary if u_t^π are identical, say u, for all t. For brevity, we refer to such a policy as the stationary policy u. Following [4, Vol 2, Chap. 1], the content caching problem assumes an optimal stationary policy.

Restless multi-armed bandit formulation The Markov decision problem described above presents a challenge due to its high dimensionality. However, we can make the following observations:

1. The evolution of the popularities of the contents is independent when considering their caching statuses. Their popularity changes are connected solely through the caching actions, specifically the capacity constraint of the cache.
2. The total cost can be divided into individual costs associated with each content.

We thus see that the optimal caching problem is an instance of the *restless multi-armed bandit problem* (RMAB) with each arm representing content. We show in Sect. 3 that this problem is *indexable*. This allows us to develop a Whittle index policy for the joint caching problem.

By recognizing the similarities between the optimal caching problem and the *restless multi-armed bandit problem* (RMAB), where each arm corresponds to a content, we can conclude that the optimal caching problem can be framed as an RMAB instance. In Sect. 3, we establish that this problem is *indexable*, enabling us to devise a Whittle index policy to tackle the joint caching problem efficiently.

Remark 1. In practice the popularity evolution could be unknown. The authors in [14, 21–23] have proposed reinforcement learning (RL) based approaches to learn Whittle indices in case of Markov chains with unknown dynamics. But these works consider only one-dimensional Markov chains. Thanks to the switching costs, we have a two-dimensional Markov chain at our disposal which renders convergence of the RL algorithms and calculation of the Whittle indices much harder. This constitutes our future work.

3   Whittle Index Policy

We outline our approach here. We first solve certain caching problems associated with each of the contents. We argue that these problems are indexable. Under indexability, the solution to the caching problem corresponding to a content yields Whittle indices for all the states of this content. The Whittle index measures how rewarding it is to cache that content at that particular state. The Whittle index policy chooses those M arms whose current states have the largest Whittle indices and, among these caches, those with positive Whittle indices.

3.1   Single Content Caching Problem

We consider a Markov decision problem associated with Content i. Its state space is $\{0, 1\} \times \mathbb{Z}_+$ and its action space is $\{0, 1\}$. Given $x_i(t) = (\bar{a}_i, \bar{r}_i)$ and action

$a_i(t) = a_i$, the state evolves as described in Sect. 2 (see (5)). The expected single-stage cost is

$$c_{i,\lambda}(\bar{a}_i, \bar{r}_i, a_i) = \lambda a_i + da_i(1 - \bar{a}_i) + (1 - a_i)T^{a_i}C_i(r_i). \tag{6}$$

Observe that a constant penalty λ is incurred in each slot in which Content i is stored in the cache. Here a policy π is a sequence $\{u_t^\pi, t = 1, 2, \cdots\}$ where $u_t^\pi : \{0,1\} \times \mathbb{Z}_+ \to \{0,1\}$. Given initial state (a_i, r_i) the problem minimizes

$$V_{i,\lambda}^\pi(a_i, r_i) := \mathbb{E}\left[\sum_{t=1}^\infty \beta^t c_{i,\lambda}(x_i(t), u_t^\pi(x_i(t))) \Big| x_i(0) = (a_i, r_i)\right]$$

over all the policies to yield the optimal cost function $V_\lambda(a_i, r_i) := \min_\pi V_{i,\lambda}^\pi(a_i, r_i)$. We analyze this problem below. However, we omit the index i for brevity. The single content caching problem also assumes an optimal stationary policy. Moreover, following [4, Vol 2, Chap. 1], the optimal cost function $V_\lambda(\cdot, \cdot)$ satisfies the following Bellman's equation.

$$V_\lambda(a, r) = \min_{a' \in \{0,1\}} Q_\lambda(a, r, a'), \tag{7}$$

where

$$Q_\lambda(a, r, a') := c_\lambda(a, r, a') + \beta T^{a'} V_\lambda(a', r). \tag{8}$$

Here $T^{a'} V_\lambda(a', r)$ is defined by applying operator $T^{a'}$ to the function $V_\lambda(a', \cdot) : \mathbb{Z}_+ \to \mathbb{R}_+$. The set $\mathcal{P}(\lambda)$ of the states in which action 0 is optimal, referred to as the *passive set*, is given by

$$\mathcal{P}(\lambda) = \{(a, r) : Q_\lambda(a, r, 0) \le Q_\lambda(a, r, 1)\}.$$

The complement of $\mathcal{P}(\lambda)$ is referred to as the *active set*. Obviously, the penalty λ influences the partition of the passive and active sets.

Definition 2. (*Indexability*) An arm is called indexable if the passive set $\mathcal{P}(\lambda)$ of the corresponding content caching problem monotonically increases from $\emptyset$ to the whole state space $\{0,1\} \times \mathbb{Z}_+$ as the penalty λ increases from $-\infty$ to ∞. An RMAB is called indexable if it's every arm is indexable [3].

The minimum penalty needed to move a state from the active set to the passive set measures how attractive this state is. This motivates the following definition of the Whittle index.

Definition 3. (*Whittle index*) If an arm is indexable, its Whittle index $w(a, r)$ associated with state (a, r) is the minimum penalty that moves this state from the active set to the passive set. Equivalently,

$$w(a, r) = \min\{\lambda : (a, r) \in \mathcal{P}(\lambda)\}. \tag{9}$$

Before we establish the indexability of the arm (content) under consideration, we define threshold policies and show that the optimal policy for the single content caching problem is a threshold policy.

Definition 4. (*Threshold Policies*) A stationary policy u is called a threshold policy if it is of the form

$$u(a,r) = \begin{cases} 0 \text{ if } r \leq r^a, \\ 1 \text{ otherwise,} \end{cases}$$

for some $r^a \in \mathbb{Z}_+, a = 0, 1$. In the following, we refer to such a policy as the threshold policy (r^0, r^1).

3.2   Optimality of a Threshold Policy

Observe that the optimal cost function $V_\lambda(\cdot, \cdot)$ is obtained as the limit of the following *value iteration* [4, Vol 2, Chap. 1]. For all $(a, r) \in \{0,1\} \times \mathbb{Z}_+, V_\lambda^0(a,r) = 0$, and for $n \geq 1$,

$$V_\lambda^n(a,r) = \min_{a' \in \{0,1\}} Q_\lambda^n(a,r,a'), \tag{10}$$

where

$$Q_\lambda^n(a,r,a') := c_\lambda(a,r,a') + \beta T^{a'} V_\lambda^{n-1}(a',r). \tag{11}$$

We start by arguing that $V_\lambda^n(a,r)$ is concave and increasing in r for all a and $n \geq 0$. But it requires the following assumption.

Assumption 3.

$$p^0 \Big(C(3) - C(2) \Big) - (2p^0 + q^0 - 1) \Big(C(2) - C(1) \Big) + (p^0 + 2q^0 - 1) \Big(C(1) - C(0) \Big) \leq 0.$$

Lemma 1. $V_\lambda^n(a,r)$ *is concave and non-decreasing in* r *for all* a *and* $n \geq 0$.

Proof. Please refer to our extended version [24]   ☐

Remark 2. We require Assumption 3 merely to prove that $V_\lambda^1(a,r)$ is concave. It follows via induction that $V_\lambda^n(a,r), n \geq 2$ are also concave.

Lemma 2. *For all* $n \geq 1$,

1. $Q_\lambda^n(a,r,0) - Q_\lambda^n(a,r,1)$ *are non-decreasing in* r *for* $a = 0, 1$.
2. $V_\lambda^n(0,r) - V_\lambda^n(1,r)$ *are non-decreasing in* r.

Proof. Please refer to our extended version [24]   ☐

The following theorem uses Lemma 1 and 2 to establish that there exist optimal threshold policies for the single content caching problems.

Theorem 1. *For each* $\lambda \in \mathbb{R}$ *there exist* $r^0(\lambda), r^1(\lambda) \in \mathbb{Z}_+$ *such that the threshold policy* $(r^0(\lambda), r^1(\lambda))$ *is an optimal policy for the single content caching problem with penalty* λ. *Also,* $r^0(\lambda) \geq r^1(\lambda)$.

Proof. Please refer to our extended version [24].   ☐

3.3 Indexability of the RMAB

We now exploit the existence of an optimal threshold policy to argue that the RMAB formulation of the content caching problem is indexable.

Lemma 3. *For all $n \geq 1$,*

1. $Q_\lambda^n(a,r,1) - Q_\lambda^n(a,r,0)$ *are non-decreasing in λ for $a = 0,1$.*
2. $V_\lambda^n(1,r) - V_\lambda^n(0,r)$ *are non-decreasing in λ.*
3. $V_\lambda^n(a,r+1) - V_\lambda^n(a,r)$ *are non-decreasing in λ for $a = 0,1$.*

Proof. Please refer to our extended version [24].   □

Theorem 2. *Under Assumptions 1, 2 and 3 the content caching problem is indexable.*

Proof. Please refer to our extended version [24].   □

Remark 3. A more common approach to show indexibility of a RMAB have been arguing that the value function is convex, e.g., see [7,25]. But it can be easily verified that the value functions in our problem will not be convex even if the content missing costs are assumed to be convex.

Remark 4. Theorems 1 and 2 require Assumption 3. Many works in literature have relied on such conditions on transition probabilities for indexibility of RMABs (see [26,27]).

3.4 Whittle Index Policy for the RMAB

We now describe the Whittle index policy for the joint content caching problem. As stated earlier, it chooses those M arms whose current states have the largest Whittle indices and among these caches the ones with positive Whittle indices. It is a stationary policy. Let $u^W : \mathcal{A} \times \mathbb{Z}_+^K \to \mathcal{A}$ denote this policy. Then

$$u_i^W(a,r) = \begin{cases} 1 \text{ if } w(a_i,r_i) \text{ is among the highest } M \text{ values} \\ \quad \text{in } \{w(a_i,r_i), i \in \mathcal{C}\} \text{ and } w(a_i,r_i) > 0, \\ 0 \text{ otherwise.} \end{cases}$$

Holding cost There can also be a holding cost for keeping a content in the cache. Let h denote this fixed holding cost per content per slot. The content caching problem remains unchanged except that single stage cost associated with Content i becomes

$$c_i(\bar{a}_i, \bar{r}_i, a_i) = ha_i + da_i(1 - \bar{a}_i) + (1 - a_i)T^{a_i}C_i(r_i).$$

Comparing it with (6), we see that the penalty λ can be interpreted as the fixed holding cost. Obviously, in the presence of the holding cost, the content caching problem can be solved following the same approach as above.

Table 1. Choices of $\hat{C}(0)$ and $\hat{C}(1)$ that render the problem indexable; empty cells indicate absence of suitable choices.

Case	Costs
$p^0 + 2q^0 \leq 1$	$\hat{C}(1) = C(1),\ \hat{C}(0) = \min\left\{C(0), C(1) - \frac{F}{p^0+2q^0-1}\right\}$
$p^0 + 2q^0 > 1, 2p^0 + q^0 < 1$	
$p^0 + 2q^0 > 1, 2p^0 + q^0 \geq 1, q^0 \leq p^0$	$\hat{C}(1) = C(2) - \frac{p^0(C(3)-C(2))}{p^0-q^0},\ \hat{C}(0) = 2\hat{C}(1) - C(2)$
$p^0 + 2q^0 > 1, 2p^0 + q^0 \geq 1, q^0 > p^0$	

where $F = p^0\Big((C(2) - C(1)) - (C(3) - C(2))\Big) - (1 - p^0 - q^0)\Big(C(2) - C(1)\Big).$

4   Noncompliance with Assumption 3

We have so far assumed that the costs and the transition probabilities satisfy Assumption 3 to ensure indexability of the content caching problem. We now explore a novel approach of manoeuvring the content missing costs so that the modified content caching problem is "close" to original problem and is indexable. We obtain the Whittle index policy for the modified problem and use it for the original problem.

More specifically, let us consider a particular content for which Assumption 3 is not met. We investigate the possibility of tinkering only $C(0)$ and $C(1)$ to achieve indexability.[3] In other words, we consider content missing costs $\hat{C} : \mathbb{Z}_+ \to \mathbb{R}_+$ with $\hat{C}(r) = C(r), r \geq 2$ and other costs and popularity evolution also unchanged. We demonstrate that in certain special cases adequate choices of $\hat{C}(0)$ and $\hat{C}(1)$ render the modified problem indexable. Our findings are summarized in Lemma 4 and Table 1.

Lemma 4. *If (a) $p^0 + 2q^0 \leq 1$ or (b) $p^0 + 2q^0 > 1, 2p^0 + q^0 > 1, q^0 \leq p^0$ then, with $\hat{C}(0)$ and $\hat{C}(1)$ as in Table 1,*

1. *$\hat{C} : \mathbb{Z}_+ \to \mathbb{R}_+$ is non-decreasing,*
2. *$\hat{C} : \mathbb{Z}_+ \to \mathbb{R}_+$ is concave,*
3. *the modified costs satisfy Assumption 3.*

In other cases, there do not exist $\hat{C}(0)$ and $\hat{C}(1)$ such that $\hat{C} : \mathbb{Z}_+ \to \mathbb{R}_+$ satisfies all these three properties.

Proof. Please refer to our extended version [24].   □

Typically the number of requests remains much higher than 0 or 1, and so the optimal caching policy and the cost for the amended problem are close to those for the original problem. Consequently, the Whittle index policy for the modified problem also performs well for the original problem. We demonstrate it in Sect. 6 though theoretical performance bounds have eluded us so far.

---

[3] As in Sect. 3.1, we omit the content index.

5   Popularity Evolution Oblivious to the Caching Action

If the popularity evolution is independent of the caching action, $p^0 = p^1$ and $q^0 = q^1$. In this case one can easily show via induction that $V_\lambda(1,r) - V_\lambda(0,r)$ is non-decreasing in λ, and consequently, the associated restless bandit problem is indexable. The proofs of these assertions follow from similar steps as in the proofs of the second part of Lemma 3 and of Theorem 2, respectively.

Remark 5. When popularity evolution does not depend on the caching action the above indexability assertion does not rely on the the special transition structure of Fig. 1. In other words, the restless bandit problems corresponding to the caching problems with arbitrary Markovian popularity evolutions are indexable as long as the evolutions do not depend on the caching action.

Below we generalize the above assertion by deriving a condition on the difference of popularity evolution with and without caching for indexability. Towards this, we define $\delta := 2\max\{|p^0 - p^1|, |q^0 - q^1|\}$. We prove the following indexability result.

Theorem 3. *If $\beta \leq \max\{\frac{1}{1+\delta}, \frac{1}{2}\}$, the content caching problem is indexable.*

Proof. We argue that

1. $Q_\lambda^1(a,r,1) - Q_\lambda^1(a,r,0)$ is nondecreasing in λ,
2. If $Q_\lambda^n(a,r,1) - Q_\lambda^n(a,r,0)$ for $a = 0,1$ are nondecreasing in λ, so is $V_\lambda^n(1,r) - V_\lambda^n(0,r)$,
3. If $V_\lambda^n(1,r) - V_\lambda^n(0,r)$ is nondecreasing in λ and $\beta \leq \max\{\frac{1}{1+\delta}, \frac{1}{2}\}$, then $Q_\lambda^{n+1}(a,r,1) - Q_\lambda^{n+1}(a,r,0)$ is also nondecreasing in λ.

Hence, via induction, $Q_\lambda(a,r,1) - Q_\lambda(a,r,0)$ is nondecreasing in λ which implies that the problem is indexable. Please see [24] for the details.   □

Observe that, for $\beta \leq 1/2$, the problem is indexable for arbitrary p^0, p^1, q^0 and q^1. For $\beta \in (1/2, 1)$, the problem is indexable if $\delta \leq \frac{1-\beta}{\beta}$. Assumptions 1, 2 or 3 are not needed in these cases.

Remark 6. Meshram et al. [27] have considered a restless single-armed hidden Markov bandit with two states and have shown that under certain conditions on transition probablities, the arm is indexable for $\beta \in (0, 1/3)$. More recently, Akbarzadeh and Mahajan [28] have provided sufficient conditions for indexability of general restless multiarmed bandit problems. One can directly infer from [28, Theorem 1 and Proposition 2] that the caching problem is indexable for $\beta \leq 1/2$. On the other hand, Theorem 3 implies that the caching problem can be indexable even for $\beta \in (1/2, 1)$. In Sect. 6, we numerically show that the caching problem can be indexable even when $\beta > 1/(1 + \delta)$.

6   Numerical Results

In this section, we numerically evaluate the Whittle index policy for a range of system parameters. We demonstrate a variation of Whittle indices with various parameters. We also compare the performance of the Whittle index policy with those of the optimal and greedy policies. We compute Whittle indices using an algorithm proposed in [29]. We assume $C_i(r) = 3\sqrt{r}$ for all $i \in \mathcal{C}$. We use $p^{a_i}, q^{a_i}, a \in \{0, 1\}$, for all $i \in \mathcal{C}$ which satisfy Assumptions 1 and 3.

Whittle indices for different caching costs We consider $K = 40$ contents and a cache size $M = 16$. We assume transition probabilities $p^0 = 0.06082, q^0 = 0.38181, p^1 = 0.63253, q^1 = 0.26173$ for all the contents and discount factor $\beta = 0.95$. We plot the Whittle indices for two different values of the caching costs $d = 10$ and $d = 400$ in Figs. 2(a) and 2(b), respectively. As expected, $w(0, r)$ and $w(1, r)$ are increasing in r. We also observe that, for a fixed r, $w(1, r)$ does not vary much as the caching cost is changed but $w(0, r)$ decreases with the caching cost. This is expected as increasing caching costs makes the passive action (not caching) more attractive.

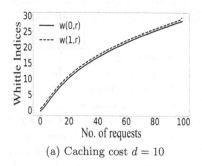
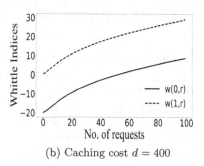

(a) Caching cost $d = 10$ (b) Caching cost $d = 400$

Fig. 2. Whittle indices for different caching costs

Whittle indices for different discount factors We plot the Whittle indices for two different values of discount factors $\beta = 0.3$ and $\beta = 0.9$ in Figs. 3(a) and 3(b), respectively. Other parameters are the same as those for Fig. 2 except caching cost $d = 10$. Here also, we observe that, for a fixed r, $w(1, r)$ does not vary much as the β is changed, but $w(0, r)$ increases with β.

Whittle indices for different transition probabilities We plot the Whittle indices for two different sets of transition probabilities

1. $p^1 > q^1$ and $p^0 > q^0$ e.g., $p^0 = 0.0093, q^0 = 0.0061, p^1 = 0.3274, q^1 = 0.0030$
2. $p^1 < q^1$ and $p^0 < q^0$ e.g., $p^0 = 0.0007, q^0 = 0.9362, p^1 = 0.0021, q^1 = 0.8902$

Assuming caching cost $d = 10$ and $\beta = 0.95$, we note that in the first scenario, whether the content is cached or not (active or passive action), the number of requests is likely to increase. Similarly, in the second scenario, the number of

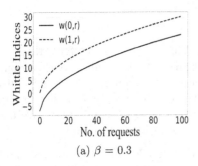

(a) $\beta = 0.3$

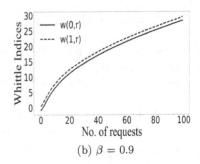

(b) $\beta = 0.9$

Fig. 3. Whittle indices for different discount factors

requests is likely to decrease regardless of caching status. Figure 4 illustrates the Whittle indices for both cases. It is evident that the Whittle indices are higher in the first case compared to the second case. This outcome is expected since when the number of requests is more likely to increase, caching is anticipated. The Whittle index policy selects the M contents with the highest current state Whittle indices and caches those with positive indices. Thus, as the likelihood of request increases for content to be cached, the corresponding Whittle indices are expected to rise.

Performance of the Whittle index policy for a problem conforming to Assumptions 1 and 3 In our comparison, we evaluate the performance of the Whittle Index Policy against the optimal policy obtained through value iteration and the greedy policy. The greedy policy selects the action that minimizes the total cost outlined in Sect. 2, considering all possible actions while satisfying the constraints at each moment. However, the optimal policy is only feasible for small values of K, M. Therefore, we set $K = 3$ and $M = 1$ for our analysis. The parameters $\beta = 0.95$, caching cost $d = 10$, and the probabilities $p^{a_i}, q^{a_i}, a \in \{0, 1\}$, for all $i \in \mathcal{C}$, are chosen to satisfy Assumptions 1 and 3. Our findings indicate that the Whittle index policy outperforms the greedy policy and approaches the performance of the optimal policy, as depicted in Fig. 5.

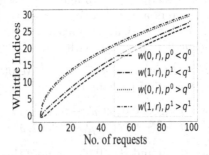

Fig. 4. Whittle indices for different transition probabilities

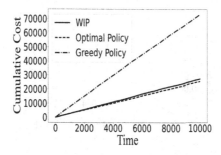

Fig. 5. Performance of Whittle Index Policy for a problem conforming to Assumptions 1 and 3

Performance of the Whittle index policy for a problem not conforming to Assumption 3 We manipulate the content missing costs of such a problem as suggested in Sect. 4 to make it indexable. In other words, we choose $\hat{C}(1)$ and $\hat{C}(0)$ as in the Table 1. We obtain the Whittle indices of the modified problem and use them for the original problem. Then we compare the performances of the Whittle index policy, the optimal policy and the greedy policy for the original problem. We see that the Whittle index policy still performs better compared to the greedy policy and is close to the optimal policy and is shown in Fig. 6

Indexability of the caching problem when $\delta > \frac{1-\beta}{\beta}$ The caching problem 4 is seen to be indexable when $\delta \leq \frac{1-\beta}{\beta}$. Here we numerically check indexability when $\delta > \frac{1-\beta}{\beta}$. We use $p^0 = 0.1855, p^1 = 0.2137, q^0 = 0.7719, q^1 = 0.6280$ and $\beta = 0.95$, resulting in $\delta = 0.2878$ and $\frac{1-\beta}{\beta} = 0.0526$. We run value iteration for different values of λ to find $Q_\lambda(a, r, a')$ $\forall a', a, r$ and plot $Q_\lambda(a, r, 1) - Q_\lambda(a, r, 0)$ vs λ. For indexability $Q_\lambda(a, r, 1) - Q_\lambda(a, r, 0)$ should be non-decreasing in λ as argued in the proof of Theorem 2. From Fig. 7, we can see that $Q_\lambda(a, r, 1) - Q_\lambda(a, r, 0)$ is indeed non-decreasing in λ. Hence the caching problem is indexable even when $\delta > \frac{1-\beta}{\beta}$.

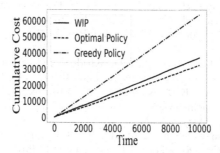

Fig. 6. Performance of Whittle Index Policy for a problem not conforming to Assumption 3

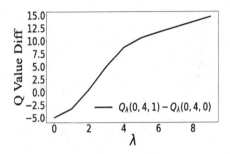

Fig. 7. Indexability of caching problem when $\delta > \frac{1-\beta}{\beta}$.

7 Conclusion

We considered optimal caching of contents with varying popularity. We posed the problem as a discounted cost Markov decision problem and showed that it is a an instance of RMAB. We provided a condition under which its arms is indexable and also demonstarted the performance of the Whittle index policy.

Our future work entails deriving performance bounds of the Whittle index policy. We plan to consider more general popularity dynamics. We also aspire to augment RMAB model with reinforcement learning to deal with the scenarios where the popularity dynamics might be unknown.

References

1. https://www.cisco.com/c/en/us/solutions/collateral/executive-perspectives/annual-internet-report/white-paper-c11-741490.pdf
2. Puterman, M.L.: Markov Decision Processes: Discrete Stochastic Dynamic Programming. Wiley (1994)
3. Whittle, P.: Restless bandits: activity allocation in a changing world. J. Appl. Prob. **25**(A), 287–298 (1988)
4. Bertsekas, D.: Dynamic Programming and Optimal Control, I and II, Athena Scientific, Belmont, Massachusetts. New York-San Francisco-London (1995)
5. Glazebrook, K., Mitchell, H.: An index policy for a stochastic scheduling model with improving/deteriorating jobs. Naval Res. Logistics (NRL) **49**(7), 706–721 (2002)
6. Glazebrook, K.D., Ruiz-Hernandez, D., Kirkbride, C.: Some indexable families of restless bandit problems. Adv. Appl. Probab. **38**(3), 643–672 (2006)
7. Ansell, P., Glazebrook, K.D., Nino-Mora, J., O'Keeffe, M.: Whittle's index policy for a multi-class queueing system with convex holding costs. Math. Methods Oper. Res. **57**(1), 21–39 (2003)
8. Li, S., Xu, J., Van Der Schaar, M., Li, W.: Popularity-driven content caching. In: IEEE INFOCOM 2016-The 35th Annual IEEE International Conference on Computer Communications. IEEE, pp. 1–9 (2016)
9. Sadeghi, A., Sheikholeslami, F., Giannakis, G.B.: Optimal and scalable caching for 5G using reinforcement learning of space-time popularities. IEEE J. Selected Topics Signal Process. **12**(1), 180–190 (2017)

10. Gao, J., Zhang, S., Zhao, L., Shen, X.: The design of dynamic probabilistic caching with time-varying content popularity. IEEE Trans. Mob. Comput. **20**(4), 1672–1684 (2020)
11. Abani, N., Braun, T., Gerla, M.: Proactive caching with mobility prediction under uncertainty in information-centric networks. In: Proceedings of the 4th ACM Conference on Information-Centric Networking, pp. 88–97 (2017)
12. Traverso, S., Ahmed, M., Garetto, M., Giaccone, P., Leonardi, E., Niccolini, S.: Temporal locality in today's content caching: why it matters and how to model it. ACM SIGCOMM Comput. Commun. Rev. **43**(5), 5–12 (2013)
13. ElAzzouni, S., Wu, F., Shroff, N.,Ekici, E.: Predictive caching at the wireless edge using near-zero caches. In: Proceedings of the Twenty-First International Symposium on Theory, Algorithmic Foundations, and Protocol Design for Mobile Networks and Mobile Computing, pp. 121–130 (2020)
14. Xiong, G., Wang, S., Li, J., Singh, R.: Model-free reinforcement learning for content caching at the wireless edge via restless bandits (2022). arXiv preprint arXiv:2202.13187
15. Le Ny, J., Feron, E.: Restless bandits with switching costs: linear programming relaxations, performance bounds and limited lookahead policies. In: 2006 American Control Conference, p. 6 (2006)
16. Aalto, S., Lassila, P., Osti, P.: Whittle index approach to size-aware scheduling with time-varying channels. In: Proceedings of the 2015 ACM SIGMETRICS International Conference on Measurement and Modeling of Computer Systems, pp. 57–69 (2015)
17. Anand, A., de Veciana, G.: A whittle's index based approach for QoE optimization in wireless networks. In: Proceedings of the ACM on Measurement and Analysis of Computing Systems **2**(1), 1–39 (2018)
18. Duran, S., Ayesta, U., Verloop, I.M.: On the whittle index of markov modulated restless bandits. Queueing Syst. (2022)
19. Sadeghi, A., Wang, G., Giannakis, G.B.: Deep reinforcement learning for adaptive caching in hierarchical content delivery networks. IEEE Trans. Cognit. Commun. Netw. **5**(4), 1024–1033 (2019)
20. Wu, P., Li, J., Shi, L., Ding, M., Cai, K., Yang, F.: Dynamic content update for wireless edge caching via deep reinforcement learning. IEEE Commun. Lett. **23**(10), 1773–1777 (2019)
21. Avrachenkov, K.E., Borkar, V.S.: Whittle index based Q-learning for restless bandits with average reward. Automatica **139**, 110186 (2022)
22. Fu, J., Nazarathy, Y., Moka, S., Taylor, P.G.: Towards Q-learning the whittle index for restless bandits. In: Australian & New Zealand Control Conference (ANZCC). IEEE, vol. 2019, pp. 249–254 (2019)
23. Robledo, F., Borkar, V., Ayesta, U., Avrachenkov, K.: QWI: Q-learning with whittle index. ACM SIGMETRICS Performance Eval. Rev. **49**(2), 47–50 (2022)
24. Pavamana, K.J., Singh, C.: Caching contents with varying popularity using restless bandits (2023). https://arxiv.org/pdf/2304.12227.pdf
25. Larranaga, M., Ayesta, U., Verloop, I.M.: Index policies for a multi-class queue with convex holding cost and abandonments. In: The ACM International Conference on Measurement and Modeling of Computer Systems **2014**, 125–137 (2014)
26. Liu, K., Zhao, Q.: Indexability of restless bandit problems and optimality of whittle index for dynamic multichannel access. IEEE Trans. Inf. Theory **56**(11), 5547–5567 (2010)

27. Meshram, R., Manjunath, D., Gopalan, A.: On the whittle index for restless multiarmed hidden Markov bandits. IEEE Trans. Autom. Control **63**(9), 3046–3053 (2018)
28. Akbarzadeh, N., Mahajan, A.: Conditions for indexability of restless bandits and an $\mathcal{O}(k^3)$ algorithm to compute whittle index. Adv. Appl. Probab. **54**(4), 1164–1192 (2022)
29. Gast, N., Gaujal, B., Khun, K.: Testing indexability and computing whittle and gittins index in subcubic time. Math. Methods Oper. Res. **97**(3), 391–436 (2023). https://doi.org/10.1007/s00186-023-00821-4

Tools

dSalmon: High-Speed Anomaly Detection for Evolving Multivariate Data Streams

Alexander Hartl$^{(\boxtimes)}$ ⓘ, Félix Iglesias ⓘ, and Tanja Zseby ⓘ

TU Wien—Institute of Telecommunications, 1040 Wien, Austria
{alexander.hartl,felix.iglesias,tanja.zseby}@tuwien.ac.at

Abstract. We introduce dSalmon, a highly efficient framework for out-lier detection on streaming data. dSalmon can be used with both Python and C++, meeting the requirements of modern data science research. It provides an intuitive interface and has almost no package dependencies. dSalmon implements main stream outlier detection approaches from lit-erature. By using pure C++ in its core and making the most of available parallelism, data is analyzed with superior processing speed.
We describe design decisions and outline the software architecture of dSalmon. Additionally, we perform thorough evaluations on benchmark-ing datasets to measure execution time, memory requirements and energy consumption when performing outlier detection. Experiments show that dSalmon requires substantially less resources and in most cases is able to process datasets between one and three orders of magnitude faster than established Python implementations.

Keywords: Outlier detection · Data streams · Unsupervised learning · Python · C++

1 Introduction

In a world of ever-increasing transmission rates, performing knowledge discovery on data streams becomes more and more challenging. A particularly important and well-known data mining task is detecting anomalies and outliers. A variety of methods have been proposed for Outlier Detection (OD) on static datasets [8,17], but also for online OD on a live stream of arriving data samples [18].

While algorithm implementations with low processing speed might pose a problem for practical online processing of data streams, it is even more challeng-ing for researchers. Performing feature selection or fitting algorithm parameters using, e.g., grid search, randomized search or Bayesian optimization, involves

This work was supported by the project MALware cOmmunication in cRitical Infras-tructures (MALORI), funded by the Austrian security research program KIRAS of the Federal Ministry for Agriculture, Regions and Tourism (BMLRT) under grant no. 873511.

E. Kalyvianaki and M. Paolieri (Eds.): VALUETOOLS 2023, LNICST 539, pp. 153–169, 2024.
https://doi.org/10.1007/978-3-031-48885-6_10

a vast amount of algorithm runs on a captured data stream, which naturally should cover a period that is as long as possible. Additionally, researchers often have the requirement to test algorithms on multiple datasets. Hence, the computational ability to process a data stream in real time is far from sufficient for research and slow algorithm implementations become a burden for researchers or even prevent them from considering specific methods for a given task.

With this paper, we specifically target *evolving* data streams, i.e. streams whose properties and structures in feature space change over time. Models therefore have to be continuously updated or retrained to avoid declining detection performance due to outdated models. This characteristic of data streams is also frequently referred to as *concept drift*. When it comes to algorithm run times, we note a basic systematic difference for processing evolving streaming data compared to the processing of static datasets considering opportunities for batch processing in scripting languages. Due to the lack of an inherent ordering, for static datasets, blocks of data samples can be evaluated against one and the same model, in many cases yielding opportunities for batch processing and, hence, fast processing. The same cannot be said about evolving streaming data. Since algorithms continuously adapt to newly seen data, the model relevant for mining data sample n is potentially influenced by all data samples $0, \ldots, n-1$. Any attempt for faster processing by evaluating a block of data against the same model would therefore yield inaccurate results compared to production use, where data samples are processed one at a time at the time of their arrival.

We present our **D**ata **S**tream **A**nalysis Algorithms for the Impatient (dSalmon)[1], a framework for performing OD on multivariate evolving streams of data, which has been specifically designed to process data as efficiently as possible with respect to both execution time and memory footprint. dSalmon provides a simple and intuitive Python interface to allow rapid development by data scientists, but performs processing in C++, achieving substantial performance benefits compared to existing implementations. It is easily extendable by deploying software for automatically generating boilerplate code and has almost no package dependencies. We perform a thorough comparison of dSalmon to PySAD [35], the only Python framework for performing OD on streaming data to date. To provide a comprehensive evaluation, we measure run time, memory usage and energy consumption when applying stream OD algorithms on three different publicly available benchmarking datasets. Our findings show that dSalmon provides substantial benefits for all resources. Execution time improvements of up to three orders of magnitude can be obtained with dSalmon.

The remainder of this paper is structured as follows. After highlighting related software projects in Sect. 2, we provide a brief introduction into the foundations of modern stream OD approaches in Sect. 3, particularly considering challenges when processing high-rate data streams. In Sect. 4, we then discuss design objectives, our resulting architectural design and the interface of dSalmon. To demonstrate that substantial performance benefits can be obtained with our

---

[1] https://github.com/CN-TU/dSalmon.

deployed architecture, we proceed in Sect. 5 with a comprehensive experimental evaluation and comparison of resource consumption when using our framework. Section 6 concludes the paper.

2 Related Work

The most important software project related to dSalmon is the recent PySAD [35] framework, which similarly targets OD on streaming data in Python. PySAD provides several methods for OD on data streams and is entirely written in Python. Some of the outlier detectors PySAD provides wrap existing Python solutions, like, e.g., from the PyOD [36] framework or scikit-learn [24]. In this paper, we compare runtime performance with PySAD, since algorithms implemented in PySAD are similar to the ones we provide.

For OD tasks, PyOD [36] or scikit-learn [24] can also be used directly. PyOD is a popular Python package that provides several methods for OD. Unlike dSalmon, it targets methods for processing static datasets rather than streaming data. Several outlier detectors for static datasets are also provided by scikit-learn, the most popular Python framework for machine learning and data mining.

A well-known software project for processing streaming data is the MOA [7] framework implemented in Java. Algorithms provided by MOA are not limited to OD, but cover several fields of data mining like clustering and classification. Outlier detectors for streaming data implemented in MOA are, however, limited to a distance-based outlier definition and provide only binary labels instead of outlier scores. In dSalmon, we additionally implement several recent approaches for stream OD like ensemble-based methods. MOA is meant to be used as a stand-alone application rather than a programming library. Since implemented algorithms additionally differ severely from algorithms implemented in dSalmon, we do not include MOA in our experimental evaluations.

In the Java community, also the ELKI [27] framework is worth mentioning. ELKI provides a comprehensive selection of data mining algorithms. However, similar to PyOD and scikit-learn, it focuses on the processing of static datasets instead of streaming data processing.

3 Outlier Detection on Evolving Data Streams

Detection of outliers in evolving data streams is an important data mining problem. Several techniques have been proposed in the literature [18]. Coarsely classified, OD can be performed based on distances to nearest neighboring samples [3,16,19,34], deploying histograms [25], relying on tree structures [12,29] or by performing density estimations in feature space [22,26].

In data stream analysis, the underlying technique for handling concept drift is as critical as computing outlier scores. This aspect of algorithm construction is of substantial importance, since it determines whether the memory length, i.e. the duration for which patterns in the data stream should be remembered, has a strong influence on the algorithm's resource consumption. Particularly in the context of high-rate processing, this property if of substantial relevance.

	SW-DBOR	SW-KNN	SW-LOF	LODA [25]	RS-Hash [26]	RRCF [12]	HS-Trees [29]	xStream [22]	SDOstream [16]
Windowing mechanism	SW	SW	SW	SW	SW	SW	RW	RW	EW
Constant space complexity	✗	✗	✗	✗	✗	✗	✓	✓	✓
Constant time complexity	✗	✗	✗	✗	✓	✗	✓	✓	✓
Ensemble-based	✗	✗	✗	✓	✓	✓	✓	✓	✗
Parallelizable in dSalmon	✗	✗	✗	✓	✓	✓	✓	✓	✗

Fig. 1. Methods for streaming OD from related work available in dSalmon.

For handling concept drift, several methods follow a *sliding window* (SW) approach [3,12,19,25,26,34], where the most recently seen N data samples are stored and used for assessing outlierness of newly arriving data samples, $N \in \mathbb{N}$ denoting the window length. The use of a SW has the effect that space complexity depends linearly on memory length, rendering SW-based algorithms impractical for high-rate data streams. In addition, as a general rule, time complexity is significantly influenced by memory length.

For this reason, some modern OD methods adopt a *reference window* (RW) approach [22,29]. In this case, a model is trained from observed data samples without performing outlier scoring on the observed data. After having observed N data samples, the trained model is deemed the RW and used for scoring outlierness of newly arriving data samples, while a new model is trained from newly observed data. Hence, for scoring outlierness of points $kN \ldots (k+1)N$ with $k \in \mathbb{N}$ and the window length $N \in \mathbb{N}$, data samples $(k-1)N \ldots kN - 1$ are used as RW. RW methods typically achieve space and time complexity $\mathcal{O}(1)$ with respect to memory length.

Another approach for achieving $\mathcal{O}(1)$ complexity is the use of an *exponential window* (EW) [16,26]. In this case, models use an exponentially weighted moving average for internal counters, avoiding the need to store data samples.

In Fig. 1, we show OD methods implemented in dSalmon and several characteristics relevant for execution time.

4 Architectural Design and Interface

We now describe how we engineered dSalmon to optimize usability for research on streaming data processing. To motivate our architectural design, we start by depicting software goals and resulting design decisions.

4.1 Design Decisions

We primarily target researchers working with streaming data who aim to develop or optimize systems and algorithms and therefore possess offline datasets of captured data streams. Here we present the objectives that motivated our design decisions for dSalmon.

- **High Speed Data Processing.** A primary goal is the optimization of run times of the algorithms provided by dSalmon. This is especially important for researchers who conduct tests with different algorithms and parameters, aiming to make an informed decision about the best parameterization.
  Design Decision: To achieve high-speed processing, the core of dSalmon is implemented in C++. Furthermore, a spatial indexing data structure is used to reduce execution times of nearest neighbors and range queries.

- **Straightforward Usability.** In the field of data science, Python is a commonly used language. Many tools provide Python interfaces and researchers often develop algorithms in Python. While largely implemented in C++, we thus aimed to provide an interface that is familiar in the Python community.
  Design Decision: For outlier detectors, we adhere to the known interface of scikit-learn, which also has been adopted by PyOD.

- **Processing of Recorded Data.** While in the application phase data samples have to be processed one at a time, during algorithm development and parameter tuning researchers commonly can make use of datasets consisting of previously collected streaming data. If desired, dSalmon allows providing blocks of data as input to achieve superior processing speed. In such cases, to accomplish a behavior equivalent to application phases, the implementation must guarantee to be invariant of the used block size.
  Design Decision: To provide block size invariance, we process block samples sequentially within our fast C++ backend. Hence, block size has no effect on the returned results.

- **Support for Efficient Ensemble Learning.** In recent research, it has become common to construct data mining algorithms by pooling the results of an ensemble of weak learners, providing opportunities for embarrassingly parallel processing. These opportunities for parallelization have to be passed on the user, allowing a substantial speedup on modern computing hardware.
  Design Decision: We leverage available parallelism in the core of dSalmon, allowing the user to simply set an n_jobs parameter to reduce run time.

- **Reproducibility.** To support reproducibility of results, results obtained from randomized algorithms have to be parameterized by a random seed, so that results are deterministic and reproducible when providing the same seed value. Changing the used block size or the number of parallel computing threads has to leave the obtained results unaffected.
  Design Decision: We support parameterization of randomized algorithms by a random seed and engineered algorithm implementations to be invariant of block size or requested parallelism.

- **Simple Installation and Maintenance.** To reduce the surface for version incompatibilities and provide an uncomplicated installation, it is highly beneficial to keep the number of software dependencies small.
  Design Decision: For installing dSalmon, we only require NumPy [14]. While dSalmon uses SWIG [6] for generating Python wrapper code and makes intensive use of Boost [13], the permissive licenses of SWIG and Boost allow us to ship any code required for compilation together with dSalmon.

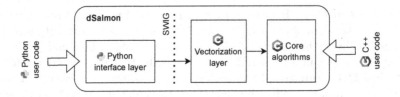

Fig. 2. Architecture of dSalmon.

Besides the above goals, it is also worth elaborating on some tasks that we explicitly constrain in the development of dSalmon.

- **Algorithm Fidelity.** A clear non-goal is the optimization of any of the implemented algorithms for OD accuracy. Such improvements inherently depend on the specific problem under investigation and, hence, are difficult to be made in an objective way. Rather, we follow the descriptions of the respective algorithm authors as closely as possible, so that users of our framework can be confident to deploy an established, well-tested method for their research tasks.
- **Maximum Code Reuse.** We see the focus of our framework in filling an important gap by providing highly efficient processing for streaming data. On the other hand, for several recurring tasks of data analysis and processing, well-functioning and comprehensive tools are provided by existing frameworks like NumPy [14], scikit-learn [24] or SciPy [30], or can trivially be implemented in a fast, vectorized manner. We explicitly avoid reimplementing tools that are already provided by established software projects to keep our code base narrow and relieve the user from having to choose between competing implementations. For instance, comprehensive metrics for evaluating the quality of an obtained outlier scoring are provided by scikit-learn, like, e.g., the ROC-AUC score or the P@n score.

4.2   Architecture

Considering design decisions in the previous Sect. 4.1, it was of importance for us to allow use of dSalmon from a programming language that is known and used by data science researchers. For this reason, we targeted the Python programming language, which allows efficient and swift data science development.

Traditional data mining algorithms for static data in many cases have at least limited opportunities for batch processing. Therefore, algorithms for static data often allow efficient implementations from an interpreted language like Python directly. However, when processing a data stream the model has to be adapted for each processed point, inherently making batch processing hardly feasible, if not impossible. To provide superior processing speed while allowing use from Python directly, dSalmon therefore implements core algorithms in C++, but provides interfaces to the algorithms from both C++ and Python.

Listing 1.1. A toy example for finding the 5 most outlying points using dSalmon.

```python
from dSalmon.outlier import HSTrees
import numpy as np
detector = HSTrees(window=500, n_estimators=100, n_jobs=4)
data = np.load('data.npy')
outlier_scores = detector.fit_predict(data)
print('Outliers:', np.argsort(outlier_scores)[-5:].tolist())
```

Figure 2 depicts the architecture of dSalmon. Hence, the core algorithms layer depicted in Fig. 2 is implemented in C++. We use C++ template programming for instantiating single and double precision floating point variants of all algorithms. Researchers can thus achieve a smaller memory footprint and faster processing times by falling back to single precision processing if required. Since loop iterations are fast in C++, the core algorithms C++ interface accepts individual samples instead of blocks of data.

On the other hand, looping over individual samples in Python would incur a substantial performance penalty. Hence, the C++ vectorization layer in Fig. 2 accepts blocks of streaming data and iterates over samples within each block when passing on the data to core algorithms. To account for the dynamic nature of data streams, we allow the user to use differently sized blocks or even to vary the number of passed samples at each iteration. Additionally, the vectorization layer ensures that opportunities for parallel processing are efficiently taken by, for example, executing base detectors of ensemble methods in parallel.

For generating the actual interface between Python and C++, we deploy SWIG [6], a tool for automatically generating Python bindings by parsing C/C++ header files. The benefits of deploying SWIG are that the code base of dSalmon can easily be extended, leaving the generation of boilerplate interface code to SWIG. Since SWIG supports a wide range of target languages, our approach additionally yields the possibility to create bindings for further programming languages like, for instance, R without having to rewrite core algorithms.

The Python interface layer depicted in Fig. 2 finally accepts blocks of streaming data from user code. It accomplishes the task of ensuring a clean interface familiar in the Python community. Additionally, it performs several sanity checks on the provided data blocks.

We genuinely believe that source code should be publicly available and therefore distribute dSalmon under the LGPL 3.0 license, which permits widespread use, but requests developers to keep modified versions open-source.

4.3   Using dSalmon for Outlier Detection

Listing 1.1 shows an example of performing OD with dSalmon. In this example, the rows of **data** are interpreted as sequentially arriving samples of a data stream. As alternative to the depicted listing, a user might similarly call fit_predict() sequentially with blocks of consecutive rows, or even iterate over rows in data individually. Since data rows are iterated by dSalmon, all three approaches provide equal results. Choosing a too small block size, however, might result in substantially slower processing. As described in Sect. 4.1, block size invariance is crucial for evaluating algorithms in a realistic manner.

4.4   M-Tree Indexing

When developing algorithms for data mining, a frequent task is finding nearest neighbors in a large set of points. In literature, this requirement gave rise to the development of various indexing data structures for performing nearest neighbor and range queries efficiently. However, many indexing trees are optimized for tree construction from bulk data and do not allow removing points and inserting new points once the tree has been built. In particular, this limitation applies to the popular KDTree and BallTree data structures provided by scikit-learn [24].

dSalmon implements an M-Tree [9] spatial indexing data structure for its internal use, which allows efficient nearest neighbor and range queries in metric spaces. By using an M-Tree, dSalmon thus allows to modify the tree after it has been built. To additionally allow algorithm development from Python, we provide a Python interface for directly using an M-Tree in custom algorithms. Similar to our further implementations, we ensured that parallel processing capabilities can efficiently be made use of and allow partially parallelized tree building and fully parallelized tree querying in an uncomplicated way by simply setting respective parameters.

5   Experimental Evaluation

In what follows, we present results from an extensive experimental evaluation that we have performed to evaluate dSalmon's resource consumption. We have performed our algorithm benchmarks on desktop machines equipped with Intel i7-4770 processors, 16GiB of main memory and no configured swap space. All machines used for evaluation have an equal setup. We used CPython version 3.7.3 and Debian Buster with kernel version 4.19.0. To avoid distorted measurements, we avoided any simultaneous use of the machines and shut down background processes as far as possible. For measuring energy consumption, we used the Running Average Power Limit (RAPL) [11] feature of our Intel CPUs, and sum memory and processor power consumption. Reported execution times do not include the time needed for loading the dataset into memory.

For performing realistic benchmarks, we selected publicly available datasets representing multivariate streaming data:

- The SWAN-SF [4] dataset provides measurement data on solar flares. To follow established preprocessing steps for SWAN-SF, we used preprocessing scripts available on the Internet [2], extracting the same features that the repository authors used in their examples. The preprocessed dataset consists of 331,185 data samples with 12 features per sample. For assessing outlier scores, we assigned a normal label to the majority class and marked remaining classes as outliers.

- The KDD Cup'99 [1] dataset is an established dataset for OD, containing host-based and network-based features for detecting attacks in computer networks. We marked attack samples as outliers over normal traffic and used one-hot encoding for nominal features. The resulting dataset has 4,898,431 data samples with 52 features each.

- The CIC-IDS-2017 [28] dataset similarly aims at detecting network attacks, but only provides network traffic, making unsupervised attack detection substantially harder. We used an established feature vector for network traffic [32] together with publicly available preprocessing scripts [23] and consider network attacks as outliers over normal traffic. The resulting preprocessed dataset has 2,317,922 data samples and 33 features.

We selected PySAD as framework to compare it against dSalmon and performed all benchmarks using double-precision floating point processing. As described in Sect. 2, further software projects exist for OD tasks. However, the majority of these projects do not provide methods for processing streaming data. Furthermore, as well as with dSalmon, PySAD can be used from Python.

5.1 Nearest-Neighbors Algorithms

A simple approach for establishing the outlierness of arriving data points is counting the number of nearest neighbors within a pre-determined radius. Hence, in many traditional publications [3,19,34] an arriving data point is declared to be an outlier if less than $k \in \mathbb{N}$ points of the current SW lie within a radius $R \in \mathbb{R}^+$. While modern approaches for OD frequently outperform this simple nearest-neighbors-based approach in both, detection accuracy and execution time, the importance of a simple nearest-neighbors-based approach lies in its unrivaled interpretability of reported outlier scores, making its availability cru-

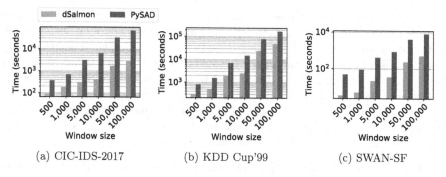

Fig. 3. Execution time comparison for nearest-neighbors-based streaming outlier detection.

cial for dSalmon. Interpretability is crucial in various fields of application like, e.g., medicine [20,31], or network intrusion detection [5,15,21].

While providing a binary label (inlier/outlier) in some cases is sufficient in practice, for research and parameter selection it is usually necessary to obtain a score for outlierness for data samples. When requiring an outlier score instead of a binary label, distance-based OD can be performed in two flavors:

1. When implementing a SW-based k nearest neighbors (kNN) rule, OD can be parameterized by the neighbor count k, providing the distance to the kth nearest point as outlier score.
2. Alternatively, OD can be parameterized by the search radius R, providing the number of neighbors within R as inverse outlier score.

dSalmon allows OD using both flavors (1) and (2), termed SW-KNN and SW-DBOR, respectively, and deploys M-Tree indexing to reduce execution time.

PySAD supports nearest-neighbors-based OD only in flavor (2), adopting the name ExactStorm from [3] for this model. We thus used this operational mode also for dSalmon, resulting in execution times as shown in Fig. 3 for different lengths of the SW. To provide a meaningful comparison, for each individual window size we used grid search on a logarithmic scale for finding the radius R that optimizes the ROC-AUC score when applying the algorithm to the complete dataset, and used the resulting R for performing the benchmark.

Execution time benefits demonstrated in Fig. 3 can be explained by two effects: On the one hand, for small window lengths execution time is dominated by interpretation overhead of the Python language for PySAD, which dSalmon avoids due to its C++ core implementation. However, PySAD sensibly performs distance computations for each processed data sample in a vectorized manner, diminishing the interpretation overhead as the window length increases. As shown in Fig. 3, dSalmon is able to retain a substantial speedup even as window size increases. This observation demonstrates execution time benefits of M-Tree indexing compared to straight per-sample distance computations.

5.2 Ensemble-Based Outlier Detectors

In recent research, an increasingly popular approach for OD, which sets new records in detection accuracy, is to construct algorithms by pooling outlier scores obtained by an ensemble of weak learners. Beneath yielding good accuracy, this approach is intrinsically embarrassingly parallel, as the processing of distinct base detectors can trivially be distributed to several workers. dSalmon allows to easily leverage this feature by simply setting an n_jobs parameter.

When evaluating execution performance, for the sake of providing a fair comparison, we chose algorithms whose specification leaves little room for interpretation. In particular, we selected the following methods:

---

[1] Missing results for RRCF using PySAD indicate experiment runs that failed due to reaching Python's recursion limit.
[2] xStream for KDD Cup'99 using PySAD with 50 random projections failed due to running out of memory.

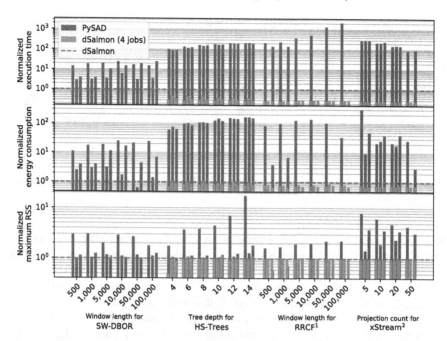

Fig. 4. Overall comparison of the resource consumption of several outlier detectors implemented by dSalmon and PySAD. For each parameter setting, values are normalized to results obtained by single-threaded dSalmon for better comparison. Bars depicted for each algorithm parameterization indicate results for SWAN-SF, KDD Cup'99 and CIC-IDS-2017 in this order.

- Robust Random Cut Forest (RRCF) [12] uses an ensemble of dynamically constructed trees, where each tree performs random cuts based on the feature space of observed samples. Concept drift is taken care of using a SW approach. We perform runs with varying window sizes to show dependence when varying this parameter.
- Half-Space-Trees [29] similarly constructs a tree ensemble, but performs tree construction statically at the time of algorithm initialization. Concept drift is considered based on a RW approach. In our experiments, we vary the depth of the constructed trees to evaluate influence of tree depth on resource usage.
- xStream [22] is a recent method for OD, which introduces half-space-chains, which establish an anomaly score by splitting randomly selected features with varying precisions. xStream combines half-space-chains with the technique of random projections. For benchmarking, we set the chain length to 15 as used for the evaluations in [22] and vary the number of projections to show dependence on this parameter.

In our experiments, we use an ensemble size of 100 for all algorithms, which is similarly used as default value for ensemble methods by scikit-learn. Using 100 base estimators as ensemble size is a natural choice and is likely to reduce

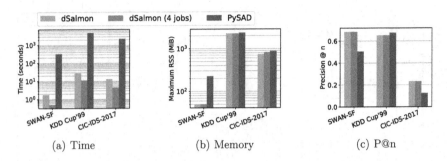

Fig. 5. HS-Trees: Resource consumption and OD performance using a tree depth of 10.

statistical variation of outlier scores to an acceptable level. For dSalmon, we evaluate performance for both single-threaded operation and when utilizing four processor cores. Multi-threaded operation in not supported by PySAD.

In Fig. 4 we depict a summarized comparison of resource consumption that we measured while performing OD with dSalmon and PySAD on the SWAN-SF, KDD Cup'99 and CIC-IDS-2017 datasets, also including the results already presented in Sect. 5.1. We depict execution time, memory usage as maximum Resident Set Size (RSS) and energy consumption. Since we aim to depict relative performance when using both frameworks, we normalize all measurements by results obtained when using dSalmon on one processor core.

Figure 4 shows that, particularly for modern ensemble-based algorithms, dSalmon yields substantial execution time benefits. For most algorithm runs, a speed-up by a factor of more than 100 can be obtained. From Fig. 4 we can additionally conclude that dSalmon makes highly efficient use of parallel processing capabilities. Execution time indicates that, by using four simultaneous jobs, a speed-up of almost 4 can be obtained in most cases. Furthermore, memory consumption does not increase when relying on parallel processing, allowing highly efficient operation on modern multi-core desktop machines or servers. It is also interesting to note that by relying on multi-threaded processing considerable energy savings can be obtained.

In what follows, we will analyze behavior for specific algorithms in more detail. We skip RRCF for closer analysis, as for RRCF many PySAD runs failed due to reaching the maximum recursion limit, which cannot be fixed safely [33]. RRCF results that we obtained for SWAN-SF indicate that dSalmon shows markedly low runtimes, especially if longer memory lengths are required.

Half-Space-Trees Figure 5 shows the absolute measurement readings that we obtained for HS-Trees with a tree depth of 10. In the light of execution times in Fig. 5 (a), we can generally attest HS-Trees' outstanding run time performances, since HS-Trees is able to process millions of data samples in about 10 s.

It is worth noting that, besides obtaining markedly different execution times, we also obtained deviating results for detection performance when deploying both implementations, as shown in Fig. 5(c). This can be explained by PySAD basing the reported outlier score on all tree nodes traversed for one sample, while dSalmon computes outlier scores only from terminal nodes as suggested by Tan et al. [29] when introducing HS-Trees. Figure 5(c) additionally demonstrates reproducibility of obtained results for dSalmon. Hence, for both independent algorithm runs – one utilizing one CPU core and another utilizing four cores – the precise same outlier scores are reported, since the same seed value has been provided as parameter. This holds true even though both runs differ in their parameterization for parallel processing. We have verified this property also for all further runs depicted in Fig. 4.

In Fig. 6, we depict absolute execution times as function of tree depth. Hence, dSalmon obtains an approximately 100 times speed-up and execution time shows only a slight increase when increasing the tree depth. In fact, rather memory occupation is limiting the usable maximum tree depth, since for HS-Trees tree structures are statically created, resulting in memory consumption that increases exponentially with tree depth.

xStream Figure 7 shows absolute execution times und maximum RSS as function of the number of projections for xStream. As discussed by the algorithm authors [22], execution time depends linearly on ensemble size, chain length and the number of projections. Hence, observed behavior for our dSalmon runs is reasonable. We notice that PySAD shows a less pronounced dependency of the number of projections. Consequently, execution time differences of dSalmon range between 20 and 200. dSalmon proves to make highly efficient use of parallel processing, allowing a 4-times speed-up by using 4 parallel jobs.

Memory consumption as a function of the number of projections, as depicted in Fig. 7, is particularly striking. While PySAD's memory consumption shows no clear dependence of the number of projections for SWAN-SF, for KDD Cup'99 a clear monotonic dependence can be observed, and the algorithm run eventually fails on our 16GiB machine due to running out of memory for 50 projections. xStream authors [22] suggest using a Count-min sketch (CMS) [10] for counting bin frequencies to ensure constant space complexity. In dSalmon, we adopt the

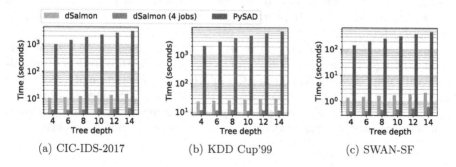

(a) CIC-IDS-2017   (b) KDD Cup'99   (c) SWAN-SF

Fig. 6. Runtimes of HS-Trees in response to variations of the tree depth.

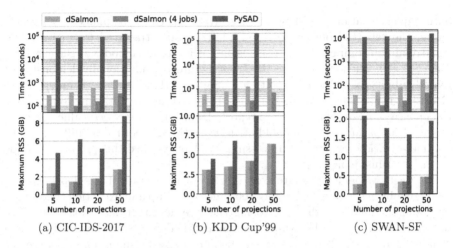

Fig. 7. xStream: Resource consumption in response to variations of the number of projections.

approach of using CMSs, while PySAD uses classical hash tables. The use of hash tables for this purpose provides an explanation for the data-dependent memory consumption observable in Fig. 7, since memory consumption in this case is reduced if the majority of data samples shares a small number of bins. In dSalmon, memory requirements for storing CMS structures are independent of the projection count. The increase of memory consumption can be explained by the memory requirements for storing projected values for a given block of data.

6   Conclusions

We have introduced and presented dSalmon, a highly efficient framework for OD on multivariate evolving data streams. Due to the nature of streaming data, data samples frequently accumulate to a substantial volume within short time, making efficient processing crucial. We have presented dSalmon's architecture, which allows easy extension and enables researchers and practitioners to add algorithms for OD or even implementing entirely different methods for analyzing streaming data.

In a thorough evaluation, we have shown that dSalmon was able to outperform existing Python stream outlier detectors by up to three orders of magnitude with respect to execution time. Combined with the selection of a recent OD method optimized for processing high-rate data streams, gigabytes of data can be processed in few seconds, paving the way for analyzing comprehensive datasets, which increasingly become available due to advances of modern technology.

References

1. Kdd cup 1999 data. https://kdd.ics.uci.edu/databases/kddcup99/kddcup99.html (1999), accessed: 2023-07-04
2. Ahmadzadeh, A., Aydin, B.: Multivariate Timeseries Feature Extraction on SWAN Data Benchmark (SWAN_Features) (2020), GSU Data Mining Lab
3. Angiulli, F., Fassetti, F.: Detecting distance-based outliers in streams of data. In: Proceedings of the 16th ACM Conference on Information and Knowledge Management, pp. 811–820, CIKM'07, ACM, New York, NY, USA (2007)
4. Angryk, R.A., Martens, P.C., Aydin, B., Kempton, D., Mahajan, S.S., Basodi, S., Ahmadzadeh, A., Cai, X., Filali Boubrahimi, S., Hamdi, S.M., Schuh, M.A., Georgoulis, M.K.: Multivariate time series dataset for space weather data analytics. Sci. Data **7**(227) (2020)
5. Bachl, M., Hartl, A., Fabini, J., Zseby, T.: Walling up backdoors in intrusion detection systems. In: Big-DAMA '19, pp. 8–13. ACM, Orlando, FL, USA (2019)
6. Beazley, D.M.: SWIG: An easy to use tool for integrating scripting languages with C and C++. In: Proceedings of the 4th Conference on USENIX Tcl/Tk Workshop, 1996 - Volume 4, p. 15, TCLTK'96, USENIX Association, USA (1996)
7. Bifet, A., Holmes, G., Kirkby, R., Pfahringer, B.: Moa: massive online analysis. J. Mach. Learn. Res. **11**, 1601–1604 (2010)
8. Campos, G.O., Zimek, A., et al.: On the evaluation of unsupervised outlier detection: measures, datasets, and an empirical study. Data Mining and Knowl. Discovery **30**(4), 891–927 (2016), ISSN 1573–756X
9. Ciaccia, P., Patella, M., Zezula, P.: M-tree: An efficient access method for similarity search in metric spaces. In: Proceedings of the 23rd International Conference on Very Large Data Bases, pp. 426–435, VLDB '97, Morgan Kaufmann Publishers Inc., San Francisco, CA, USA (1997), ISBN 1558604707
10. Cormode, G., Muthukrishnan, S.: An improved data stream summary: the count-min sketch and its applications. J. Algorithms **55**(1), 58–75 (2005)
11. David, H., Gorbatov, E., Hanebutte, U.R., Khanna, R., Le, C.: Rapl: memory power estimation and capping. In: 2010 ACM/IEEE International Symposium on Low-Power Electronics and Design (ISLPED). IEEE, pp. 189–194 (201)
12. Guha, S., Mishra, N., Roy, G., Schrijvers, O.: Robust random cut forest based anomaly detection on streams. In: Proceedings of The 33rd International Conference on Machine Learning, Proceedings of Machine Learning Research, vol. 48, pp. 2712–2721, PMLR, New York, New York, USA (2016)
13. Gurtovoy, A., Abrahams, D.: The boost C++ metaprogramming library, p. 22 (2002)
14. Harris, C.R., Millman, K.J., van der Walt, S.J., Gommers, R., Virtanen, P., Cournapeau, D., Wieser, E., Taylor, J., Berg, S., Smith, N.J., Kern, R., Picus, M., Hoyer, S., van Kerkwijk, M.H., Brett, M., Haldane, A., del Río, J.F., Wiebe, M., Peterson, P., Gérard-Marchant, P., Sheppard, K., Reddy, T., Weckesser, W., Abbasi, H., Gohlke, C., Oliphant, T.E.: Array programming with NumPy. Nature **585**(7825), 357–362 (2020)
15. Hartl, A., Bachl, M., Fabini, J., Zseby, T.: Explainability and adversarial robustness for RNNs. In: 2020 IEEE Sixth International Conference on Big Data Computing Service and Applications (BigDataService), pp. 148–156. IEEE, New York, NY, USA (2020a)
16. Hartl, A., Iglesias, F., Zseby, T.: SDOstream: Low-density models for streaming outlier detection. In: ESANN 2020 proceedings, pp. 661–666 (2020b)

17. Iglesias, F., Hartl, A., Zseby, T., Zimek, A.: Are network attacks outliers? a study of space representations and unsupervised algorithms. In: Joint European Conference on Machine Learning and Knowledge Discovery in Databases, pp. 159–175. Springer (2019)

18. Iglesias Vázquez, F., Hartl, A., Zseby, T., Zimek, A.: Anomaly detection in streaming data: A comparison and evaluation study. Expert Syst. with Appl. **233**, 120994 (2023), ISSN 0957-4174

19. Kontaki, M., Gounaris, A., Papadopoulos, A.N., Tsichlas, K., Manolopoulos, Y.: Continuous monitoring of distance-based outliers over data streams. In: IEEE 27th International Conference on Data Engineering, pp. 135–146 (2011)

20. Lakkaraju, H., Rudin, C.: Learning cost-effective and interpretable treatment regimes. In: Proceedings of the 20th International Conference on Artificial Intelligence and Statistics, pp. 166–175, PMLR, Fort Lauderdale, FL, USA (2017)

21. Lundberg, H., Mowla, N.I., Abedin, S.F., Thar, K., Mahmood, A., Gidlund, M., Raza, S.: Experimental analysis of trustworthy in-vehicle intrusion detection system using explainable artificial intelligence (xai). IEEE Access **10**, 102831–102841 (2022)

22. Manzoor, E.A., Lamba, H., Akoglu, L.: xStream: outlier detection in feature-evolving data streams. In: 24th ACM SIGKDD International Conference on Knowledge Discovery and Data Mining (2018)

23. Meghdouri, F.: Datasets Preprocessing (2021). https://github.com/CN-TU/Datasets-preprocessing, gitHub repository

24. Pedregosa, F., Varoquaux, G., Gramfort, A., Michel, V., Thirion, B., Grisel, O., Blondel, M., Prettenhofer, P., Weiss, R., Dubourg, V., Vanderplas, J., Passos, A., Cournapeau, D., Brucher, M., Perrot, M., Duchesnay, E.: Scikit-learn: machine learning in Python. J. Mach. Learn. Res. **12**, 2825–2830 (2011)

25. Pevný, T.: Loda: Lightweight on-line detector of anomalies. Mach. Learn. **102**(2), 275–304 (2016)

26. Sathe, S., Aggarwal, C.C.: Subspace outlier detection in linear time with randomized hashing. In: 2016 IEEE 16th International Conference on Data Mining (ICDM), pp. 459–468 (2016)

27. Schubert, E., Zimek, A.: Elki: A large open-source library for data analysis—elki release 0.7.5 "heidelberg". arXiv preprint arXiv:1902.03616 (2019)

28. Sharafaldin, I., Habibi Lashkari, A., Ghorbani, A.A.: Toward generating a new intrusion detection dataset and intrusion traffic characterization. In: ICISSP, pp. 108–116, SCITEPRESS, Funchal, Madeira, Portugal (2018)

29. Tan, S.C., Ting, K.M., Liu, T.F.: Fast anomaly detection for streaming data. In: Twenty-Second International Joint Conference on Artificial Intelligence (2011)

30. Virtanen, P., Gommers, R., Oliphant, T.E., Haberland, M., Reddy, T., Cournapeau, D., Burovski, E., Peterson, P., Weckesser, W., Bright, J., van der Walt, S.J., Brett, M., Wilson, J., Millman, K.J., Mayorov, N., Nelson, A.R.J., Jones, E., Kern, R., Larson, E., Carey, C.J., Polat, İ., Feng, Y., Moore, E.W., VanderPlas, J., Laxalde, D., Perktold, J., Cimrman, R., Henriksen, I., Quintero, E.A., Harris, C.R., Archibald, A.M., Ribeiro, A.H., Pedregosa, F., van Mulbregt, P., SciPy 1.0 contributors: SciPy 1.0: fundamental algorithms for scientific computing in Python. Nature Methods **17**, 261–272 (2020)

31. Weng, S.F., Reps, J., Kai, J., Garibaldi, J.M., Qureshi, N.: Can machine-learning improve cardiovascular risk prediction using routine clinical data? PLoS ONE **12**(4), 1–14 (2017)

32. Williams, N., Zander, S., Armitage, G.: A preliminary performance comparison of five machine learning algorithms for practical IP traffic flow classification. SIG-COMM Comput. Commun. Rev. **36**(5), 5–16 (2006)

33. Wouters, T.: Answer to "what is the maximum recursion depth in python, and how to increase it?" (2010). https://stackoverflow.com/a/3323013, stackoverflow discussion

34. Yang, D., Rundensteiner, E., Ward, M.O.: Neighbor-based pattern detection for windows over streaming data. In: Proceedings of the 12th International Conference on Extending Database Tech.: Advances in Database Tech., pp. 529–540, EDBT'09, ACM, New York, NY, USA (2009)

35. Yilmaz, S.F., Kozat, S.S.: Pysad: a streaming anomaly detection framework in Python (2020). arXiv preprint arXiv:2009.02572

36. Zhao, Y., Nasrullah, Z., Li, Z.: Pyod: a python toolbox for scalable outlier detection. J. Mach. Learn. Res. **20**(96), 1–7 (2019)

REALYST: A C++ Tool for Optimizing Reachability Probabilities in Stochastic Hybrid Systems

Joanna Delicaris[1(✉)] , Jonas Stübbe[1] , Stefan Schupp[2] ,
and Anne Remke[1]

[1] Westfälische Wilhelms-Universität, 48149 Münster, Germany
{joanna.delicaris,jonas.stuebbe,anne.remke}@uni-muenster.de
[2] TU Wien, 1040 Wien, Austria
stefan.schupp@tuwien.ac.at

Abstract. This paper presents the open-source C++ tool REALYST for effectively computing optimal time-bounded reachability probabilities for subclasses of hybrid automata extended with random clocks. The tool explicitly resolves the underlying nondeterminism and computes reachable state sets exactly. The error of the computed results solely stems from the multi-dimensional integration. The architecture of REALYST is extensible and allows to easily integrate other classes of hybrid automata extended by random clocks. REALYST relies on the HYPRO library to perform flowpipe construction, and on GSL for multi-dimensional integration.

Keywords: Tool · (Optimal) reachability probabilities · Stochastic hybrid automata

1 Introduction

Stochastic hybrid systems (SHS) combine discrete, continuous and stochastic behavior. Especially in systems which affect humans or where humans are in the loop, safety is of major importance and formal approaches, such as time-bounded reachability analysis allow to make validated statements about the safety of a system. The reachability analysis of SHS poses a diverse set of challenges, rooted in the combination of discrete-continuous behavior with stochasticity. Nondeterminism, which arises naturally e.g., in concurrent systems, is often resolved probabilistically in (purely) stochastic models [1,6,20], and is usually not explicitly resolved in non-stochastic hybrid systems. Maintaining the discrete and continuous nondeterminism present, e.g., in initial sets, dynamic behavior or time delays in a stochastic hybrid system, enables us to optimize reachability probabilities, leading to *maximum* and *minimum* reachability probabilities.

Supported by DFG project 471367371.

E. Kalyvianaki and M. Paolieri (Eds.): VALUETOOLS 2023, LNICST 539, pp. 170–182, 2024.
https://doi.org/10.1007/978-3-031-48885-6_11

REALYST is an open-source tool that is specifically designed to optimize discrete and continuous nondeterminism in SHS. The tool is taylored for stochastic variants of subclasses of hybrid automata, namely *singular automata with random clocks (SAR)* [22,26] and *rectangular automata with random clocks (RAR)* [11]. Currently, REALYST resolves discrete and continuous nondeterminism via maximum prophetic schedulers and computes optimal time-bounded reachability probabilities. The computations performed in REALYST rely on the library HYPRO for geometric operations on convex polytopes and the construction of the reachable state space as a flowpipe [3]. By using the rational number format GMP, these state sets are guaranteed to be exact. Multi-dimensional integration is currently done via Monte Carlo VEGAS as provided by GSL [12] which computes a probability and statistical error for a predefined number of samples.

We illustrate the capabilities of REALYST on an existing case study [11] with considerably improved computation times.

Related Work The tool HPNMG [18] is a model checker for hybrid Petri nets with general transitions (HPnGs) [14], which exhibit discrete and continuous behavior, as well as stochasticity in the form of *general transitions* modeling random delays. Earlier work resolved the inherent discrete nondeterminism of HPnGs via weights [14], and has later been optimized for both prophetic and non-prophetic schedulers in [21]. FAUST^2 [27] only supports *discrete-time* stochastic systems. Its successor STOCHY [8] then performs quantitative analysis of *discrete-time* SHS by constructing abstractions in the form of (interval) Markov decision processes (MDPs). The MODEST toolset [16] is a collection of tools for the analysis of stochastic timed and hybrid systems. Using PROHVER [15] as a backend, MODEST analyses reachability in stochastic hybrid systems with general probability distributions and (nonlinear) continuous dynamics. It performs a discretization of the support of continuous stochastic delays and an abstraction for discrete probabilistic behaviour. Together this results in an overapproximation of the actual reachability probabilities. PROBREACH [25] provides algorithms to analyse *parametric* SHS that allow for nonlinear continuous dynamics, where parameters can be random as well as nondeterministic. Here, bounded reachability analysis is encoded as a first-order logic formula and solved using DREACH [19], which provides a rigorous enclosure that includes the sought reachability probability. Recent computations within the ARCH competition [2] show that PROBREACH is not competitive with REALYST on small examples. UPPAAL [5] offers a wide range of tools and verification techniques for networks of timed automata. Stochastic extensions for more expressive models can be evaluated with *statistical model checking* and optimal strategies can be identified and constructed using STRATEGO [10] and TIGA [4].

Outline After introducing the class of models in Sect. 2, the tool is described in Sect. 3. The evaluation of the case study is presented in Sect. 4 and the paper is concluded in Sect. 5.

2   Model Classes

Hybrid automata (HA) [3] are a modeling formalism for systems which exhibit mixed discrete-continuous behavior. A subclass of HA are rectangular automata [17], where rates and conditions are described via intervals.

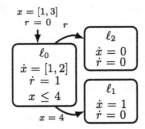

Fig. 1. RAR with random clock r.

Recently, rectangular automata with random clocks (RAR) have been proposed as a stochastic extension for this subclass of HA, where the duration of random delays is measured explicitly via stopwatches and constraints on the syntax ensure that the resulting probability space is sound. We refer the interested reader to [11] for a detailed presentation of their syntax and semantic.

REALYST implements the algorithm proposed in [11] to maximize reachability probabilities in rectangular automata with random clocks (RAR) for history-dependent prophetic schedulers. RAR allow for (i) *initial nondeterminism* in the choice of the initial state, (ii) *time nondeterminism* when time can elapse but also jumps are enabled during the whole flow, and (iii) *rate nondeterminism* when continuous variables can evolve with different rates. In addition to these continuous types of nondeterminism, RAR also contain (iv) *discrete nondeterminism* when different jumps are enabled simultaneously. An example RAR with random clock r is shown in Fig. 1, see Appendix A for explanation. We use prophetic schedulers [9] to resolve nondeterminism, which have full information not only on the history but also on the future expiration times of all random clocks, as introduced in [22]. While prophetic scheduling may seem unrealistic, it is well-suited to perform a *worst-case* analysis, especially when uncontrollable uncertainties are modeled nondeterministically.

For a bounded number of jumps, reachability is decidable for non-initialized rectangular automata (RA) [3]. Hence, forward flowpipe construction computes exact reachable state-sets, e.g. using convex polytopes as a state-set representation. Jump-bounded reachability can also be computed for RAR,, when stochasticity is disregarded, i.e., stochastic edges that represent the expiration of a random delay are interpreted as regular edges without guard. Since it has been shown that RA can be transformed into singular automata (SA), stopwatch automata (SWA) and timed automata (TA), respectively [3,17], all of those model classes can be extended with random clocks, similarly to RAR.

3   The REALYST Tool

We present REALYST, an open source C++ tool available online via go.unims.de/realyst, for the efficient computation of optimal reachability probabilities in stochastic hybrid automata. Currently, REALYST relies on the state-space representation in terms of convex polytopes. While this representation is exact for the classes of hybrid automata that are currently supported by REALYST, the geometric operations are computationally involved. Hence, the tool architecture is extensible and can easily include other state-space representations like zonotopes or support functions, in the future [23], as well as more efficient multi-dimensional integration [28].

This section is further organized as follows: Sect. 3.1 presents the overall program flow, Sect. 3.2 the necessary details on backward refinement and integration and Sect. 3.3 introduces dependendicies and usage parameters.

3.1   Program Flow

Figure 2 illustrates the program flow for a given automaton.

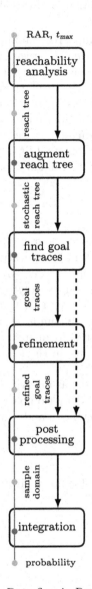

RAR, t_{max}

reachability
analysis

reach tree

augment
reach tree

stochastic
reach tree

find goal
traces

goal
traces

refinement

refined
goal
traces

post
processing

sample
domain

integration

probability

Fig. 2. Data flow in REALYST.

0. Initially, a rectangular automaton with random clocks, a time bound t_{max} and a goal specification is given.
1. The `reachabilityAnalysis` results in a *reach tree* up to the time bound t_{max}, where *nodes* link to state sets represented by convex polytopes. Here, random clocks are treated as continuous variables. The computed reachable state space then contains all possible valuations of the random clocks, regardless of their distributions' domain.

2. The method `augmentReachTree` augments the *reach tree* with stochastic information. Each random delay is modeled as a *stochastic edge* with a corresponding random clock, which is *active* in the source location of that edge. This information from the model is embedded in the nodes of the reach tree, resulting in a *stochastic reach tree*.

3. Next, `selectGoalStates` identifies traces of the *(stochastic) reach tree* that reach the goal. Each node containing goal states then induces a *goal trace* starting from the root of the reach tree, and links to the *refined segment*, which results from the intersection of the nodes state set with the goal.

4. The `backwardRefinement` starts from the refined segments and effectively computes a scheduler partitioning on the state space regarding their ability to reach the goal. This results in *refined* goal traces, which hold a sequence of convex polytopes representing all states that lead to the goal.

5. Method `findIntegrationBounds` prepares the obtained state sets for integration by (i) projection onto the stochastic domain, (ii) adaptation of upper bounds to incorporate later expiration of random delays, (iii) intersection of all resulting constraints per trace. For each goal trace, we obtain a (possibly unbounded) convex polytope that contains all sample values that allow to follow that trace to the goal. The *sample domain* is given by the union of these polytopes.

6. The `numericalIntegration` over the union of polytopes is done via Monte Carlo VEGAS and results in a optimal reachability probability, as well as a *statistical* error and an *integration* error.

3.2   Backward Refinement and Integration

Backward refinement restricts the reachable state space to the fragment from which the goal can be reached. This iterative process alternates the computation of *refined segments* and *intermediate goal segments* on all traces in the reach tree that lead to goal states. A scheduler that stays in the refined segment hence resolves all continuous nondeterminism, effectively creating a purely stochastic version of the model. A partitioning of the schedulers is then given by each trace in the refined segments: all schedulers that make similar choices and enable the same trace in the reach tree belong to the same equivalence class. Note that backward refinement is only needed if the model contains continuous nondeterminism, e.g., in the initial set, dynamics, or time delays. Otherwise, e.g. as in the *urgent* version of SAR (c.f. [26]), the backward refinement step can be skipped.

Integration and error. Multidimensional integration over unbounded polytopes is not possible in general. Hence, we restrict the integration domain by a predefined *integration bound* $t_{int} \geq t_{max}$. This results in a new integration region $\mathcal{P}_{max}$, computed by intersection of the union of possibly unbounded polytopes with $[0, t_{int}]^d$. Further, we obtain an overapproximative error:

$$e_\infty = 1 - \int_{[0,t_{int}]^d} G(s)ds.$$

Here, $G = \prod_{r_n} Distr(r_n)$ is the joint probability density function for all random delays r_n with probability density functions $Distr(r_n)$. This error is exact if: (i) no random clock has ever expired upon reaching the goal set on all traces, or (ii) the support of all random clocks that have not expired upon reaching the goal is finite. Otherwise, e_∞ overapproximates the actual error. Clearly, increasing t_{int} decreases e_∞. REALYST implements Monte Carlo VEGAS for multi-dimensional integration, which introduces an additional statistical error e_{stat}, depending on the number of integration samples. This error is estimated based on the weighted average of independent samples and provided directly by GSL [12].

VEGAS uses *importance sampling* and *stratified sampling*, where a multidimensional weight function is used to concentrate the samples in regions with the highest peaks. VEGAS suffers from the curse of dimensionality, because it uses *rejection sampling* on the *bounding box* to obtain samples that are uniformly distributed over the polytopes.

3.3 Dependencies and Usage

REALYST is designed as a command line tool for Linux and our experiments have been run on the *Windows Subsystem for Linux*. The tool mainly depends on the libraries HYPRO [24], GSL [12], and GMP [13]. Further dependencies include SPDLOG (logging), CEREAL (serialization), CLI11 (command line interface), and GTEST (unit testing) that are automatically fetched during configuration.

For state-set representations (e.g., convex polytopes), as well as reachability analysis, we rely on HYPRO. By using a rational number format provided by GMP, the computation of the state sets is guaranteed to be exact. Integration via Monte Carlo VEGAS with GSL [12] leads to optimal reachability probabilities.

A command-line interface provides the option to analyze programmatically constructed models with different parameters such as the reachability time bound, the integration precision, as well as model-specific configurations. The models are specified in C++ files.[1]

REALYST can be invoked via `./realyst [OPTIONS]` where the major parameters in [OPTIONS] are:

-h displays a complete help message with all parameters
-t sets the global timebound t_{max} for the reachability analysis
-d sets the bound for the jump depth for all traces
-i sets the considered intergration bound t_{int}
-s sets the number of samples for Monte Carlo integration
-b chooses a benchmark, requires further parameters based on choice
-l allows to choose a logging level
-p enables plotting, requires specifications of which dimensions to plot.

Depending on the chosen benchmark, further sets of parameters may be required. Apart from compiling the source, a user additionally can access a DOCKER container which holds a compiled version.[2] Once started, the tool will printout the

---

[1] See https://go.uni-muenster.de/iozrb for an exemplary model file.
[2] https://hub.docker.com/r/realyst/realyst.

chosen parameter settings as well as the final result, and, depending on the logging level, further output during the analysis.

4 Evaluation

We recompute results for the case study presented in [11] to illustrate the improved capabilities of REALYST. The case study models the state of charge of an e-car (c.f. Appendix B). The model contains random *charging* and *driving times*, as well as a scalable number of *detours*. In contrast to [11] we consider uniformly distributed charging and driving times, both following $\mathcal{U}(0, 15)$.

Table 1 shows the results for different model variants evaluated with REALYST and PROHVER [15]. The dimensionality of the variants is given by $K = (|Var_R|, |R|, |I_S|)$, where $|Var_R|$ is the number of random delays in the model, $|R|$ is the number of nodes in the reach tree and $|I_S|$ is the number of traces leading to the goal set. Using $1 \cdot 10^5$, $2 \cdot 10^6$ and $1 \cdot 10^7$ integration samples for $0, 1, 2$ detours respectively, REALYST computes maximum reachability probabilities for all model variants with 0 and 1 detour in less than 2 minutes.

For 2 detours the complexity of the model increases significantly. The computations in REALYST takes less than 45 minutes for the variant singular **A** and about 2 hours for rectangular **A**. In variants **AB** and **ABC** with 2 detours, the size of the state space becomes very large. REALYST is only able to complete the singular variant of **AB**, which takes about 13 hours instead of 83 hours as in [11]. For rectangular **AB** and both versions of **ABC**, flowpipe construction does not terminate anymore for 2 detours.

Table 1. Maximum reachability probabilities for benchmark from [11] with uniformly distributed *charging* and *driving time*, i.e., $c, d \sim \mathcal{U}(0, 15)$. Computation times t_{comp} provided for REALYST (R) with error e_{stat} and PROHVER (P). $K = (|Var_R|, |R|, |I_S|)$.

			0 detours			1 detour			2 detours
		Var.	A	AB	ABC	A	AB	ABC	A
		K	$(2,8,2)$	$(2,12,3)$	$(2,16,4)$	$(5,38,10)$	$(5,88,19)$	$(5,167,39)$	$(8,128,34)$
Rectangular	R	p_{max}	0.318 970	0.335 863	0.341 218	0.407 734	0.425 624	0.428 865	0.407 632
		e_{stat}	$1.193 \cdot 10^{-3}$	$4.363 \cdot 10^{-4}$	$5.984 \cdot 10^{-4}$	$4.031 \cdot 10^{-4}$	$5.066 \cdot 10^{-4}$	$1.636 \cdot 10^{-3}$	$4.122 \cdot 10^{-3}$
		t_{comp}	0.27 s	0.41 s	0.55 s	8.41 s	38.53 s	115.09 s	7260.44 s
	P	p_{max}	0.351 074	0.367 676	0.371 582	0.625 977	0.660 687	0.660 969	0.862 513
		t_{comp}	568.03 s	1162.00 s	1605.56 s	9907.90 s	21 373.98 s	38 688.62 s	23 273.99 s
Singular	R	p_{max}	0.319 275	0.337 199	0.341 095	0.407 481	0.424 928	0.431 253	0.406 746
		e_{stat}	$1.028 \cdot 10^{-3}$	$4.216 \cdot 10^{-4}$	$4.480 \cdot 10^{-4}$	$3.948 \cdot 10^{-4}$	$1.825 \cdot 10^{-3}$	$1.772 \cdot 10^{-3}$	$9.040 \cdot 10^{-4}$
		t_{comp}	0.33 s	0.41 s	0.51 s	6.78 s	24.67 s	61.90 s	2643.05 s
	P	p_{max}	0.351 074	0.367 676	0.371 582	0.623 630	0.643 771	0.652 361	0.862 513
		t_{comp}	368.76 s	535.77 s	674.30 s	7869.98 s	14 334.37 s	25 710.70 s	13 688.28 s

Due to more efficient memory allocation in REALYST, the computed results are on average 10 times faster than in [11]. Note that the impact of the chosen distributions on the computation times is negligible. See Appendix C for further details on computation times. The charging rates in the singular variant equal the *lower bounds* of the rectangular interval. Due to the setup of the case study, the resulting maximum reachability probabilities are almost identical. This serves as further validation and illustrates the smaller computation times of the singular variant.

Similar to [11], results are validated by PROHVER and have been recomputed for the uniform distribution. While REALYST results are well supported by the overapproximation computed by PROHVER, computation times of PRO-HVER are considerably slower. Note that PROHVER is not able to refine its discretization for 2 detours, resulting in a significant overapproximation.

All experiments have been conducted on a machine equipped with an Intel® Core™ i7 with 1.70 GHz and 64 GiB RAM.

5   Conclusion and Future Work

With REALYST we present a tool that is able to optimize reachability probabilities in different types of SHS, potentially containing discrete and continuous nondeterminism, as well as stochastic behavior via random delays. The results of the feasibility study show that REALYST performs very well for up to five random variables. Reachability probabilities are highly accurate and obtained fast in comparison to PROHVER.

Future work includes the computation of *minimum* reachability probabilities, as well the integration of a dedicated analysis for a restricted version of SAR (c.f. [22]), where prophetic and non-prophetic schedulers are used to compute maximum and minimum reachability probabilites. Furthermore, we aim to improve scalability via other state set representations and include established input formats for SHS,, such as the JANI format [7].

Appendix A

Figure 1 illustrates an exemplary RAR with three locations that has two variables: random clock r and continuous variable x. The model contains initial nondeterminism in the valuation of x, which can be chosen from the interval $[1, 3]$. According to the syntax as presented in [11], the random clock r behaves as a stopwatch and has to be 0 initially.

The evolution of r is always either 1 or 0, since it can be *active* or *inactive*. In the given model, r is only active in location ℓ_0. Hence, it evolves with rate 1 in ℓ_0 and there is a stochastic transition from ℓ_0 to ℓ_2 modelling the expiration of the random delay. The continuous variable x, however, can evolve with a rate $\in [1, 2]$ in ℓ_0, which again models nondeterministic behavior. If it reaches a valuation of 4, location ℓ_0 has to be left, either with the stochastic transition or with the transition from ℓ_0 to ℓ_1. In ℓ_1, x is evolving with rate 1 and r is inactive and hence cannot expire anymore.

Appendix B

For completeness, we have included Fig. 3 illustrating the RAR model of the case study evaluated in Sect. 4. Note that the figure is taken from [11].

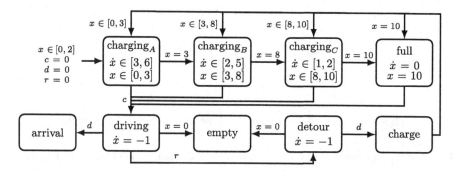

Fig. 3. Car model with detours. Random clock c is active ($\dot{c} = 1$) in the charging locations, d is active in locations *driving* and *detour* and r is active in location *driving*. The state of charge x is restricted to $[0, 10]$ in all locations unless stated otherwise. No time is spent in location *charge* due to invariants not shown.

Appendix C

Figure 4 shows the computation times of the different model variants, where rectangular model variants are indicated with R and singular model variants with S. The computation times are separated for flowpipe construction (step 1), refinement (step 2 and 3), extraction of the sample domain (step 4) and the multi-dimensional integration (step 5). As the figure illustrates, REALYST is considerably quicker for all model variants in comparison to the computations from [11], and especially the flowpipe construction and integration perform much better.

Note that due for to the absence of peaks in the uniform distribution, VEGAS is unable to perform importance sampling. This particularly occurred during the variant singular AB for 2 detours, hence a larger number of integration samples had to be used in the computation. This resulted in a probability of 0.425 528 with $e_{stat} = 1.203 \cdot 10^{-05}$.

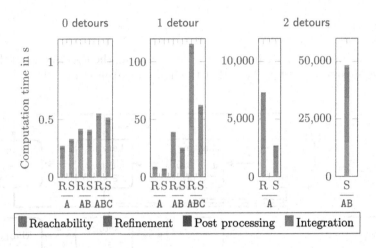

Fig. 4. Computation times for different models and number of detours with REALYST.

References

1. Abate, A., Prandini, M., Lygeros, J., Sastry, S.: Probabilistic reachability and safety for controlled discrete time stochastic hybrid systems. Automatica **44**(11), 2724–2734 (2008). https://doi.org/10.1016/j.automatica.2008.03.027
2. Abate, A., Blom, H., Cauchi, N., Delicaris, J., Haesaert, S., van Huijgevoort, B., Lavaei, A., Remke, A., Schön, O., Schupp, S., Shmarov, F., Soudjani, S., Willemsen, L., Zuliani, P.: ARCH-COMP23 Category report: stochastic models. In: 10th International Workshop on Applied Verification of Continuous and Hybrid Systems (ARCH23). EPiC Series in Computing, EasyChair (2023), accepted for publication
3. Alur, R., Courcoubetis, C.A., Halbwachs, N., Henzinger, T.A., Ho, P., Nicollin, X., Olivero, A., Sifakis, J., Yovine, S.: The algorithmic analysis of hybrid systems. Theoret. Comput. Sci. **138**(1), 3–34 (1995). https://doi.org/10.1016/0304-3975(94)00202-T
4. Behrmann, G., Cougnard, A., David, A., Fleury, E., Larsen, K.G., Lime, D.: Uppaal-tiga: Time for playing games! In: Computer Aided Verification, pp. 121–125. Springer, Berlin Heidelberg, Berlin, Heidelberg (2007). https://doi.org/10.1007/978-3-540-73368-3_14
5. Bengtsson, J., Larsen, K., Larsson, F., Pettersson, P., Yi, W.: Uppaal—a tool suite for automatic verification of real-time systems. In: Hybrid Systems III, pp. 232–243. Springer (1996)
6. Bertrand, N., Bouyer, P., Brihaye, T., Menet, Q., Baier, C., Größer, M., Jurdzinski, M.: Stochastic timed automata. Logical Methods Comput. Sci. **10**(4), 1–73 (2014). https://doi.org/10.2168/LMCS-10(4:6)2014
7. Budde, C.E., Dehnert, C., Hahn, E.M., Hartmanns, A., Junges, S., Turrini, A.: JANI: quantitative model and tool interaction. In: Tools and Algorithms for the Construction and Analysis of Systems—23rd International Conference, TACAS 2017, Held as Part of the European Joint Conferences on Theory and Practice of Software, ETAPS 2017, Uppsala, Sweden, April 22–29, 2017, Proceedings, Part II.

Lecture Notes in Computer Science, vol. 10206, pp. 151–168 (2017). https://doi.org/10.1007/978-3-662-54580-5_9

8. Cauchi, N., Abate, A.: Stochy—automated verification and synthesis of stochastic processes: Poster abstract. In: Proceedings of the 22nd ACM International Conference on Hybrid Systems: Computation and Control, pp. 258–259. Association for Computing Machinery (2019). https://doi.org/10.1145/3302504.3313349

9. D'Argenio, P.R., Gerhold, M., Hartmanns, A., Sedwards, S.: A hierarchy of scheduler classes for stochastic automata. In: Proceedings of FOSSACS'18. LNCS, vol. 10803, pp. 384–402. Springer (2018)

10. David, A., Jensen, P.G., Larsen, K.G., Mikučionis, M., Taankvist, J.H.: Uppaal stratego. In: Tools and Algorithms for the Construction and Analysis of Systems, pp. 206–211. Springer (2015). https://doi.org/10.1007/978-3-662-46681-0_16

11. Delicaris, J., Schupp, S., Ábrahám, E., Remke, A.: Maximizing reachability probabilities in rectangular automata with random clocks. In: 17th International Symposium on Theoretical Aspects of Software Engineering. LNCS, vol. 13931, pp. 1–19. Springer (2023)

12. Galassi, M., Davies, J., Theiler, J., Gough, B., Jungman, G., Alken, P., Booth, M., Rossi, F., Ulerich, R.: GNU Scientific Library Reference Manual (3rd Ed.), http://www.gnu.org/software/gsl/

13. Granlund, T.: The GNU Multiple Precision Arithmetic Library Reference Manual. https://gmplib.org/gmp-man-6.2.1.pdf

14. Gribaudo, M., Remke, A.: Hybrid petri nets with general one-shot transitions. Perform. Eval. **105**, 22–50 (2016). https://doi.org/10.1016/j.peva.2016.09.002

15. Hahn, E.M., Hartmanns, A., Hermanns, H., Katoen, J.P.: A compositional modelling and analysis framework for stochastic hybrid systems. Formal Methods Syst. Des. **43**(2), 191–232 (2013)

16. Hartmanns, A., Hermanns, H.: The modest toolset: an integrated environment for quantitative modelling and verification. In: Tools and Algorithms for the Construction and Analysis of Systems, pp. 593–598. Springer (2014)

17. Henzinger, T.A.: The theory of hybrid automata. In: Verification of Digital and Hybrid systems, NATO ASI Series, vol. 170, pp. 265–292. Springer (2000). https://doi.org/10.1007/978-3-642-59615-5_13

18. Hüls, J., Niehaus, H., Remke, A.: hpnmg: A C++ tool for model checking hybrid petri nets with general transitions. In: Lee, R., Jha, S., Mavridou, A. (eds.) NASA Formal Methods—12th International Symposium, NFM 2020, Moffett Field, CA, USA, May 11–15, 2020, Proceedings. Lecture Notes in Computer Science, vol. 12229, pp. 369–378. Springer (2020). https://doi.org/10.1007/978-3-030-55754-6_22

19. Kong, S., Gao, S., Chen, W., Clarke, E.: dreach: δ-reachability analysis for hybrid systems. In: Tools and Algorithms for the Construction and Analysis of Systems, pp. 200–205. Springer (2015)

20. Lygeros, J., Prandini, M.: Stochastic hybrid systems: a powerful framework for complex, large scale applications. Eur. J. Control. **16**(6), 583–594 (2010). https://doi.org/10.3166/ejc.16.583-594

21. Pilch, C., Hartmanns, A., Remke, A.: Classic and non-prophetic model checking for hybrid petri nets with stochastic firings. In: HSCC '20: 23rd ACM International Conference on Hybrid Systems: Computation and Control, Sydney, New South Wales, Australia, April 21–24, 2020, pp. 10:1–10:11. ACM (2020). https://doi.org/10.1145/3365365.3382198

22. Pilch, C., Schupp, S., Remke, A.: Optimizing reachability probabilities for a restricted class of stochastic hybrid automata via flowpipe-construction. In: Quantitative Evaluation of Systems—18th International Conference, QEST 2021, Paris, France, August 23–27, 2021, Proceedings. Lecture Notes in Computer Science, vol. 12846, pp. 435–456. Springer (2021). https://doi.org/10.1007/978-3-030-85172-9_23

23. Schupp, S.: State Set Representations and Their Usage in the Reachability Analysis of Hybrid Systems. Ph.D. thesis, RWTH Aachen University, Aachen (2019). https://doi.org/10.18154/RWTH-2019-08875

24. Schupp, S., Ábrahám, E., Makhlouf, I.B., Kowalewski, S.: HyPro: A C++ library of state set representations for hybrid systems reachability analysis. In: Proceedings of the 9th NASA Formal Methods Symposium (NFM'17). LNCS, vol. LNCS, pp. 288–294. Springer (2017). https://doi.org/10.1007/978-3-319-57288-8_20

25. Shmarov, F., Zuliani, P.: Probreach: verified probabilistic delta-reachability for stochastic hybrid systems. In: Proceedings of the 18th International Conference on Hybrid Systems: Computation and Control, pp. 134–139 (2015)

26. da Silva, C., Schupp, S., Remke, A.: Optimizing reachability probabilities for a restricted class of stochastic hybrid automata via flowpipe-construction. Trans. Modeling Comput. Simul. (2023), accepted for publication

27. Soudjani, S.E.Z., Gevaerts, C., Abate, A.: FAUST ^{2} : Formal abstractions of uncountable-state stochastic processes. In: Tools and Algorithms for the Construction and Analysis of Systems—21st International Conference, TACAS 2015, Held as Part of the European Joint Conferences on Theory and Practice of Software, ETAPS 2015, London, UK, April 11–18, 2015. Proceedings. Lecture Notes in Computer Science, vol. 9035, pp. 272–286. Springer (2015). https://doi.org/10.1007/978-3-662-46681-0_23

28. Stübbe, J., Remke, A.: Monte-Carlo integration on a union of polytopes. In: 19th Cologne-Twente Workshop on Graphs and Combinatorial Optimization, Garmisch-Patenkirchen, Germany, June 20–23, 2023 (2023), accepted for publication

Author Index

Published by Springer Nature Switzerland AG 2024. All Rights Reserved
E. Kalyvianaki and M. Paolieri (Eds.): VALUETOOLS 2023, LNICST 539, p. 183, 2024.
https://doi.org/10.1007/978-3-031-48885-6

Printed in the United States
by Baker & Taylor Publisher Services